T0306037

The Rural to Urban Transition in Developing Countries

Increasing urbanisation and industrial development is occurring at the expense of shrinking forest cover and agricultural land in South Asia. Various land uses compete with each other, reducing forests and farmlands. This book addresses urbanisation and peri-urban land markets, with a special focus on Bangalore, one of the fastest growing cities in South Asia.

It contributes to historic perspectives on the spatial transformation of peri-urban locales, as well as providing much-needed empirical evidence. The book discusses issues related to the context of peri-urban land use, land transactions, demand supply relationships and land prices in the peri-urban land market. The steep rise in land prices of the periphery, rapid changes in land use patterns, active land transactions, growth of the real estate market and the challenge to implement efficient land use regulations are explored with the help of field evidence. Insights and challenges to land administration addressed in this book are common to other metropolitan cities, and the key message is that a separate peri-urban land policy is required for the major metropolitan cities of India and other developing countries. The book contributes to the understanding of how these spatial markets function in order to work towards an improved implementation of land policy in the context of dynamic rural-urban periphery.

As such, it will appeal to researchers, scholars and students of regional, urban and agricultural economics, economic geography, urban and regional planning and environmental science. It will also be of great interest to city planners and policy makers, and action-based think tanks focused on urban governance.

Amrutha Mary Varkey is a researcher and teacher of Development Economics at the Faculty of Economic Sciences, University of Warsaw, Poland.

Routledge Advances in Regional Economics, Science and Policy

For more information about this series, please visit: www.routledge.com/series/RAIRESP

The Rural to Urban Transition in Developing Countries

Urbanisation and Peri-Urban Land Markets

Amrutha Mary Varkey

LONDON AND NEW YORK

First published 2023
by Routledge
4 Park Square, Milton Park, Abingdon, Oxon OX14 4RN

and by Routledge
605 Third Avenue, New York, NY 10158

Routledge is an imprint of the Taylor & Francis Group, an informa business

© 2023 Amrutha Mary Varkey

British Library Cataloguing-in-Publication Data
A catalogue record for this book is available from the British Library

Library of Congress Cataloging-in-Publication Data
Names: Varkey, Amrutha Mary, author.
Title: The rural to urban transition in developing countries : urbanisation and peri-urban land markets / Amrutha Mary Varkey.
Description: Abingdon, Oxon ; New York, NY : Routledge, 2023. | Series: Routledge advances in regional economics, science and policy | Includes bibliographical references and index.
Identifiers: LCCN 2022049256 (print) | LCCN 2022049257 (ebook) | ISBN 9781032423364 (hardback) | ISBN 9781032423357 (paperback) | ISBN 9781003362333 (ebook)
Subjects: LCSH: Urbanization—India—Banglalore. | Rural-urban migration—India—Banglalore. | Land use—India—Banglalore.
Classification: LCC HT384.I42 B368 2023 (print) | LCC HT384.I42 (ebook) | DDC 307.760954/87—dc23/eng/20221212
LC record available at https://lccn.loc.gov/2022049256
LC ebook record available at https://lccn.loc.gov/2022049257

ISBN: 978-1-032-42336-4 (hbk)
ISBN: 978-1-032-42335-7 (pbk)
ISBN: 978-1-003-36233-3 (ebk)

DOI: 10.4324/9781003362333

Typeset in Bembo
by codeMantra

Dedicated to my father, Varkey a progressive liberal and a communist whose values and principles moulded me and *to my mother, Alice* whose love survived me.

Contents

Figures

Tables

Foreword by Professor S. Irudaya Rajan

I am pleased to write foreword to this book as I know Amrutha Varkey as a motivated scholar in the field of urbanisation and innovation. I find the debates on peri-urban interesting; it evokes the discourse on rural-urban fringe from a spatial perspective. This book initiates debates and discussions on rural-urban transition, sustainable urbanisation in developing countries.

India with the second largest urban population in the world provides a pertinent backdrop to examining the issues of population and sprawling nature of metropolitan peripheries. The challenges associated with urban and peri-urban growth echo the demographic pressure. The major metropolitan cities in India constitute 28% of urbanites in the total population. In 2001, there were 35 metropolises with more than a million inhabitants, representing 38% of the total urban population in India; among them six mega cities accounted for more than 5 million inhabitants. The rate of urbanisation in India shows a moderate progression from 1981 to 2011, according to the Census 2011.

Various demographic, economic and socio-cultural factors contribute to urban population growth. In the context of global competition, peri-urban areas create growth nodes, especially IT hubs in the peripheries of major metropolises of India, such as Bangalore, Hyderabad and Chennai. Bangalore metropolitan city exhibits peri-urbanisation in all the corners. This book analyses the peri-urban scenario by identifying various issues related to land uses and land prices. The skyrocketing land prices of the periphery, rapid changes in the land use pattern, active land transactions and the difficulty to implement efficient land use regulations are brought out with the help of primary research. The issues identified in this book are common to other metropolitan cities of India and beyond. This is of great interest to urban planners and policy makers since it addresses on the relevant socio-economic issue of the present era of smart cities mission.

The data used in this book include Land Use/Land Cover (LU/LC) data from Landsat series, primary survey of land transactions and land prices collected from official sources. This book is organised into seven chapters narrating the Peri-urban Portrait, Elucidation of Land Use Changes, Econometric Analysis of Land Use Changes, Land Transactions in Peri-Urban, Land Prices, Peri-Urban Land Governance and Sustainable Urbanisation. This book offers a significant contribution to the existing literature on rural-urban transition with an in-depth case study approach.

I wish Amrutha Varkey good luck in her academic career and future endeavours with the publication of this book. I hope this book will contribute adequately to the peri-urban literature and invite more debates on rural-urban continuum in the coming years. My sincere appreciation for her academic enthusiasm and diligent effort. I wish her all the best!

Professor S. Irudaya Rajan
Chairman
The International Institute of Migration and Development

Foreword by Professor Julio D. Dávila

This book deals with an important but often forgotten policy and planning issue: the interface between cities and their rural hinterland. As humanity becomes progressively urban, access to affordable and well-located land for housing, industrial production, services and the myriad of activities necessary for an urban society to thrive becomes increasingly urgent. As land becomes scarcer, prices rise such that new developments are increasingly directed to environmentally fragile areas in the urban periphery, such as steep hills or floodplains, or to distant locations from the urban core where land prices are lower. This leads to a broad range of environmental consequences, including risks arising from landslides, increased runoff from man-made hard surfaces and potential for flooding, destruction of valuable natural habitats such as wetlands and forests, and a lower capacity to absorb the increased rainfall or rising temperatures likely to result from climate change. The urban sprawl resulting from seeking ever more distant locations from the urban core is, in turn, associated with increased energy consumption for transport, higher levels of harmful greenhouse gas emissions and longer commuting times for residents and workers.

For analytical, policy and planning purposes, a distinction between urban and rural areas is not terribly useful, especially in a context of rapid urbanisation. Some residents in areas that might be traditionally considered rural perform what is conventionally seen as "urban" occupations such as small manufacturing production, teaching, even remote working via the internet. Many residents of cities in Sub-Saharan Africa, for example, spend only part of their time there, migrating seasonally or daily to rural farms. In Latin America, the United States, Europe and India upper and middle-class households in semi-rural, low-density "gated communities" commute regularly into the city for work, education, shopping and leisure.

Following on from this, the peri-urban interface should not be seen as the meeting point of the two ends of a conceptual dichotomy. It is rather the context in which people, commodities, finance, waste and energy, among others, flow from the urban core to areas marked by lower population densities conventionally dominated by farming or extractive activities.

In this book, Varkey examines the consequences of some of these flows, focusing on their impact on land markets. This illustrates the imbalances arising from the meeting of powerful urban-based interests such as IT firms and real estate developers, and weak rural communities. Conventional planning mechanisms are largely unable to cope both with a rapidly changing landscape and with blurred administrative and disciplinary boundaries in what is, in effect, a high-stakes, complex and irreversible process of changes in land-use, social profiles and a worsening environment. The benefits often accrue to a few, mainly in the form of rapid land prices. In many contexts, the absence of mechanisms to capture surplus land values as a form of collective compensation is a tragic political reality.

With illustrations from India and to a lesser extent from Europe, the preoccupations of this book lie at the core of the future sustainability of cities and, therefore, of humanity.

Julio D. Dávila
Professor of Urban Policy and International Development
Development Planning Unit
University College London

Preface

This book elucidates the scenario of urbanisation and peri-urban land markets in the developing country setting of industrialisation and IT developments. The rural-urban fringe in developing countries is distinctive in its terms of physical and spatial characteristics to those of the cities in Europe. It is based on a comparative perspective of per-urbanisation of developed countries "north" and developing countries "south". I have found championing of peri-urban portrait from the cities of Europe and explain how the developing world differs in its spatial manifestations and metamorphosis. The aspect of peri-urban development is illustrated by portraying the scenarios of fast urbanisation, real estate and the growth of land markets in Bangalore Metropolitan city. The perspective of peri-urban is demonstrated with the patterns of spatial development in Warsaw, Toulouse, Amsterdam and Utrecht. I seek the evidence of peri-urbanisation in developing countries with its specific characteristics, industry and IT lead growth in recent years. The dynamic growth of the rural-urban fringes in the developing world is owing to the economic development and rapid urbanisation.

Projections show that urbanisation, the progressive shift in dwelling of the human population from rural to urban areas, combined with the overall growth of the world's population could add another 2.5 billion people to urban zones by 2050, with near 90% of this expansion occurring in Asia and Africa. Asia is home to 54% of the world's urban populace, trailed by Europe with 13%. A comparative perspective of peri-urban of leading cities of Europe with the Asia's fastest growing IT city Bangalore reveals the challenges of land administration and the problems of land markets in the developing country.

Urban expansion is by far the speediest type of land use change in Europe. The periphery of the cities of Europe is considered as well planned through efficient land use planning, but the periphery of the million cities like Bangalore is known for its rapid industrialisation and remarkable population growth and fast urban development due to IT sector led growth and real estate boom which is a unique pattern of urbanisation in Asia. Evidence from the urban fringes of post-industrial cities like Toulouse, Amsterdam – a tech gateway of Europe, Utrecht – The Canal City, Warsaw a hub of IT and businesses tells the specific pattern of peri-urban development in Europe.

I interpret the "Global South" and "Global North" perspective of peri-urban by describing the issues and challenges of peri-urbanisation of India's major metropolitan city, Bangalore, and intensely talks about the urbanisation and peri-urban land market in Indian context. By 2050, it is expected that India will have additional 416 million urban dwellers. About 34% of India's population presently lives in urban areas. This is an increase of 3% since the 2011 Census (DESA, 2012). Urban development in India will occur at a speed very dissimilar to anything the country or the world has seen previously. It took about 40 years (from 1971 to 2008) for India's urban population to ascend by almost 230 million; it will set aside just a large portion of that effort to include the next 250 million. This extension will influence pretty much every state. For the first time in India's history, five of its major states will have a greater amount of their populace living in villages. This offers a guide of urbanisation by state and notes which cities are ready to outperform the 4-million imprint in populace (McKinsey, 2010). The increase in urban expansion prompts the growth of cities and creates pressure to land resources.

Today land in the peri-urban faces major challenge. Unequal infrastructural growth all across the country has led to the rural-urban dichotomy. This rural-urban divergence is blatantly apparent with regard to the electric supply, quality of education and health facilities, transportation, drinking water and basic facilities. Most of all, the limited supply of land is a significant problem in the context of urbanisation, especially in major metropolitan cities of India. Various issues related to land use, land transactions, land value and demand supply relation in the peri-urban land market in Bangalore are addressed in this book. The skyrocketing land prices of the periphery, rapid changes in the land use pattern, active land transactions in the periphery and the difficulty to implement efficient land use regulations are brought out with the help of field evidence.

I debate on peri-urban land markets and the relationship between urban land use and land value models, impact of urban land use and land value and the role of institutions in the land policy, administration and management. It contributes to the understanding of how these spatial markets function in order to work towards an improved implementation of land policy in the context of dynamic rural-urban periphery. Land policy must pay close attention to the way that supply and demand interact to determine prices and the demarcation between rural and urban periphery. At this context of rapid urbanisation, the important questions are: What helps some metropolitan cities more successful than others? How does urban policy integrate peri-urban land as well? In an urban economic model, individuals and firms are presumed to behave rationally, choosing locations based on the accessibility and affordability. The correct solution to the land problem is of balanced and comprehensive land use; each type of land use is allocated to its best suited use.

Land use and land value models often consist of agents interacting in markets for locations (i.e. housing, commercial space or land). These are supposed to be in a spatial equilibrium where prices adjust to ensure that supply equals demand for each location. Mapping land transactions gives an idea about the pattern of land sale and land purchase. Further experience at the field shows the need of an improved implementation of peri-urban policy. To mitigate the strains that will develop as cities expand, and to amplify the potential economic opportunity that well-managed cities can offer, India urgently needs a fresh, proactive approach to addressing the challenges of urbanisation. The results contribute to the theoretical literature in urban economics that relies on the spatial equilibrium assumption such as intra-urban models of the Alonso (Vonthunen, 1826; Alonso, 1964).

I take close look at the role of institutions in land policy, administration and management. Land administration and policy has not clearly demarcated land markets both in urban and rural areas as well as in the peri-urban areas in most of the Indian cities. Illegal transfers of land and lack of coherent management of restrictive land and their updated information, boundary dispute, ownership rows, land re-measurements, payment of land taxes, land possession and non-encumbrance certificates are vexatious issues in Indian context. The land-related conflicts that lead to court cases and litigations resulting in social cost, creation of fake documents where single property is sold to several persons, encroachments and illegal constructions are the major loopholes. Therefore, more control at the official level is required to tackle these irregularities. The E-governance in the context of complicated land management practices is an innovative remedy.

How does peri-urban land policy impact on rural urban governance is a debatable issue in the context of land policy, administration and management is addressed in this book. To provide theoretical answers to these, I include the field insights from the peri-urban areas and analysis on spatial and temporal changes in land use and land value and throw light on an integrated peri-urban land policy in the context of sustainable land administration of the state.

Acknowledgements

I am grateful to the many people without whom this book would not have been possible. A lot of people provided immense support to whom I am especially beholden. I would like to thank those worthy of note in this journey. With a grateful heart, I acknowledge Prof. S. Irudaya Rajan, Chairman, International Institute of Migration and Development, Former Professor Centre for Development Studies(CDS), India and Prof. Julio D Davila, Professor of Urban Policy and International Development at University College London (UCL) for sparing their valuable time and for their kind support. I gratefully acknowledge Prof. Zofia Barbara Liberda, Faculty of Economic Sciences, University of Warsaw, for her valuable feedback.

Insights from cities and cosmopolitan cultures were truly insightful and instrumental in writing this book; it was a remarkable learning experience in understanding the urbanisation and peri-urban pattern both in developed and developing countries. Life in various Indian cities Bangalore, Chennai, Delhi and Ghaziabad, visits to countries Nepal, Athens – Greece, Italy, cities of France Paris, Toulouse, Tarbes, Lourdes and Nancy and the Netherlands cities Amsterdam and Utrecht were helpful in understanding the pattern of sprawling and urban growth from the field. My life in Poland as a researcher at the University of Warsaw helped me a lot in understanding the nature of urban growth in Warsaw and Krakow. It was during the time of League of European Research Universities (LERU) summer school (Urban Futures Studio, Utrecht University, the Netherlands, 2022), I decided to proceed with this book. Discussions with researchers from different parts of the world enriched the process of writing.

This research is based on the field survey conducted in Bangalore when I was a research scholar at the Institute for Social and Economic Change (ISEC), Bangalore (2015–21). I thank my advisor Dr. S. Manasi, Prof. M.V. Nadkarni, Prof. Sunil Nautiyal, Prof. Meenkshi Rajeev, Prof. Kala S. Sridar, Prof. K. Gayithri, Prof. Parmod Kumar, Prof. S. Madheswaran, B.P. Vani for their valuable suggestions and comments to improve my research during days of intellectual pursuit at ISEC.

I thank the distinguished faculty, Dr. Bahman Jabbarian Amiri, Department of Regional Economy and Environment of the University of Lodz, Poland, Dr. Mahalaya Chatterjee, Director, Centre for Urban Economic Studies, Calcutta University, Professor – Urban Economics, Urban Planning for the timely support.

I thank Dr. Lakshmi Kanth KSRSAC, Ms. Geethanjali (KSRSAC) and Mr. Adarsh (World Wildlife Institute) for their immense support for LU/LC data acquisition, officials of BMRDA, Hoskote Taluk and Kanakapura, Mr. Nagabhoosashan (BMRDA, Hoskote) and Dr. Lakshmi Pathi (Joint Director, Kanakapura, BMRDA), Srinivasa, ISEC for their valuable inputs.

A special thanks to farmers from the field and Mr. Jayaguru Venketesh who enhanced the process of data and information collection and helped me to interpret and understand the field dynamics. I am so grateful to the landlords, builders and particularly the villagers of Hoskote and Kanakapura for their support and the warmth they extended to me during my time in the villages.

Warm thanks to the editorial assistants Kristina Abbotts and Christiana Mandizha for helping me to navigate the world of international publishers, while always finding the time to provide encouraging comments and support.

I would like to thank my friend, colleague Eby Johny, University of Warsaw for the vital steering of the ship, his commitment and charm helped me to accomplish this successful journey.

Author

Amrutha Mary Varkey is a researcher in the Faculty of Economic Sciences, University of Warsaw, Warsaw, Poland. She worked in the FIRMINREG – Gospostrateg VI research project in the Faculty of Economic Sciences and Ministry of Finance, Poland (grant from the National Centre for Research and Development). Currently, she teaches Development Economics and Inequalities and Development at the University of Warsaw, Poland. She is awarded the Dekaban Liddle Fellowship and engages in research in the Adam Smith Business School, University of Glasgow, Scotland, 2022–2023. She has been at the leading edge of research in urbanisation, land markets, innovation and new technology. She was an assistant professor of Economics at Christ University and Alliance University, Bangalore, India (2013–21) and other organizations in India. She was a First Rank Gold Medalist – M.A. Economics, Stella Maris College, Chennai, India, in 2012. She authored articles on urbanisation, land policy and innovation in newspapers and journals.

Abbreviations

AEZ	Agriculture Export Zone
ALMA	Agent Based Land Market Model
APZ	Area Planning Zone
BBMP	Bruhat Bengaluru Mahanagara Palike
BDA	Bangalore Development Authority
BEL	Bharat Electronics Limited
BHEL	Bharat Heavy Electricals Limited
BIA	Bangalore International Airport
BMR	Bangalore Metropolitan Region
BMRDA	Bangalore Metropolitan Region Development Authority
BOT	Build Operate Transfer
BWSSB	Bangalore Water Supply and Sewerage Board
CBD	Central Business District
CDCZ	Corridor Development Control Zone
CDP	Comprehensive Development Plan
CPI	Consumer Price Index
CPWD	Central Public Works Department
DBT	Direct Benefit Transfer
DESA	Department of Economics and Social Affairs
ERDAS	Earth Resources Data Analysis System
FAO	Food and Agricultural Organisation
FDI	Foreign Direct Investment
GIS	Geographic Information System
GOK	Government of Karnataka
HAL	Hindustan Aeronautics Limited
HMT	Hindustan Machine Tools Limited
IRR	Inner Ring Road
IT	Information Technology
ITI	Indian Telephone Industries Limited
ITRR	Individual Town Ring Road
KAVERI	Karnataka Valuations and E-Registration Integrated
KIADB	Karnataka Industrial Areas Development Board
KMC	Karnataka Municipal Corporation

KPTCL	Karnataka Power Transmission Corporation Limited
KSCB	Karnataka Slum Clearance Board
KSRTC	Karnataka State Road Transport Corporation
KSWAN	Karnataka State Wide Area Network
KTCP	Karnataka Town and Country Planning
LDC	Less Developing Countries
LGAF	Land Governance Assessment Framework
LPA	Local Planning authority
LU/LC	Land Use/ Land Cover
MNC	Multi National Company
NABARD	National Bank for Agriculture and Rural Development
NH	National Highway
NHAI	National Highways Authority of India
NICE	Nandi Infrastructure Corridor
ODP	Outline Development Plan
OLS	Ordinary Least square
ORR	Outer Ring Road
PLUREL	Peri-urban Land Use relationships
PLUREL	Peri-Urban Land Use Relationship
PPP	Public Private Partnership
PRR	Peripheral Ring Road
PUA	Peri-Urban Area
PUI	Peri-Urban Interface
PWD	Public Works Department
R.T.C	Record of Rights, Tenancy and Crops
RR	Ring Road
RUR	Rural Urban Region
SBD	Second Business District
SEZ	Special Economic Zone
SRO	Sub Registrar Office
SSI	Small Scale Industrial Units
STRR	Satellite Town Ring Road
TCS	Tata Consultancy Services
TMC	Town Municipal Council
US	The United States
UAS	University of Agricultural Sciences
UN	United Nations
UPOR	Urban Property and Ownership Rights

1   The Peri-Urban Portrait

The Peri-Urban Debate

Great divergence is a term made popular by Kenneth Pomeranz book titled European Miracle, coined by Eric Jones in 1981. Scholars have proposed a wide variety of theories to establish great divergence in the context of urbanisation, geography, culture, colonialism, resources, etc. Changes in the divergent fringe areas of the cities are widely studied in the United States and Western States since 1940. The term urban fringe was coined by American geographers describing changes in the population composition of Louisiana, during the 1940s and 1950s. It has been projected that by 2050, over 66% of the worldwide populace will live in urban territories and urban expansion will happen more in Asia, Africa and Latin America (DESA, 2014). Further projections show that 40–50% of India's population, 30–40% Latin American, 20–60% in Arab countries and 50–80% in Sub-Saharan African cities will live in informal settlements. This implies that developing countries will experience a rapid expansion of large cities. Subsequently, small urban centres and villages around cities are turned into peri-urban zones due to changes of city and civil limits to oblige to the urban developments (Nuhu, 2019).

The Global Plan of Action for Sustainable Development adopted by the Rio Conference 1992, Agenda 21 pointed out the major issues the world faces at present. They are poverty, problems of sustainable settlement, deforestation and environmental degradation; these are directly related to the land. The major problems are related to access to land for the urban and rural poor, to create efficient and accessible land markets, increase in land prices and the lack of proper land records in certain states. There is mounting competition for peri-urban land located adjacent to towns and cities by people of diverse backgrounds. As a result of these pressures and rapid socio-economic change, space in the peri-urban area is becoming scarce and conflicts over land are also becoming very noticeable. In the last decade, urbanisation of these rural fringes has proceeded with high momentum due to the growth of IT corridors in major cities of the world. The peri-urban locale in the context of contested land is a major debatable research issue.

The question of peri-urban is associated with the changes in the population; the urban portion of a nation's populace increasing over time with an

DOI: 10.4324/9781003362333-1

expanding proportion of urban and rural population. This differs from the concept of urban growth, which refers to a rise in the absolute level of an urban population. More recently, there has been more prominent attention focused on the potential that peri-urbanisation has for advancing growth, with concentrated populace and infrastructure providing opportunities for raising efficiency through economies of scale, innovation and knowledge spill-overs (Locke & Henley, 2016).

Peri-urban areas are usually beyond the purview of city jurisdiction and are sites with competing governance claims. In peri-urban areas (PUAs), the interface between urban and rural areas is common. Peri-urban areas are transitional spaces that are subject to rapid and profound changes, in a given environment, population and socio-economic activities (Dupont, 2005). Differentiation of "urban fringe" and "rural fringe" will assist longitudinal studies of the urban invasion of rural areas, particularly in relation to Burgess' zone theory, exhibiting a density of occupied dwellings lower than the median density of the total rural-urban fringe (Burgess, 1925).

The question of peri-urban development cannot be addressed outside the framework of balanced development of both the rural and urban areas (He et al., 2012). The simple dichotomy between "rural" and "urban" has "long ceased to have much meaning in practice" (Simon, 2008). Perhaps, the areas can be seen as rural locations that have become more urban in character (Morton et al., 2014). Characteristics of the fringe need not be intermediate nor on a continuum between rural and urban; yet distinctive location and internal heterogeneity and transition do make possible a unitary if not uniform definition. The rural-urban fringe is a complex transition zone on the periphery of growing urban areas in Western countries. T. L. Smith's discussion of the "urban fringe" around Louisiana in 1937 marked the first use of this term signifying the built-up area just outside the corporate limits of the city (Pryor, 1968). Two characteristic features of the literature on urban fringe over the past 30 years are the general absence of explicit references to the subject outside North America, although there have been studies, and clear delineation in case studies. The urban periphery is defined as the transition zone between the city or urban zones and the surrounding countryside. Thomas L. Daniels depicts the urban periphery as the territory inside 5–50 miles of a city that has dispersed, low-density advancement less than 500 individuals for each square mile-normally on 1–10 section of land parts. Ralph E. Heimlich and William D. Anderson characterise the urban periphery as low-thickness settlement 0.5 section of land parcels or bigger in metropolitan areas (Theobald, 2001). Differentiation of "urban fringe" and "rural fringe" will assist longitudinal studies of the urban invasion of rural areas, particularly in relation to Burgess' zone theory, exhibiting a density of occupied dwellings lower than the median density of the total rural-urban fringe (Pryor, 1968).

Another most cited distinguishing feature of sprawl is discontinuous or leapfrog development. Most empirical studies of sprawl are based on aggregate measures of urban density that fail to account for the non-contiguous and dispersed aspects of development patterns that many associate with sprawl (Fulton et al., 2001). Rural–urban interactions show that populations and activities described either as "rural" or "urban" are more closely linked both across space and across sectors than is usually thought, and that distinctions are often arbitrary. What is defined as an "urban centre" may vary from one country to another. Flows of people, goods and wastes and the related flows of information and money act as linkages across space between cities and countryside. However, while the nature of these changes is global, they are also characterised by great diversity at the local level (Tacoli, 1998).

Peri-urban areas tend to be areas of rapid transition with overlapping or fragmented land administration frameworks. The changes that these peri-urban areas experience as they urbanise frequently and within this process, changes in land administration and governance can unequivocally impact urbanisation. In spite of peri-urban zones being the focal point of transition, land issues in peri-urban regions generally deserve special mention. Peri-urban areas are characterised by different land use, population density, frequent land transactions and high land values. This cutting edge of transition leads to land markets extending and land turning out to be progressively commoditised. Therefore, land transactions in peri-urban areas become more frequent, and pressure tends to sub-divide land into smaller parcels in order to increase supply and monetary returns. It is hypothesised as a primary determinant of this development pattern and there is some empirical evidence supporting this. Sprawl is defined as a new urban development that occurs in a fragmented and dispersed pattern across the landscape.

The land conversion in rural–urban is from agriculture to residential land uses, and therefore, a model of land-use conversion with two land uses are agriculture and residential uses are used. The loss of agricultural land is caused by conversion to urban land uses particularly low-density residential and commercial use at the urban fringe. A dynamic model of the urban residential market shows both the supply and the demand sides as cities grow by attaining a sequence of short run equilibrium. Microeconomic theory of the urban land market pioneered by Alonso (1964). This approach has been reached out in a few significant ways through the works of Muth, Mills, Beckmann, Solow and others. Each has depended, similar to the original Alonso model, on static concepts of analysis (Anas, 1978). Several researchers have statistically explored the importance of various factors in determining urban land values or agricultural land values (Chicoine, 1981).

What influences the choice of an individual when he selects property in a particular residential area? Unquestionably, land price is a significant factor determining land value. Since land supply is fixed, land value in an urban community is determined by the demand for space. Demand is a function of the site's accessibility, amenity level, topography, certain historical factors and the value of the land in non-urban uses (Brigham, 1965). Economic transactions are at the core of well-functioning market economies. As emphasised by North, winner of the 1993 Nobel Prize in Economics, "the inability of societies to develop effective, low-cost enforcement of contracts is the most important source of both historical stagnation and contemporary underdevelopment in the Third World" (Knack, 2001). Cross-country empirical studies show where the social and legal institutions that support land and real estate transactions are weak, as in Africa, Latin America and South Asia, the most urgent urban land policy issue may be to establish rule of law that facilitate economic transactions and lower transaction costs. The critical question at this context is what happens to the land rights as the local peri-urban communities themselves become part of the city; as their farmlands are turned into urban built-up properties and as the area become residence to large number of urbanities both formally and informally. For instance, the peri-urban land market research seeks to reveal the nature of a demand for and supply of land located in the fringe areas of the metropolitan city of Bangalore where IT industries are located in the peripheral areas of the city.

The conversion of land from agriculture to urban and industrial development is a critical process of change being witnessed in the peripheries. Conversion of cultivated land to non-agricultural uses is shown to contribute to economic growth, particularly in cities with more than 5 million people, strong agricultural land constraints, secondary industrial or service dominance (He et al., 2012). It is also consistent with the long-run evidence of Kuznets (1966) concerning the decline of agriculture's employment share, the rise and then fall of the manufacturing share and the rise in the service share.

It is evidence for the rural-urban dichotomy of major metropolitan cities of the world which undergo a structural transition (Moore & Lawrence, 1970). Changes in the land use pattern led to the changes in the structure of many cities across the globe. Thus, land use change, considered the outcome of economic growth and structural change aligns itself with the neoclassical growth model in which land plays a decreasing role in economic growth. Peripheral spaces are subject to frequent changes because of industrial, residential and commercial land uses with land price being a significant determinant of land use types. Societies are becoming increasingly multifaceted due to urban sprawl, leading to scarcity of land, its price tends to rise because local governments invest in infrastructure, transportation, education and health sectors. Every land use shows different price lines across urban services and facilities, land use types, accessibility and social and environmental factors.

At this context, it is important to understand reasons and the extent of rising demand of land for non-agricultural land in the peripheries and extent of competition for land resources for agricultural and non-agricultural purposes. The unprecedented growth of urban population causes an exceptionally rapid increase in the demand for urban land. The rising demand for urban land, therefore, tends to be met primarily by converting peri-urban agricultural land at the periphery of the existing built-up area. There are several factors underlying the increased demand. A fairly high rate of economic growth from the early 2000s has undoubtedly been a significant contributor. The real estate boom has led to a significant role in supporting industries such as cement, steel and paint – during the construction phase, as it has been abetted by government policies related to credit and foreign direct investment in the real estate. Peri-urban villages of major metropolitan cities of India are subject to frequent land transaction in the past two decades. This drives up the land prices and the land markets are thriving in the peripheral locations. In this process, peripheries driven by increasing land prices become part of the core areas due to spatial expansion. There exists a strong relationship between land use change, demand and land price.

Why the price of land has risen so rapidly in the last decade and why is the land in core and peripheries so expensive? The most direct explanation is that while the demand for urban land has increased, its supply has not increased commensurately. The mismatch between demand and supply has driven up land prices, and since the demand has increased rapidly, price has increased rapidly. Since urban land is more expensive, agents in the land market are increasingly focusing their attention on peripheries where they can purchase land at affordable prices. The land markets are now flush with money, increasing demand and money supply is sufficient to explain the very rapid rise in the land prices, especially in cities like Mumbai, Delhi and Bangalore. Moreover, the establishment of IT and development corridors in the peripheral areas of the metropolitan cities is mainly responsible for land prices shooting up. There is a mass influx of people from the different parts of the country to the areas for employment, and as a result, the demand for housing, transportation and infrastructural facilities is on the increase. Given that the supply of urban land is limited and expensive, the demand for industrial commercial and residential land is growing in the peripheries. Although peripheral areas are relatively less expensive than the core regions, the land markets drive up land prices considerably. As populace in PUAs rise and city outskirts are broadened. This can show itself in expanded land-related conflicts and disputes, haphazard changes from land use, illegal land transactions and proliferation of informal settlements.

The physical limits of urban territories frequently don't harmonise with their managerial limits, and urban and peri-urban regions regularly fall under discrete authoritative locales with various assets, property rights systems can differ significantly between rural and urban areas, frequently (Locke & Henley, 2016). A microeconomic model of individual choice is significant. In this scheme, individual rational actors decide to migrate because a cost-benefit calculation leads them to expect a positive net return, usually monetary, from movement. The new economics of migration in recent years has arisen to challenge many of the assumptions and conclusions of neoclassical theory (Stark & Bloom, 1985). This new approach refers to the migration decisions that are not made by isolated individual actors, but by collective factors such as search for new employment and income in the cities, gradually (Massey et al., 1993). This rural-urban migration is the cause of peri-urban transition. We investigate the rural-urban transition and analyse the economic impact of this transition. Why this transition in a regional context and focuses its attention on peri-urban areas in metropolitan city to understand what land market issues emerges right now. It investigates what role land policy, planning and governance can play to facilitate an efficient peri-urban land policy in the context of dynamic land use changes and high land prices. Land in the peri-urban interface is of vital importance and it is impacted by frequent land use changes, while being part of the city's hinterland, its economic as well as ecological role in the sustenance of both the urban and rural zones assumes importance. The global portrait of peri-urban assumes a different scenario across various geographic regions; it is important to understand the concept of peri-urban.

Definition of Peri-Urban

The inner ring represents the core of the city consisting of the Central Business Districts with and urban amenities (Figure 1.1). The intermediary ring exemplifies the buffer zone between rural and urban area, where the flow of resources and movement of people from rural to urban areas take places. The outer ring depicts the hinterlands; the land away from the city includes forests, farmlands and natural resources. In developing countries particularly, the transition takes places quickly; the rural areas transform to the peri-urban and the peri-urban to the urban .

Structural Transition in conjunction with Push and Pull factors: In an effort to identify the significance of the transition concept, we deepen our perception of the underlying processes causing a dynamic transition in developing countries (Figure 1.2). These push and pull factors of development are the key drivers of peri-urban transition. The rural areas are characterised by agriculture, cultivation and forests; but, the peri-urban transition zone consists of new developments related to businesses and technology with a rapidly

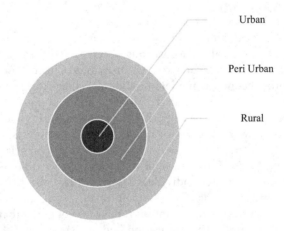

Figure 1.1 Peri-urban concept. Compilation by the author.

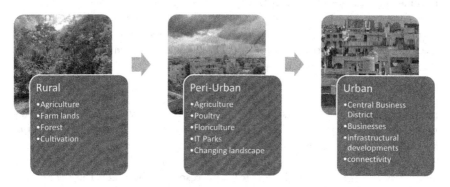

Figure 1.2 Structural transition. Compilation by the author.

changing landscape caused by the urban sprawl. Employment is a major pull factor leading to movement of people from villages to cities; however, drivers on multiple levels can be identified. In order to recognise how the contextual and case-specific effect this dynamic transition process, it suggests that they can be viewed as "push or pull factors". Some good examples of pushes and pulls for peri-urban development can be given. Increasing mobility and expanding IT developments enable the frequent use changes and bring new urban structures in the periphery. Push factors emerge with the growth of real estate in the periphery as the peri-urban areas often provide accessible and affordable living conditions. Peri-urban areas are dynamic transition zones with changing landscapes, rapid structural changes, distinctive features, assimilating the rural-urban population with force of a push or pull factors of development. To identify the distinctive features of the peri-urban, a graphical representation of the peri-urban is provided based on the developing economy context.

The urban fringe: "The space into which the town extends as the process of dispersion operates an area with distinctive characteristics which is only partly assimilated into the growing urban complex" (Adell, 1999).

As a lacking area: "Usually characterized by the loss of rural aspects e.g. fertile soil, agricultural land, natural landscape or the lack of urban attributes such as services or infrastructure" (Allen, 2003).

A transition zone: It is a zone of interaction between urban and rural socio-economic systems, a zone of rapid economic, social structural change (Adell, 1999).

A new kind of rural-urban hybrid: It is "a dramatic new species of urbanism" (Davis, 2004).

A challenging periphery: It is subject to ambiguity, informality, and illegality "...but also encompassing unconventional or unorthodox alternatives to dominant planning and management perspectives". Smith's conception of the peri-urban was based on the concentration of non-village, rural non-farm population and the characteristics of land use outside the city limits. Land use along the city limits is evident of the change over from urban land use patterns to the rural. In other words, it can be considered as the urban land use, which is residential, commercial and industrial in nature compared to the rural particularly agricultural land use before.

Place, process and concept: Peri-urban is a term used in three different ways to connote a place, process and concept. As a place-based term, it is the rural-urban fringe and transitional zone around the city characterised by intense interactions, flows and linkages between the rural and urban areas. It is an intermediary geographical space with rural areas meeting the urban areas. As a process, based definition, it refers to the transition of rural to urban areas as well as the flow of goods, services and resources between the urban and rural areas. In terms of concept, based definition, the proximity of the zone to urban centres is less significant; it is the co-existence of both rural and urban characteristics, linkages and the flow of goods and services between them that matter (Narain & Nischal, 2007). There are three characteristics that make peri-urban zone distinctive. They include changing locations, population and weak institutional structure. The peri-urban interface can be characterised as a natural ecosystem affected by the material and energy flows demanded by both the urban and rural.

Peri-Urbanisation – Global and Indian Context

Peri-urban is considered "mixed spaces" which are "mid-way between urban centres and rural spaces" (Dupont, 2005). Dupont argues that peri-urban areas transitional zone and these areas are subject to rapid and profound changes. Several writers point out peri-urbanisation in association with industrialisation. Stephan Haggard provides a comprehensive comparison of the political economy of industrialisation in selected East Asian and Latin American countries in the context of different growth paths (Haggard, 1991). Peri-urban phenomenon is common in industrialised countries. Cadène (2005) states peri-urban lying between cities and the countryside; but the midway is never defined theoretically or geographically. There exist striking differences in the characteristics of the periphery of different countries. But these characteristics change from time to time and one country from another (Iaquinta & Drescher, 2000). In the European countries, the growth of peri-urban areas is projected to be 3.7 times as high as in urban areas. European-wide projections of built development in peri-urban areas are at 1.4–2.5% per annum if such trends continue. Total built development in peri-urban areas could double between the years 2040 and 2060, (Piorr, 2011). In France, the suburbs are transitional zones with largely middle-class and poor groups in an uneasy competition.

In the United States, the suburbs are rich and powerful; the dialogue in the United States concerns suburbs development or with pejorative connotations, suburban sprawl (Drier et al., 2001). In the United States, the peripheral development in metropolitan areas consists of a planned development of single-family homes catering to higher income households. Secondly, office parks and clean industries relocate to reduce land costs and reduce the commuting time of already suburbanised employees. In the context of the United States, peripheries are often defined in contradiction to the concept of central city. The situation of the U.S metropolitan region is at odds with most of the rest of the world. The phenomenon of sprawl in Ohio shows rural-to-urban land conversion and sprawl in two ways. To start with, spatial statistics is used to measure the degree of fragmentation and dispersion of development and to determine the model predicted to contribute to a sprawl pattern of development. Next, the problem of spatial error autocorrelation, a problem exists in any model of land use or land values due to the spatial nature of the data. The neighbouring positive spillover effects suggest that, ceteris paribus, new residential development is more likely to occur next to existing development (Carrion-Flores & Irwin, 2004). Urban growth and the price of land and housing prices vary dramatically among metropolitan areas in North America. One such example is Santiago metropolis that houses nearly 5.2 million residents with a share of 50% of Chilean urban population (82%). In 1981, the average house price in San Diego was twice the average house price in Detroit ($48,500). Similarly, the average price of a house in Calgary was more than twice that in Winnipeg (Helsley & Strange, 1990). Santiago supports growth in the north, incorporating some satellite towns, but the bulk of metropolitan growth has occurred on the southern fringe. Most fringe residents are recent low-income migrants from rural areas or provincial towns or villages; Fringe areas are transitional economic and social spaces, articulated to both rural and urban economies and as such, stimulating growth in both the sectors.

In the case of China, the peri-urban zone begins just beyond the contiguous built-up urban area and, sometimes, extends to 150 kilometres from the core city, even as far as 300 km. The role of the Hukou[1] system in the complicated administration of rural-urban migration in mainland China. Hukou conversion process is quite complicated and has significance for the understanding of reforms and problems in the 1980s and 1990s (Chan & Zhang, 1999). The land that can be characterised as peri-urban shifts over time as cities, and the transition zone itself expands outward. What frequently results is a constantly changing mosaic of both traditional and modern land use. Peri-urbanisation does not necessarily result in an end-state that resembles conventional urban or suburban communities.

Studies on Bangkok and Jakarta (Browder et al., 1995) have examined the socio-economic composition and structure of settlements on the metropolitan fringe in some cities in developing countries. Literature shows peri-urban metropolitan fringe as dynamic zones linked to both rural and urban areas, with different aid activities stimulating economic growth of both the areas. Bangkok had approximately 6 million inhabitants in 1985, while its metropolitan area exceeded 8 million. The city suffers the lack of a systematic and enforced planning, its shape being the result of market forces, which have driven the growth towards the urban fringe for the last 20 years. In Jakarta, during the 1970s and the 1980s, rural-urban migration outpaced governmental efforts to manage urban growth through a "closed city" policy that tried to divert growth to selected areas. The 1983 plan encouraged industrial, commercial and residential development on the eastern and western fringes of the metropolitan area, but they could not prevent most of the recent growth from occurring mostly driven by the market into the southern zone. Land markets in African cities are characterised by the co-existence of different modes of supply that originate from the different stages of their development. The land market in peri-urban Accra is an example, where land is rapidly being converted from agricultural to residential use. In peri-urban Accra, land is being converted from agricultural to residential use (Gough & Yankson, 2000). Various scholars point out that peri-urban in Asia, Africa and Europe differs significantly.

India, with the second largest urban population in the world, provides a pertinent backdrop to examining the issues of population and sprawling nature of metropolitan peripheries. The challenges associated with urban and peri-urban growth echo the demographic pressure. The major metropolitan cities in India constitute 28% of urbanites in the total population. In 2001, there were 35 metropolises with more than a million inhabitants, representing 38% of the total urban population in India, among them six mega cities accounted for more than 5 million inhabitants. The rate of urbanisation in India shows a moderate progression from 1981 to 2011 (INDIA, 2011). Various demographic, economic and socio-cultural factors contribute to urban population growth. In the context of global competition, peri-urban areas create growth nodes, especially IT hubs in the peripheries of major metropolises like Bangalore, Hyderabad and Chennai. In India, with an unprecedented population growth and migration, an increased population and urbanisation is inadvertent. Some of the underlying causes of the urbanisation include population growth, economy, patterns of infrastructure initiatives like the construction of roads and the provision of infrastructure using public money encouraging development. Metropolitan cities like Delhi and Bangalore have rapid transition; however, a political and jurisdictional distinction between the central city and rural areas is hard to find. Scholars in the global and local contexts, therefore, ought to define the peri-urban areas in geographical terms.

The transitional peripheral zone of a huge Indian city and the failure of the public sector (i.e. urban local governments) there to give the variety of services vital for the support of an acceptable quality of life because of the rapid population growth (Dahiya, 2003). Gurgaon city is developing as a significant industrial hub; its development made possible by the large-scale acquisition of agricultural lands by the government. The growth of the city has transformed patterns of resource use, social, cultural and economic changes

(Narain, 2009). "Peri-urban areas are mosaics of temporary, new residents and activities mingled with longstanding land uses and receive two flows of migrants creating wide variations in wealth and social status". Peri-urban areas of many cities have both high-value middle-class properties and poor in migrant settlements (Douglas, 2006). Between 1995 and 2004, regional political elites in Andhra Pradesh sought to transfer Hyderabad into a dynamic economic region oriented towards global growth sectors (Kennedy, 2007). Intensification of urbanisation is in the central core areas where open areas and water bodies are there, and it accommodates residential developments. The outcomes indicate that substantial Class I agricultural land was lost because of urban growth during 1997–2010, with an average annual rate of 13%. Around 77% of the accessible land in the peri-urban areas has frail or exceptionally feeble appropriateness for future urban advancement primarily basically in view of the high conservation and agriculture suitability and changing land uses. The case is similar to any other developing city and transition country of the global south and may provide valuable policy lessons (Dutta, 2012).

Studies on various Indian cities show the peri-urban dynamics in metropolitan cities using a theoretical framework of the metropolis as the new urban setup. A Western conceptualisation, the idea of the city, and especially city planning, was exported to the developing world to address its urbanisation problems of the growing cities in Indian context. At present, there is metropolitan development authorities that were established and they prepare master plans for the cities. In most instances of the city examples, "their planning strategies resulted in a conflation of the urban–rural interface into a more complex peri-urban condition, marked by heterogeneity and fragmentation" (Dahiya, 2003). Area-based knowledge deepens recent theoretical attempts to articulate a relational study of space and place (Roy, 2009). According to Schenk and Rohilla (2004), peripheral areas remain unplanned and extremely heterogenous. There arises a question whether there is a common ground in terms of a conceptual or theoretical level in the scholarly study of peri-urban development in the developing world? This can be better understood from peri-urban studies showing the self-regarding nature of the peri-urban. Self-regarding refers to small towns, rural villages or undeveloped areas where inhabitants can live and work within their borders, but these regions are inseparable from the urban economy. The analyses of various peri-urban contexts across different countries lead to the question why do countries subject to the same laws of economics and the same general principles of human relations develop such fundamentally different types of peri-urban spaces? I explore urbanisation and peri-urban land markets of the developing economies specific context of India's Silicon Valley. In the preliminary discussion, evidence of peri-urbanisation is sought from more industrialised and urbanised cities of Europe to obtain a comparative perspective of rural-urban fringes of developed countries and developing country like India.

Rural-Urban Fringe: Evidence from Europe

The traditional definition rural-urban dichotomy is no longer functional to describe these territories, which are in the continuous process of transformation due to the demographic pressure, industrialisation, urbanisation and technological innovation. Scholars have developed new methods to delineate urban and rural areas and have shed new light on the possibilities of describing peri-urban areas more accurately across globe. The rural-urban Fringe of European context is defined in the works of Ravetz et al. (2013) and Nilsson et al. (2013). The structural dynamics of European cities are not adequately understood through traditional spatial analysis. Massive suburbanisation after World War II prompted the emergence of the Compact City ideal, just as the Garden City was a reaction to the overcrowded cities of the nineteenth century (Breheny, 1996).

The global portrait displays the cities of Europe; they have different landscapes, rural-urban typologies and planning. The distinctive features of rural-urban fringe of cities of Europe are compared with India. This enables us to draw a general line in the final conclusions of rural-urban fringes in the debate about sustainable urban and peri-urban development. In order to understand the rural-urban periphery of Europe and India, we adopt a comparative perspective by portraying scenarios of European cities such as Toulouse, Amsterdam, Utrecht and Warsaw. Periphery across the globe is different, periphery of a metropolis of the same country is different in terms of the resources, heterogeneity of population, ethnicity, various social groups, type of businesses, nature of infrastructure and land uses. This perspective of the rural-urban fringe includes

1   Urban Fringes of Post-industrial city: Toulouse
2   Urban Sprawl in the Netherlands
3   Warsaw – The IT City of Poland

Urban Fringes of Post-Industrial City: Toulouse

France experienced a rapid urbanisation since the early Sixties (European Environment Agency, 2006). France is one of the populous countries in Europe. Urban region of France is expected to see its population growth by another 9 million people over the 40 years, placing its population around 72 million by 2050. With its population increasing in spite of decreases of its neighbouring countries. Toulouse is the fourth largest urban area in France. Its town has a population of 755,882 inhabitants and the city, 1.3 million inhabitants. Toulouse metropolis witnessed the speedy population growth in France in the past three decades. Desbordes (2011) points out that Toulouse's urban fabric expanded into rural areas, creating a massive metropolitan vicinity since the late 1970s. The metro area population of Toulouse in 2021 was 1,037,000, with an increase of 1.27% increase from 2020 (World Population Report).

Toulouse, in the South-Western France, experiences significant socio-economic transformations in the last century (Martin-Brelot et al., 2010). It is not only known for art, history and culture but also for the aerospace industry and education. It is the largest centre for aerospace in Europe and the centre for European Airbus and the French space agency. Another hallmark is the green space, a large number of museums, exceptional heritage sites (St Sernin Basilica and the Canal du Midi are UNESCO World Heritage sites). The significant amount of educational facility attracts a large number of international students. Moreover, the salubrious weather made this as a comfortable stay. Toulouse is far from Paris, it has a particular independence and it attracts several industries. The fringe area consists of a "rural" landscape with a predominance of agricultural land uses. It is characterised by its demographic dynamism, notably in the peri-urban area, and its geographical extension (453 municipalities, 4000 km^2). The specific drivers for peri-urban developments include

- Salubrious Weather
- Sufficient landscape available for development
- Better Educational Facilities
- Stability and quality of the urban environment
- Diverse Demography
- Transportation and connectivity – Metro, Train & Tramway
- Accessibility to airport
- Inflow of Immigrants in search of opportunities
- Ethnic Diversities

Peri-Urban Transition of Toulouse Metropolis

Eurostat describes the urban area of Toulouse as the functional urban areas of economic units identified on the base of population density and it includes the "inner city" of a high-density cluster and the "commuting zone", which is the peri-urban ring. Sustainable development of peri-urban areas is a challenge for European cities as well (Antrop, 2005); farming in peri-urban areas deserves deliberate attention as the changes in the land uses are frequent. In urban centres of Europe, there are major differences in languages, wealth, resources and an agglomeration of various social groups. Toulouse residential area consists of young and qualified various ethnic groups, and they settle in Toulouse and gradually less well-off try to settle in the suburbs. But for the planners, stability and quality of the urban environment is critical (Perrin et al., 2013; Salvati & Carlucci, 2014; Duvernoy et al., 2018). The geographic area of the suburbs consists of farming and well known for the cultivation. The vast area from the suburbs of the Toulouse till Tarbes consists of farmlands. Toulouse exhibited the peri-urban transition since 1970s. In 2010, the metropolitan area extended up to 5,400 km^2 (Martin-Brelot et al., 2010); these cluster focus on the highest number of jobs in the region.

French metropolitan regions in common consider agricultural activities for securing metropolitan food systems (Bonnefoy & Brand, 2014) in the context of frequently changing in farming scenario in the European peri–urban fringes (Rothwell et al., 2015). According to the agricultural census, 2010 arable area cultivated nearly 65% of the existing 6,000 metropolitan farms. It provides ecosystem services and reconnects nature and city life (Lévy & Hajek, 2017). Toulouse metropolitan area is an elegant example of local governance and metropolitan farming systems with cultivable crops in the rural landscapes. Across various years, Toulouse has emerged as a cluster of Aerospace industries and hub of education.

Toulouse as Hub of Aerospace Companies

The Toulouse metropolis region dates to World War I is well known for civil and aviation industries though it has invited several start–ups in the recent years in the fields of mobility, drones and technology. Today, it is considered as the hub of Europe's aeronautics and aerospace industry. The economy is based on three major pillars such as large industries, research labs and inflow of students and highly skilled workers. At present, this ecosystem fosters innovation in fields of aviation, artificial intelligence and robotics particularly. Toulouse is an established cluster of commercial aircraft in the world (Insee, 2011); it had a giant leap in the last decade.

Airbus Industrie is a European consortium, and it is based in Toulouse founded in 1969 with a Franco–German lead initially and later by British and Spanish (Niosi & Zhegu, 2005). Toulouse has become a major aerospace cluster, with hundreds of firms.[2] The firms in Toulouse include Turbomeca (turbines), Messier-Dowty – landing gear for 30 airframers both civil and military, including Airbus and EADS Socata, the French member of the European consortium. EADS produces small aircraft and structures for Airbus in Toulouse. Toulouse has attracted several other aerospace producers, the aerospace cluster in the fringes off the city of Toulouse comprises 80% of French aerospace exports and over 9% of all French exports, about €39 billion.[3] According to IHS Global insight (2011), the Aerospace cluster exports €23 billion to the rest of the world excluding trade within the EU and imports nearly €7 billion.

Government plays a significant role in fostering research and development. The Aerospace Valley IFC established by the government is for coordinating scientific research, promoting the cluster and building ties with related clusters in the area. It is a cluster of various prominent universities, Grandes Écoles, including the French Civil Aviation University (ENAC) and Higher Institute of Aeronautics and Space (ISAE); they train hundreds of engineers and conduct advanced research on subjects related to aerospace. Several other lead research centres are located in this cluster including the French Aerospace Lab (ONERA) and the Toulouse branch of the National Centre for Scientific Research (CNRS) (Porter & Takeuchi, 2013); it leads to the spillover effects both globally and locally.

Urban Sprawl in the Netherlands

The Netherlands is known for its relatively successful spatial planning system, managing urban development and open space preservation (Altermann, 1997; Alpkokin, 2012). Dutch word "Ommeland" suggests to the land around a town or city: a peri-urban area, a crucial spatial category (Hornis & Van Eck, 2008). Buffer zones were identified the most urbanised area of the country, the Randstad, between the major cities of Amsterdam, the Hague, Utrecht and Rotterdam. The urban sprawl in Amsterdam and Utrecht are unique as these leading metropolises built on canals particularly in the Netherlands. These locations are known for a substantial proportion of the total housing production in the Netherlands; hence, there is a significant effort in the process of sustainable urban development. The concept of city networks appears to make a contribution to the forget of peri-urban areas in spatial policy. Peri-urban areas are interdependent in many ways – the city depends on the peri-urban area for food and for labour and city is predominantly the economic, political, religious and cultural heart of the wider region. In the last few decades, the governing concept in the national spatial planning reports was to hold the anticipated urban growth while preserving rural and open areas (Faludi & Van Der Valk, 1994).

Amsterdam – A Digital Doorway to Europe

Amsterdam is the largest city in the Netherlands, with roughly 873,000 inhabitants located in the Amstel River (Figure 1.3). Amsterdam city's population increases by 11,000 a year on average, and it enables the construction

Figure 1.3 Amstel River with boats in it and building at its back. Photograph by the author.

of 52,500 new homes, primarily within the city limits, by 2025, further increases the urban sprawl.[4] The significant employment and business opportunities pave way to the transition and outgrowth to the peripheries. The remarkable growth of tech industry attracts people from other parts of the world including different European regions and developing economies.

Amsterdam's digital infrastructure and fast connections make it an easy place to start and establish businesses keeping a door opened to Europe. Amsterdam's qualified workforce, 90% English-speaking population with a global outlook help the tech growth in the city and attract significant amount of Talent pool from across the world. Amsterdam is known for its Amsterdam Science Park and start up village; moreover, it is one of the world's most friendly cities attracted tech companies and investors. Statistics shows that Amsterdam has more start-ups per person than any other place in Europe and there are more than 2,700 start-ups in Amsterdam that's 1.1 per 1,000 inhabitants.[5] It is a well-established urban settlement with the businesses that invest in the Netherlands' technology and IT sector flourish as they are a multilingual Dutch workforce with surplus digital infrastructure with open culture and strong R & D investment by the Dutch government. The Dutch is known for 98% of households having broadband connection. Amsterdam Internet Exchange is the world's leading digital data distributors. Amsterdam attracts employment opportunities by tech companies and with a multilingual culture; more English-speaking population drives the fast urbanisation and sprawling of the city.

Utrecht – The Canal City

Utrecht is the fourth largest city and a municipality of the Netherlands, capital and most populous city of the province of Utrecht (Figure 1.4). Utrecht is considered as world's most beautiful canal city. Geographically, it is in the eastern corner of the Randstad conurbation, and in the very centre of mainland Netherlands. Utrecht is a unique city in the Netherlands until the Dutch Golden Age; further it surpassed by Amsterdam as the cultural centre and most populous city. The urban development in the densely populated region of Amsterdam further sprawls to the nearby urban locales like Utrecht. At present, the urbanisation pattern is exemplified by polycentric urban structures, a strong urban concentration in Utrecht and other urban centres. It shows combination of compact growth and polycentric pattern, the demand for new residential land-use will be considerable in the coming decades. The densely populated and highly urbanised Randstad region in the western part of the country (the area including the Amsterdam, Rotterdam, The Hague and Utrecht city regions with about 7 million inhabitants) has been exposed to policy visions and measures related to urban land use (Dieleman & Musterd, 1992).

Utrecht is a transport "hub" with highways, canals and railways transecting the city (Green Surge, 2015). Utrecht facilitates urban population growth within the existing city and not to build outside the current municipal

Figure 1.4 Utrecht in early period. Photograph by the author.

Figure 1.5 Utrecht in various ages. Photograph by the author.

boundaries.[6] Utrecht is a magnificent canal city, the inner city is surrounded by canals and old forts, some of the old fortifications transformed into green parks and sidewalks, an important element of the modern urban green structure (Tjallingii, 2003).

Utrecht has a great tradition of Dutch spatial planning; it is a part of the densely populated and highly urbanised Randstad region in the western part of the country that is subjected to policy visions and measures related to urban land use (Dieleman & Musterd, 1992). Utrecht is the second most competitive region, known for EU Dom Tower, wharfs and canals (Figure 1.5). Sustainability is at the heart of Dutch spatial planning. Utrecht became the third Dutch city to declare a climate emergency in 2019. Being an attractive city to live, work, study, invest and to do business, unique known for education with a young population and highly educated workforce in the country. Utrecht is a knowledge-based economy due to the investments by innovative companies located in the city and it has an efficient labour market. Sustainable modes of transportation and green credentials are the hall marks of the Dutch model. Utrecht is a rapidly expanding city with green ambitions.

Warsaw – The IT City of Poland

City centre of Warsaw covers a surface area of 517.24 km^2, but the metropolitan area sprawls outward to nearly 6,100.43 km^2. The population density of the city is approximately 3,372 residents per square kilometre (8,730/sq mi).[7] Warsaw has a truly rich history of culture and repeated restoration after WWII and it's a place of historical attractions, museums and well-connected infrastructure. Warsaw, the capital of Poland, is well connected to other Polish cities, such as Lodz and Cracow. The Warsaw region, since the Second World War, was responsible for the self-organising developments of the peri-urban development. During the communist regime, the key driver of this development is the governmentally induced developments, but after the market reforms autonomous, market-orientated, developments were possible. The first developments in the first half are denoted by these pull factors, but during the second half, these same factors became pushes (Beeftink & de Roo, 2009). Since reforms a self-organising process involving the building of single-family houses in the surroundings of Warsaw began to influence peri-urban development. Farm land, which are relatively small in size, privately owned and run at relatively low profits, are especially vulnerable to this land use change and it is further accelerated by the acquisition of land for IT and businesses in the past few decades (Figure 1.6).

Warsaw a Hub of IT and Businesses

Warsaw is one of the largest places for IT Services in Poland attracting investments from worldwide and fostering enterprises in the city. Warsaw is well known for its extensive infrastructure, connectivity and business friendly climate. Among all, the quality of transportation is remarkable, 2019 Warsaw was considered the best location to do business.[8] It is estimated that there are nearly 65,000 IT companies operating in Poland and

Figure 1.6 Warsaw city centre and Palace of Culture. Photograph by the author.

majority registered in Warsaw. Since 2019, Warsaw is a leader in terms of the number of IT, BPO, SCC and R&D centres in Poland. Some of the global business magnets invested in Warsaw include Microsoft and Google. Tech giant Microsoft announced massive funding in the recent years in Poland, aiming to establish a technological hub for the entire Eastern Europe. The hallmark of the city is new possibilities, accessibility, affordability, better investment avenues and well connected and one of low-cost cities in Europe. The big four accounting firms that have its base in Warsaw are KPMG, Pwc, Deloitte and EY. Some of the companies that have decided to invest in Warsaw include Huawei, Johnson & Johnson, Oerlikon Business Services Europe and Sage. The smart business hub of Warsaw includes the number of firms that diligently foster businesses; they are Google Campus, the Smolna Center of Entrepreneurship, the Targowa Center of Creativity, Startup Hub Warsaw, and The City of Warsaw – Economic Development Department. Warsaw emerged as the affordable destination for the IT services and right choice for companies. For a few years now, Warsaw is in the process to carry the smart city concept, constructing an environmentally friendly community, fostering new sustainable business models and, at the same time, attracting worldwide investments. Microsoft targets to construct proposed as a digital hub – "Polish Digital Valley" in Warsaw. The significant growth of the IT and businesses leads to the expansion of city to the fringes. Poland's proximity to Germany, for as soon as in its current records, would be a big plus because it would ease the businesses and connects to the largest economy in Western Europe (Figure 1.7).

Figure 1.7 Warsaw sky, outdoor and grass. Photograph by the author.

Education and Skilled Manpower

Warsaw is a home to 15 public universities and 55 private universities; Warsaw metropolis is also an excellent hub of skilled professionals, and Warsaw draws IT professionals not only from Polish cities and from countries like India. Majority of Warsaw population are graduates and the availability of skilled labour attracts the global business tycoons to the most affordable city of Europe. Warsaw offers a well-qualified workforce as well as investment support to start ups and business enterprises.

Specific Drivers for Peri-Urban Developments

- Comfortable and affordable living conditions
- Global service economy
- Less rentals
- Development of mixed office and retail facilities
- Infrastructure and better connectivity

Peri-urban development causes conflicts between rural and urban environment and agricultural zones. It also challenges of demarcation of urban and rural areas as they are usually applied in policy and regulatory terms. Warsaw being an IT and educational hub, the further expansion of the city is becoming more tough and precarious when the chance of land sale and urban improvement increases. Loss of cultivation of land due to sale and dom developments has an impact on food self-reliance and the ability to promote any surpluses to urban dwellers. Above all, urban development of Poland, particularly Warsaw, endowed with its regional specificity: Polish culture had a landowning and rural character since the Middle Ages until almost the mid-twentieth century. The network of cities formed at that time matched the needs of economy and rural settlements across years. The specific nature of urbanisation under socialism in Central and Eastern Europe was called "controlled urbanisation" by (Musil, 1984), while forced socialist type of industrialisation was named "imposed" or Morawski (1980). Both processes helped in the rural to urban transformation process, and during 1950–55, both the urbanisation processes and the industrialisation processes were the most intensive. The migration pattern from rural to urban areas was regional in nature, i.e. it involved migration to the nearest major city. Interregional and intercity migration concerns mostly the largest urban metropolitan areas of Warsaw, which attracted the immigrants from all over the country and now from the international borders.

In the two decades (1970s and 1980s), the urbanisation process became more important than the industrialisation process despite huge investments in industry. The concept of previous socialist city in Poland is now related to the concept of industrial city in the recent decades. Currently, the challenge is making urban areas less vulnerable to political, economic and environmental changes.

Global South and Global North Perspective of Peri-Urban

The periphery of the cities of Europe is considered as well developed, known for connectivity and accessibility with better land use planning; however, the periphery of the metropolis of the developing country like India, for example Bangalore in comparison with Europe, is lagging behind in terms of its infrastructure, land policy and administration although Bangalore is considered as one of the advanced cities of South Asia. The extent of urbanisation in "Global North" is rapid with the increase in the population, but in terms of the mechanisms to cope up with the rapid urbanisation and technological developments, it lags behind. The factors influencing the peri-urban scenario of Global South and North deserve special mention. Peri-Urban transition in Developing countries and Developed countries in the following characteristics.

Global South

- Movement to cities and Rising Urban population
- Search for employment
- In search of better facilities for Education
- Shift to urban life

Global North

- Decreasing population at the city centre
- Slow population increase and rural urbanisation
- Buffer zone of agricultural and non–agricultural activities
- Amenities and quality of living

Peri-urban areas differ globally. Various studies discussed the peri-urban development across globe (Woltjer, 2014). The Peri-urban areas of developing countries significantly differ from the developed countries due to rapid growth and physical, environmental, economic and social factors. Peri-urban areas contribute to economic growth, significant amount of urbanisation and population growth. But often these pressures compromise environmental qualities and the productivity of agriculture in developing countries.

The global perspective of "north and south" peri-urban is the focal point of the discussion with the peri-urban development and planning and policies from worldwide particularly the periphery of three European countries. In the case of Indian cities, high economic growth and urbanisation have been

Table 1.1 Comparative perspective of rural urban fringes of Europe and India

	Factors Affecting Peri-Urbanisation
Europe	<ul><li>Global cities, international in nature</li><li>Cluster of industry lead growth</li><li>Low rate of population growth</li><li>Plethora of opportunities</li><li>Different ethnicity and social groups</li><li>Hubs of education</li><li>Immigrants from developing countries and other parts of Europe.</li><li>Controls for land utilisation by the government</li><li>Government sponsored developments and real estate</li></ul>
India – Bangalore	<ul><li>People from different parts of India</li><li>IT based, Industry lead growth</li><li>Rapid Population growth rate</li><li>Education hub and leading private educational institutions and state-sponsored research institutions</li><li>Rapidly growing real estate segment</li><li>Deviation in the land utilisation from the proposed pattern</li><li>Difference in the land, Governance and administration from that of Europe</li></ul>

mutually dependent in the past few decades. Fringes and cities have expanded swiftly with the increasing numbers of migrants, mostly from villages in search of employment opportunities. The demand for real estate and mobility has impacted the movement to the fringe areas. Comparative perspective of rural urban fringes of Europe and India is given in Table 1.1.

Global cities known for their planned development and controlled population growth which attracts significant global population from Europe and other parts of the world, as the tech companies provide innumerable opportunities to the rest of the world. Indian cities sprawl rapidly; however, the poor city planning leads to haphazard nature of urban and leads to the outgrowth of peripheries. Although the global South and the global North have significant amount of IT lead growth, the scenario of developing economies is a special case as the population is increasing in multiple amounts. The challenges pertaining to Global South include climate change, declining peri-urban agriculture, changing land utilisation, conversion of agricultural land for non-agricultural purposes. In order to understand the scenario in depth, we explore changing land utilisation and land conversion in the context of dynamic shift of peri-urban areas in developing economy by considering the peri-urbanisation process of India's Silicon Valley.

Peri-Urbanisation of India's Silicon Valley

One hundred years ago, approximately 15% of the world population was living in urban areas, but today it is nearly 50%. Metropolitan cities in India are growing at an unprecedented rate, especially cities like Bangalore, Chennai, Delhi, Kolkata and Navi Mumbai. A large chunk of the population from all parts of the country has migrated to cities and they live in and around peripheries of cities; similarly, there is a high demand for housing and other services and as a result agricultural land is being converted to residential, industrial and commercial activities. The establishment of industrial and IT corridors in the peripheries leads to the growth of the economy, contributing to the state domestic product. The growth of services and exports exceeds the output from primary and secondary sectors. The changing type of land use is the direct outcome of changes in land prices, ability to pay and the extent of exploitation of a given piece of land. Peri-urban centred real estate market influences land price considerably. Few studies have been undertaken, in this context, studying the peripheral land market. There is a high demand for land with a booming urban land value; land value differs across different regions of the same city. That is because the value of land in the core areas of the city is different from the land value in the periphery areas. There are fewer studies that have attempted to explore the pattern of land value and the nature of land transactions in the peri-urban land markets. In the past few decades, there has been a considerable increase in the property prices in the peripheries.

The land management practices in the peri-urban land markets have continued unplanned and unorganised. This is further aggravated by increase in the population and a large-scale migration to Bangalore City. The absence of a well-planned land management system has resulted in spiralling land prices, speculation, inflation and growth of informal settlements that unfavourable impact the overall improvement of a city. Infringement of urban land use regulations is because of the lack of valid cadastral, registration and approved tenure records resulting in a haphazard and unconstrained land use, truly affecting the efficiency of the city. In this scenario of the dynamic spatial growth of the city, transition is attributed by two important factors: first, rapid population growth due to rural–urban migration; second, rapid physical expansion of the city and absence of rural–urban administrative boundary. Given this spatial expansion and the transition nature of the city, we discuss the perspective of peri-urban Bangalore.

Bangalore is the capital city of the Karnataka state. It is one of the quickest developing urban communities in India and it has additionally been perceived as "Silicon Valley of India" for leading the development of IT-based businesses in the country. It is a fast-growing metropolitan city of India and a prominent example of urban growth. The rise and growth of IT industries started in Bangalore in the 1980s; soon, MNCs realised the value of Bangalore city and acquired land for the businesses in the periphery of the city. The IT industries located in the periphery of Southeast Bangalore led to rapid developments. South Bangalore has significant outgrowths in recent years. There are two major reasons why Bangalore periphery is identified for the study. First, there is a significant change in the land uses in the growing periphery of Bangalore. Second the growth of the city leads to spillover effects and economic impacts on land value. The periphery became a preferred destination of investment. The land value in the peripheral areas increased considerably. The real estate agents such as builders focus on the identified periphery as the channel of future investment. An attempt of analysing land values will bring more insights to the dynamic changes in the peripheral land markets. The government intervention in land market is a major focus of the study in the context of the changing land use and land value. There arises a relevant debate whether the local government policy with respect to land market in the fringe areas can overcome the problems of unplanned development especially when the existing land use pattern differs from the proposed land use pattern significantly.

The role of government intervention is debated by identifying the elements that contribute to such a policy with respect to land use planning and land values. This is an attempt to identify whether local government initiatives are essential for resolving rural–urban dichotomy amidst the unplanned development in the periphery. Another important aspect in this study is with respect to the various issues related to the land transaction, the increase in the volume of urban land transactions and changes in the land use pattern have complicated the formal process of land registration. There arises the need for a well-maintained land record system for both urban and peri-urban areas.

There are endeavours made towards this path through Bhoomi, Karnataka Valuations and E-Registration Integrated (KAVERI) and Mojini initiatives. However, there are issues that are still to be addressed. This is an attempt to explore the changing pattern of Land Use/Land Cover and land value in the peripheral areas of Bangalore Metropolitan city with specific reference to increasing land prices and active land transactions in the peripheral land markets.

With the advent of IT industries, just as various ventures in different segments and the beginning of financial advancement since the mid-1990s, Bangalore had taken lead in service-based industries fuelling considerable development of the city both economically and spatially. As per 2011 enumeration, Bangalore populace was 9.6 million and considered as India's third most crowded city and fifth most populous urban agglomeration. Bangalore had an expected populace of 10.1 million in its urban territory in 2014, and the population is 12 million[9] in 2019. It is now the one among the most populous cities in the world. Simultaneously, farmlands in and around the city were seriously affected, however, with the enhanced demand for land encourages real estate firms to acquire land in the periphery.

An overwhelming volume of literature shows that urban studies revolve around the city itself. The peri-urban areas frequently face conflicts and a relentless neglect. The blurring of an urban-rural boundary enlivened researchers from different parts of the world to explain peri-urban in various nations and in diverse contexts. The historical dichotomy of urban and rural space started to blur in Europe with the formation of nation states, industrialisation and the liberalisation of the economy in the nineteenth century (Nilsson et al., 2013). The concept of peri-urban interface belongs to the newly urbanised countries of the third world, mainly Latin America, Southeast Asia and Africa. The urban development during 1975–2000 was predominantly concentrated in these third world nations. The haphazard nature of urbanisation and unplanned migration resulted in growth of extensive peri-urban interface regions in different parts of the word. According to Kundu et al. (2003), in India, the suburbs are "degenerated peripheries", while in the United States, the suburbs are rich and incredible, and in France, the suburbs are transitional zones consisting mainly of the middle class and the poor. As we have seen above peri-urban areas around the world are different; similarly, the peri-urban areas in and around Bangalore are different. Cities like Bangalore are portrayed by a major transition in the rural-urban continuum, and as the populace and geographic extension expand, the city faces huge dangers to its future development and construction for the sake of commercial, industrial and residential projects, prompts land-use and land cover changes. It leads to the transformation of rural economy revolve around IT corridors, service trade and urban land markets. In spite of the fact that this transition process has brought about enormous pressure on peri-urban land, it additionally profited the Bangalore economy with the development of IT corridors in South Bangalore, Electronic City and North Bangalore with the foundation of the air terminal and growth of IT and business parks. However, different land uses affect economic growth differently.

I comprehend the land use dynamics around the peripheries of Bangalore City and to establish the relationship between land use and land value. I start with the assumption that the two peripheral cluster is different in terms of its growth dynamics; therefore, it is an effort to understand the divergent phenomenon. The land market analysis focuses on the two diverse peripheries of fast changing Bangalore. Peri-urban dynamics results in conflicts and challenges, on the one hand, and on the other hand, it reaps benefits to the society through the creation of external economies and growth of industries, services, exports and real estate. I draw attention to the geography and economics of the dynamic periphery of Bangalore and explain how Bangalore city growth and expansion influence the peri-urban.

Growth and Transition of Bangalore Impacting Peri-Urban Bangalore

Since independence, Bangalore city has experienced various periods of economic development. In the first stage (1951–61), growth was due to public sector undertakings with employment generation avenues businesses. The subsequent phase (1960–70) was fundamentally a result of the enterprises and state-run businesses. The third stage was because of the off shoot of private sectors since 1980s. The fourth stage is due to the growth of IT and other services. This stage proceeds till the present day of Bangalore (Sastry, 1988). A few scholars have contrasted the unprecedented development of Bangalore and the circumstances of Delhi and Paris. The transition of Bangalore is better understood by tracing its physical spread.

Physical Spread of Bangalore

The major concern is the absence of capacity to ingest mass migration populace for IT. The physical spread of the city in the initial stages is mainly attributed to the following factors.

1   *Institutional foundations:* This is a direct result of the physical spread with institutional jump frogging of IIS, along these lines the areas like Malleswaram, Srirampuram, Vyalikaval, Sheshadripuram and Sadashivanagar. So also, the institutional leapfrogging of University of Agricultural Sciences (UAS) Bangalore.
2   *Large Scale Industries:* Hindustan Aeronautics (HAL), Hindustan Machine Tools Ltd (HMT), Indian Telephone Industries limited and Bharath Electronics Limited (BEL) and the Peenya Industrial cluster.
3   *IT corridors:* The city has extended substantially in the most recent two decades due to the development of IT corridors with places like

Whitefield, Electronic City and Manyata Tech Park locales being typical examples. This, in turn, has led to developments to the prompt neighbourhood, demanding residential and infrastructural facilities.

4 *Growth of Infrastructural and transportation facilities:* The physical spread of Bangalore is attributed to the foundation of transportation facilities, air terminals, metros, etc. The recorded example of urban spread is unique in relation to the present setting, the central point is the fast populace development and movement of individuals to the core necessitated more outgrowth to the peripheries.

Spatial-Temporal Growth of Bangalore

After the period of Kempegowda, Bangalore City became extremely fast at the time of British Rule. In the first half of the twentieth century, Bangalore developed minimal greater than the British period. Post-Independence with the formation of Karnataka state between the period of 1947 and 1971, Bangalore was considered the capital town of Karnataka state. A portion of the significant territories joining the Bangalore city was Jayanagar zone, Vijayanagara, Hosakerehalli, Rajaji Nagar Industrial Area, Yeshwanthpur, Goraguntepalya, Mathikere and K R Puram. The real city growth began during the period 1981–2001. After 2001, Bruhat Bengaluru Mahanagara Palike (BBMP) twice separated the administration boundary and added some more regions to the Bangalore city and named as BBMP.[10]

Studies show developed land is expanding from 1973 to 2010 in all directions with the decline of vegetation. In 1973, built-up was high in North East directions, whereas in 2010, built-up land increased in North East, South West directions due to the compact growth of residential areas and commercial complex areas. Infilling of these places during 1973–2010 because of conversion of open spaces and vegetated regions into the built-up land. Infilling urban development in the locale and increment in built up land is because of increasingly commercial and other services activities. Land use changes during 1973–2010 demonstrate an expansion in urban land every which way because of thick neighbourhoods like Malleswaram, Jayanagar, Yeshwanthpur and small-scale industry estates like Rajaji Nagar Industrial zone and so forth (Ramachandra and Bharath, 2012). Thus, Bangalore city extended, added to this the land utilisation has changed significantly over time and population is a significant driver of the growth of the city.

Figure 1.8 shows the growth of population of Bangalore from 1950 to 2020 and projections from 2020 to 2030 based on United Nations population prospects. The United Nations populace projections are likewise included during that time 2035. The present population of Bangalore in 2020 is 12,327,000, a 3.74% expansion from 2019. The population of Bangalore in 2019 was 11,883,000, a 3.87% expansion from 2018, in 2018 was 11,440,000, a 4.09% expansion from 2017. In 2017, it was 10,990,000, a 4.1% increment from 2016 (Table 1.2).[11]

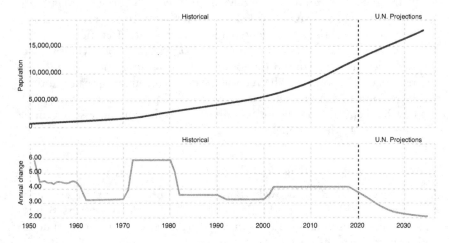

Figure 1.8 Historical trend in population growth. UN population prospects.

Table 1.2 Historical population growth of Bangalore

Bangalore – Historical Population Data

Year	Population	Growth Rate
2020	12,327,000	3.74%
2019	11,883,000	3.87%
2018	11,440,000	4.09%
2017	10,990,000	4.10%
2016	10,557,000	4.10%
2015	10,141,000	4.10%
2014	9,742,000	4.10%
2013	9,358,000	4.09%
2012	8,990,000	4.10%
2011	8,636,000	4.10%
2010	8,296,000	4.10%
2009	7,969,000	4.09%
2008	7,656,000	4.11%
2007	7,354,000	4.11%
2006	7,064,000	4.10%
2005	6,786,000	4.10%
2004	6,519,000	4.10%
2003	6,262,000	4.11%
2002	6,015,000	4.08%
2001	5,779,000	3.55%
2000	5,581,000	3.26%

Source: DESA (2014).

In the last 60 years, Bangalore witnessed an immense growth in its population. The city was home to more than 778,977 people in 1951 and Bangalore became one of the million urban communities of India since 1961. Rapid industrialisation and urban development in the city have seen an enormous growth in its population. In 1961, Population of Bangalore city was 1.2 million. The city was the sixth largest city of India with a complete of 1,207,000 people. Growth of population in Bangalore was extremely high in decades 1941–51 and 1971–81. This was the time when many manufacturing companies set up their base in Bangalore. An enormous number of immigrants from Northern Karnataka moved to Bangalore during this period between the years 1941 and 1981.

By and large, the city of Bangalore suffers from over population which leads to natural resources constraint. Bangalore population increased from 5.1 million to 8.4 million from 2001 to 2011. Bangalore is growing faster than ever, crossing the 10-million imprint in 2013. The urban locale has grown three times faster than the state, and it is now home to 16% of the state's population. The population of Bangalore increased by 2,185,452 since 2015, which represents a 3.98% yearly change. Bangalore's 2020 population is now estimated at 12,326,532 (DESA, 2014). The above estimates represent the urban agglomeration of Bangalore, which includes Bangalore's population in addition to adjacent suburban areas.[12] The above trend in the population shows the spatial expansion of Bangalore. Bangalore has developed as fast-growing city, and the significant purpose behind the progress is the development of industrial and IT corridors and migration of people to the city. This led to the active growth of land markets in the periphery.

Peri-Urban Cluster of Bangalore

Urbanisation has resulted in the sudden growth of large cities as islands of development. One such example is that of Bangalore, especially the outgrowths in the peripheries of Bangalore. Bangalore is remarkable for the authentic realities. It pulled in different classes of individuals from different parts of India. At first, this fascination was mainly direct result of trade, business and industrial purpose; however, the quick-changing nature of the city is ascribed to the development of Information Technology in the peripheries for as long as two decades. Satellite Town Ring Road (STRR) connects the peri-urban cluster of Bangalore.

There are eight peri-urban clusters in Bangalore (Figure 1.9). They are Doddaballapur, Devanahalli, Hoskote and Nelamangala, Kanakapura, Magadi and Ramanagar Taluk and Anekal Taluk. The definition of peri-urban is often difficult. As per BMRDA, the area beyond the 198 wards of BBMP is considered as the periphery. However, the peri-urban space of this city changes rapidly.

Figure 1.9 Bangalore periphery. Compilation by the author.

Southeast Industrial Corridor

Southeast periphery is known for industrial and real estate growth, and they are growth corridors. It is known for its growth for industries, strategic location, connectivity via metro, proximity to IT corridors, social infrastructure and the growth of real estate. The key belts in East Periphery are the Hoskote-Malur corridor, Hoskote-Chintamani corridor, Hoskote Kadugo-di-Whitefield corridors and Hoskote-KR Puram corridors. Hoskote has Industrial Area houses 200 industrial units. It is a home to manufacturing units of many corporate giants, VOLVO, Bando & Honda manufacturing plants, nearly 468 Japanese companies have units on the Bangalore-Chennai corridor. Hoskote comprises of industrial hub, housing auto spare parts, chassis works as well as warehousing and logistics units. Some of the major auto manufacturers have their facilities here. Hoskote is well connected to several of the other industrial areas, including Vemgal and Narsapura, and also areas emerging along the Bangalore-Chennai belt. More than 40,000 Japanese expected to work in this corridor, and it is known for Special Economic Zone (SEZ) for Electronics, hardware and IT at Bagur, Aero IT SEZ under development at Budigere to create employment for 100,000. East corridor is known for IT companies, logistics park and warehousing hub, proposed apparel park and self-contained townships and all this led to the growth of real estate in the East periphery.

Kanakapura South periphery is known for its Industrial belt in Harohalli. It is a well-known infrastructural corridor which transformed Kanakapura into a thriving real estate destination. Kanakapura is easily accessible via NICE Road, and it has improved connectivity of this area with Electronic City, Bannerghatta Road, Mysore Road and the proposed Peripheral Ring Road (PRR). Industrial growth in Kanakapura Road in South Bangalore is mainly by KIADB. KIADB's proposal is to build a multi-product industrial park encompassing about 904.86 hectares as part of combined development of phase II and III of Harohalli industrial park. And it is the residential and commercial corridor that registered exponential growth over the last few years. Kanakapura Road has witnessed bulky investments by many established corporates like Saint Gobain, Toyota, A.O Smith, Namdhari, Anthem Bio Sciences – Unit II. The Metro has created great connectivity which reduced commuting to major IT Hubs like Electronic City and Bannerghatta Road and companies like Infosys, Wipro, Bharat Heavy Electricals Limited, Tata Consultancy Services and others are just a mere 30-minute commute.

Imminent projects of the 300 acre all women Tech Park, Harohalli Industrial Estate, Jigani Industrial Estate, Metro Phase II and more has led to a major growth around South periphery. Thus, Kanakapura is a growing real estate market with the influence of above-mentioned factors. The growth of industries and infrastructural corridors in both peripheral areas leads to spillover benefits in the periphery. Hoskote and Kanakapura taluks are known for its peri-urban influence due to its significant industrial growth leading to dynamic transition.

Geographic Settings

Hoskote-East Periphery

Hoskote forms a part of the eastern side of the Bangalore Rural District and lies between the North latitude 12 degree 51' to 13 degree 15' and east longitudes 77 degree 41' to 77 degree 58'.[13] The climate of Hoskote Taluk, which is closer to Bangalore city, enjoys a pleasant and salubrious climate and free from extremes and is classified as a seasonally dry tropical climate with four seasons (Figures 1.10 and 1.11).

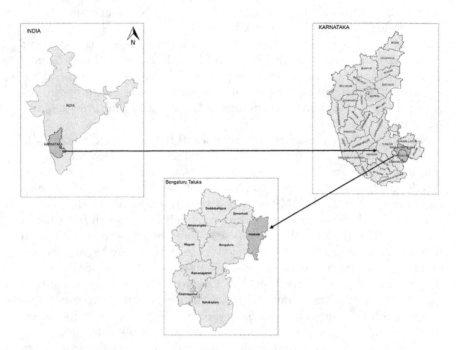

Figure 1.10 Geographical location of Hoskote. Compilation by the author.

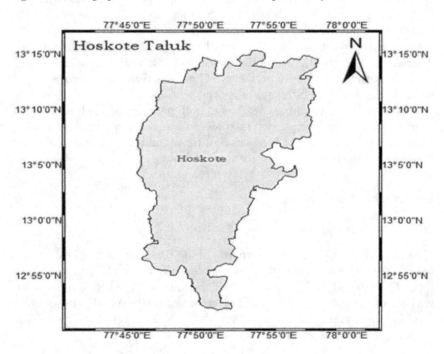

Figure 1.11 Hoskote map. Compilation by the author.

Socio-Economic Characteristics of Hoskote

Hoskote LPA comprises 316 villages out of which 300 villages and one Town Municipal Corporation (TMC) of Hoskote are in Hoskote Taluk and 16 villages in Bangalore East Taluk and five Hoblis in particular Sulibele, Nandagudi, Kasaba, Jadigenahalli and Anugondanahalli. Further, Hoskote LPA divided into a number of use zones such as Residential, Commercial, Industrial, Public and Semi Public, Park and Open space. Hoskote has potential for fast growth in various sectors such as information technology, tourism, infrastructure, agro and food-based industries and is connected to with the other urban centres viz Bangalore, Kolar, Devanahalli, Malur, Chintamani by good roads. Hoskote taluk is surrounded by Chintamani of Kolar District on the North, Kolar District on East, Malur taluk on the South and Bangalore Urban District on the west. The Taluk has witnessed an improvement in the areas of education, medical aid, drinking water and power supply. The number of inhabitants in Hoskote was predominantly relying upon Bangalore for employment opportunities.

It is one of the encompassing satellite towns of Bangalore going about as a counter magnet to Bangalore city and is inviting enterprises, ancillary developments and investments and is situated on major transport corridors. The advancement in the metropolitan zone of Bangalore created potential for regions in and around Hoskote town.[14] Hoskote, East Bangalore laying at the convergence of National Highway 4 and National Highway 207 and is more sought-after by property investor destination. There is a growing demand for housing; this is because of its vicinity to the IT centre point of Whitefield. The fringe region around Hoskote is encompassed by IT/ITeS centre points on Old Madras Road, Whitefield and commercial activities in the north-east quadrant of the Outer Ring Road (ORR). This locale is developed due to an increasing demand for residential areas. Moreover, advancement of the proposed apparel park, self-contained townships, hospitality projects and improved connectivity via metro have changed the scenario (Figure 1.12 and Table 1.3).

A considerable increase in the population of Hoskote LPA from 1981 to 2011 indicates that, because of its proximity to Bangalore, both Hoskote town and taluk are pulling in Bangalore's populace looking for budget housing and employment opportunities in view of a strong economic base of the town. It is observed that the population of Hoskote town just as different settlements in the LPA expanded from 2001 to 2011 at the pace of 19.96% on a normal, while the expansion in the population of Hoskote town alone from 2001 to 2011 is 55.85% (Master Plan, 2031)˙ The principal factors adding to the development in Hoskote are nearness to Bangalore City and consequent inducement from the BMR, commercial and industrial developments along significant roads. It incorporates two National Highways, three State Highways, seven significant area streets, two National Bank for Agriculture and Rural Development (NABARD) Roads, STRR, Intermediate ring Road and Industrial improvements by KIADB, open and private divisions. Key

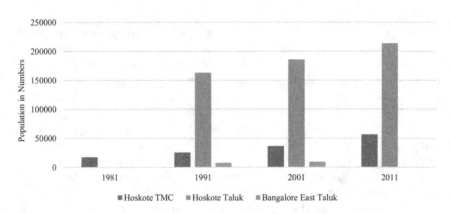

Figure 1.12 Population growth of Hoskote LPA. Compilation by the author.

Table 1.3 Population growth of Hoskote LPA (population in numbers)

Hoskote LPA	Year			
	1981	*1991*	*2001*	*2011*
Hoskote TMC	17,538	25,533	36,323	56,613
Hoskote Taluk	–	162,966	185,741	213,697
Bangalore East taluk	–	7499	9140	11,683
Total	203,594	195,998	231,204	281,993

Source: 1981–2011 Census – Govt of India, Taluk web site, Chief Officer, Hoskote TMC.

drivers of the development are (1) IT Corridors, (2) Manufacturing centre point, (3) Connectivity, (4) Social Infrastructure and (5) Land value. With the end goal of the Land Use/Land Cover examination, two Peri Villages of Hoskote Taluk are chosen. They are Devanagundi and Tavarekere, and for the land market analysis, five peri-urban villages are identified based on the Bangalore Metropolitan Region Development Authority (BMRDA) list of peripheries.

Kanakapura–South Periphery

This is an attractive real estate destination. Kanakapura is well connected to Outer Ring Road, Banashankari, JP Nagar and Uttarahalli. This area is also easily accessible from other suburbs such as Bannerghatta Road, Electronic City and Jayanagar. Connectivity and better infrastructure have fuelled the growth of real estate activity on the Kanakapura Road (Figures 1.13 and 1.14).

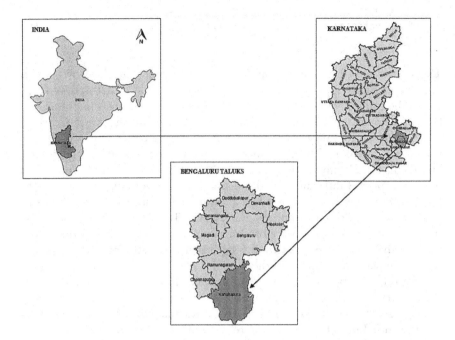

Figure 1.13 Geographical location of Kanakapura. Compilation by the author.

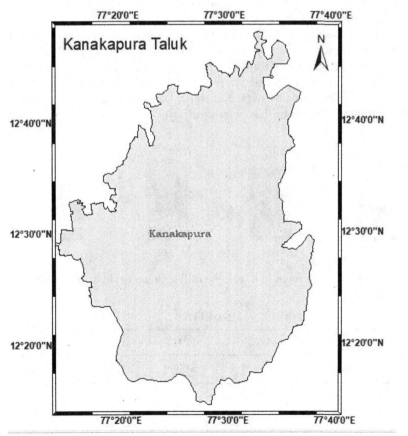

Figure 1.14 Kanakapura Taluk map. Compilation by the author.

Socio-Economic Characteristics of Kanakapura

The Kanakapura Local Planning Area was announced by the BMRDA in 2006. It is situated in the South-West part of the Bangalore Metropolitan Region. The total spread of the Taluk is 412.78 sq km and consisting of 85 villages and Kanakapura TMC. The Bangalore Mysore Infrastructure Corridor passes in close proximity to the LPA on the northeast which enhanced its development potential. There are four significant growth nodes-Kaggalipura, Harohalli, Kanakapura and Sathanur. Kanakapura is the Taluk headquarters of Kanakapura Taluk and is additionally a Town Municipal according to Census. This area is mainly residential with a few institutional structures to take into account the urban needs. Kanakapura Taluk lies in the Cauvery basin. The fundamental tributary of Cauvery, River Arkavathy, streams in the taluk. Kanakapura is secured by the sub-basin Arkavathy and drains southwards. The climatic pattern of the region is hot, moist, semi-arid ecological sub region with period of 150–180 days. Kanakapura LPA belongs to the Eastern dry agro-climatic Zone. It encounters wonderful climate practically all through the year.[15] It comprises parts of Kanakapura Taluk and the Bangalore South Taluk. It comprises 86 towns and one TMC and has an absolute population of 1.81 lakh. The total urban population of the LPA stands at 54,021, while the rustic populace 1.27 lakhs (INDIA, 2011 – *population census*; Figure 1.15 and Table 1.4).

It tends to be seen that the development of population in the Kanakapura has not been noteworthy, as compared to different regions of the BMR. The decadal development pace of Kanakapura is 6.25% (Census, 2011). The moderate development rate might be ascribed to the moderate pace of industrial growth. It is wealthy because of farm income; however, the agrobusiness has not been upheld. Migration has been significant in some of the villages of

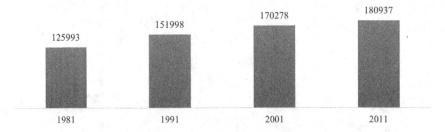

Figure 1.15 Population growth of Kanakapura LPA. Compilation by the author.

Table 1.4 Population growth of Kanakapura LPA

Year	1981	1991	2001	2011
Population (in numbers)	125,993	151,998	170,278	180,937

Source: Census 2011.

the Taluk. Significant development in this region is Intermediate Ring Road (IRR) going through Harohalli, STRR, Bangalore – Mysore infrastructure corridor towards the north and NH 209 going through the region by 2021, KIADB industrial cluster in Harohalli-Bidadi region, employment opportunities for the individuals, accessibility of groundwater, 800 modest and SSI units, 168 units in huge and medium segment, a generous level of fortune 500 organisations and different MNCs, STRR, IRR improving network to all the taluks of external BMR, Bangalore International Airport which is 75 km away and Domestic air terminal at HAL, which is 45 km away and the increase in land value in Bangalore is obliged due to non-accessibility of costly land, export potential of Granite quarrying, Agri Export Zone (AEZ) for gherkins, rose onion and blooms (CTD, 1989), Opportunity for aesthetic amenities, entertainment clubs, inns, nursing homes and scope of commercial exploitation of biotechnology. KIADB industrial estate is the major modern zone in the Kanakapura. Since the National Highway 209 is a major regional linkage, it assumes a significant role in the development (KIADB, 1995). Key Drivers of the growth of this LPA are (1) Connectivity, (2) Physical Infrastructure, (3) Social Infrastructure, (4) Affordable Housing and (5) Price of Land. The selected peri villages for the land use/land cover analysis are Harohalli and Sathanur, and for the land market analysis, five peri-urban villages are used from Kanakapura. The entire aspect of the study covers development of fringe land market of Bangalore.

Rural-Urban Migration and Real Estate Prices

Why the price of land has risen so rapidly in the last decade in Bangalore and why is the land in core so expensive? The most direct explanation is that while the demand for urban land has increased, its supply has not increased commensurately. The mismatch between demand and supply has driven up land prices and since the demand has increased rapidly, price has increased rapidly. Since urban land is more expensive, agents in the land market are increasingly focusing their attention on peripheries where they can purchase land at affordable prices. The land markets are now flush with money, increasing demand and money supply is sufficient to explain the very rapid rise in the land prices in Bangalore. The establishment of IT and development corridors in the peripheral area of East Bangalore Whitefield region and South Bangalore Electronic City is mainly responsible for land prices shooting up. There is a mass influx of people from the different parts of the country to the areas for employment, and as a result, the demand for housing, transportation and infrastructural facilities is on the increase. Given that the supply of urban land is limited and expensive, the demand for industrial commercial and residential land is growing in the periphery. Peripheral areas are relatively less expensive than the core regions, the land markets drive up land prices considerably. Frequent rural-urban migration is responsible for the peri-urban transition.

Why this transition in a regional context focuses its attention on peri–urban areas in metropolitan city? This peri–urban portrayal of Bangalore covers divergence of periphery, role of land policy and governance in the context of dynamic land use changes and high land prices. Land in the peri–urban interface is of vital importance, impacted by frequent land use changes, while being part of the city's hinterland, its economic as well as ecological role in the sustenance of both the urban and rural zones assumes importance.

Peri–Urban Land Markets of Bangalore

Bangalore is one of the most preferred investment destinations of India (Figure 1.16). Being a significant IT centre of India, it is encountering a robust real estate development. With its development of IT companies, quickly expanding high net-worth individuals and road networks are the major driving factors behind the growing real estate. The realty market of Bangalore is dominated by residential and commercial projects. The builders came up with highly advanced commercial and residential properties are giving more alternatives to the purchasers due to the mushrooming IT organisations with extending luxuries in the city. Probably, the most thriving areas of Bangalore include Electronic City, Begur Main Road, Whitefield, Bannerghatta-Road, Rajajinagar, Malleshwaram, Koramangala and Ulsoor. The demand for affordable housing originates from the price sensitive buyers; hence, such projects are developed in the peripheral areas where land acquisition cost is low. There is an expansion sought after high–end residential apartments mainly in SBD,[16] CBD,[17] ORR sub-markets, North Bangalore and Whitefield.[18] "Silicon City" is one of the most competent markets for real estate projects which

Figure 1.16 Bangalore periphery containing outdoor, real estate developments. Photograph by the author.

are generally dynamic in Northern part of the city, ORR, Sarjapur Road and Whitefield micro markets. Electronic City, Whitefield, ORR, North Bangalore have the potential to foster these requirements at competitive prices.

There is a constant demand for budget houses on the edges of the city and the accessibility of land at lower prices has led to an increase in the launch of new projects. Areas such as Mysore Road, Kanakapura, Hosur Road have witnessed a high demand. South Bangalore is the most favoured area as the majority of the reasonable and mid-housing, income segment projects are accessible. There is a considerable ascent in capital values; therefore, the developers have redesigned their projects cater to the needs of the target buyers. Whitefield, Marathahalli, Electronic City are the favourite centres amongst the professionals because of nearness to IT centre points. The normal weighted rentals of the builder floors expanded by 3% in the ongoing time frame. The significant driving forces behind the blasting interest of these areas are improved metro network; proximate city offices are increasing the value of these areas. Bangalore has extended topographically, with the suburbs and peripheries rising as new realty hotspots.

South Bangalore and North Bangalore are offering most of the affordable residential properties that are equipped with all modern amenities. East and South Bangalore have entrenched themselves as the cost-effective housing hubs with respective shares standing at 25% and 41% of the total budget. North Bangalore has come up as one of the noticeable real estate destinations which is offering residential properties at reasonable prices.[19] The significant stimulation in the realty sector has been because of its nearness of IT companies along with the key infrastructure projects. South Bangalore and North Bangalore are offering the majority of reasonable private properties that are furnished with every single modern amenity. These ideas gained popularity due to the presence of few developers like Shriram properties, Golden Gate Properties, Ozone Group, Brigade Group, Nitesh Estate and Puravankara who are predominantly centred around the reasonable client segment in Kanakapura. The demand for real estate in the periphery increases day by day and it is known for the remarkable land transactions.

Summary

I identify the pattern of peri-urbanisation in both developed countries and developing countries; the features of urbanisation in developing countries differ from those in developed countries in many ways. With the illustration of peri-urbanisation in specific regions and cities of Europe, it establishes a global perspective of bringing "north and south". Challenges such as rapid population growth, environmental issues and socio-economic changes distinguish the pattern of peri-urbanisation. Peri-urban areas reveal exceedingly globally induced pressures. The specific case of Bangalore Metropolitan city is identified to illustrate the urbanisation and peri-urban land markets in the developing context. The study starts with the assumption that the two peripheral cluster is different in terms of its growth dynamics; therefore, it is an effort to understand the divergent phenomenon. The land market analysis focuses on the two diverse peripheries of fast changing Bengaluru. Peri-urban dynamics results in conflicts and challenges, on the one hand, and on the other hand, it reaps benefits to the society through the creation of external economies and growth of industries, services, exports and real estate. It is a prelude to the peri-urban perspective, land use and land cover dynamics of land markets in the developing country context.

Notes

1   China's **hukou system** was introduced in 1958 as a modern means of population registration. It was set up as a part of the economic and social reforms of the initial years of the communist regime. In 1985, the hukou system was manifested through the provision of personal identity cards.
2   According to INSEE, in 1997 there were 494 plants in the Toulouse region directly linked to aerospace (INSEE, 1997).
3   (Ministère de l'Économie et des Finances, Ministère du Commerce Extérieur, 2013).
4   https://www.amsterdam.nl policy-urban-space
5   Dealroom Report
6   https://oppla.eu/casestudy/1931.
7   https://worldpopulationreview.com/world-cities/warsaw-population
8   ABSL Business Services Sector in Poland Report.
9   http://www.populationu.com/cities/bangalore-population
10 Palike, B. B. M. (2014). REPORT FOR.
11 https://population.un.org/wpp/
12 Indian Institute of Science - Bangalore city profile Government of India - Press Information Bureau - India stats: million plus cities in India World Urbanization Prospects - United Nations population estimates and projections of major Urban Agglomeration.
13 Master Plan (2031) provisional for Hoskote Local Planning Area, Part 1 Report.
14 Hoskote Masterplan Final Report.03.10.2013.
15 Kanakapura Local Planning Area, Draft Master Plan, 2031.
16 Secondary Business District.
17 Central Business District.
18 https://qrius.com/bangalore-real-estate/
19 https://www.99acres.com

References

Adell, G. (1999). *Theories and Models of the Peri-Urban Interface: A Changing Conceptual Landscape*, Draft, discovery.ucl.ac.uk.

Allen, A. (2003). Environmental planning and management of the peri-urban interface: Perspectives on an emerging field. *Environment and urbanization*, 15(1), 135–148.

Alonso, W. (1964). *Location and land use. Toward a general theory of land rent*. Cambridge, MA: Harvard University Press.

Alpkokin, P. (2012). Historical and critical review of spatial and transport planning in the Netherlands. *Land Use Policy*, 29(3), 536–547.

Alterman, R. (1997). The challenge of farmland preservation: Lessons from a six-nation comparison. *Journal of the American Planning Association*, 63(2), 220–243.

Anas, A. (1978). Dynamics of urban residential growth. *Journal of Urban Economics*, 5(1), 66–87.

Antrop, M. (2005). Why landscapes of the past are important for the future. *Landscape and Urban Planning*, 70(1–2), 21–34.

Beeftink, M. J., & de Roo, G. (2009). *Spatial Planning and Transitions in Warsaw's Peri Urban Area*. frw.studenttheses.ub.rug.nl.

Bonnefoy, S., & Brand, C. (2014). Régulation politique et territorialisation du fait alimentaire: de l'agriculture à l'agri-alimentaire. *Géocarrefour*, 89(89/1–2), 95–103.

Breheny, M. (1996). *Centrists, Decentrists and Compromisers: Views on the Future of Urban Form. The Compact City: A Sustainable Urban Form* (pp. 13–35). Routledge, Monograph.

Brigham, E. F. (1965). The determinants of residential land values. *Land Economics*, 41(4), 325–334.

Browder, J. O., Bohland, J. R., & Scarpaci, J. L. (1995). Patterns of development on the metropolitan fringe: Urban fringe expansion in Bangkok, Jakarta, and Santiago. *Journal of the American Planning Association*, 61(3), 310–327.

Burgess, W. (1925). The growth of the city. In R. E. Park, E. W. Burgess, and R. D. McKenzie (eds.), *The City*. Chicago: University of Chicago Press.

Cadène, P. (2005). *Dynamics of Peri-Urban Areas: From the French Case to the Developing Countries. Peri-Urban Dynamics: Population, Habitat and Environment on the Peripheries of Large Indian Metropolises. A Review of Concepts and General Issues*. New Delhi: Centre de Sciences Humaines.

Carrion-Flores, C., & Irwin, E. G. (2004). Determinants of residential land-use conversion and sprawl at the rural-urban fringe. *American Journal of Agricultural Economics*, 86(4), 889–904.

Chan, K. W., & Zhang, L. (1999). The hukou system and rural-urban migration in China: Processes and changes. *The China Quarterly*, 160, 818–855.

Chicoine, D. L. (1981). Farmland values at the urban fringe: An analysis of sale prices. *Land Economics*, 57(3), 353–362.

Dahiya, B. (2003). Peri-urban environments and community driven development: Chennai, India. *Cities*, 20(5), 341–352.

Davis, J. (2004). Scaling up urban upgrading. *International Development Planning Review*, 26(3), 305–323.

DESA, U. N. (2014). *World Urbanization Prospects, the 2011 Revision*. Population Division, Department of Economic and Social Affairs, United Nations Secretariat.

Desbordes, F. (2011). Map the evolution of suburbanization around Toulouse. South West Europe. *Geographical Review of the Pyrenees and the South-West*, 31, 11–27.

Dieleman, F. M., & Musterd, S. (1992). The restructuring of Randstad Holland. In Dieleman, F.M., Musterd, S. (eds), *The Randstad: A Research and Policy Laboratory* (pp. 1–16). Dordrecht: Springer.

Douglas, I. (2006). Peri-urban ecosystems and societies transitional zones and contrasting values. In McGregor, D., Simon, D., & Thompson, D. (eds), *Peri-Urban Interface: Approaches to Sustainable Natural and Human Resource Use* (pp. 18–29).

Dreier, P., Mollenkopf, J., & Swanstrom, T. (2001). *Place Matters: Metropolitics for the Twenty-First Century*. Lawrence: University Press of Kansas.

Dupont, V. (2005). *Peri-Urban Dynamics: Population, Habitat and Environment on the Peripheries of Large Indian Metropolises. A Review of Concepts and General Issues*. CSH Occasional Paper 14.

Dutta, V. (2012). Land use dynamics and peri-urban growth characteristics: Reflections on master plan and urban suitability from a sprawling north Indian city. *Environment and Urbanization Asia*, 3(2), 277–301.

Duvernoy, I., Zambon, I., Sateriano, A., & Salvati, L. (2018). Pictures from the other side of the fringe: Urban growth and peri-urban agriculture in a post-industrial city (Toulouse, France). *Journal of Rural Studies*, 57, 25–35.

Faludi, A., & van der Valk, A. J. (1994). *Rule and order Dutch planning doctrine in the twentieth century* (Vol. 28). Springer Science & Business Media.

Fulton, W., Pendall, R., Nguyen, M., & Harrison, A. (2001). *Who Sprawls Most. How Growth Patterns Differ Across the US*, 1. Sunday, July 1, 2001 Report.

Gough, K. V., & Yankson, P. W. (2000). Land markets in African cities: The case of peri-urban Accra, Ghana. *Urban Studies*, 37(13), 2485–2500.

Haggard, S. (1991). Review by: William R. Clark. Pathways from the periphery: The politics of growth in the newly industrializing countries. *The Journal of Asian Studies*, 50(1), 117–118.

Hajek, I., & Lévy, J. P. (2017). Urban ecology. In *Rethinking Nature* (pp. 158–165). Routledge.

He, C., Huang, Z., & Wang, W. (2012). Land use changes and economic growth in China. *Land Lines*, 24(4), 14–19.

Helsley, R. W., & Strange, W. C. (1990). Matching and agglomeration economies in a system of cities. *Regional Science and Urban Economics*, 20(2), 189–212.

Hornis, W., & Van Eck, J. R. (2008). A Typology of Peri-urban Areas in the Netherlands. *Tijdschrift voor economische en sociale geografie*, 99(5), 619–628.

Iaquinta, D. L., & Drescher, A. W. (2000). Defining the peri-urban: Rural-urban linkages and institutional connections. *Land Reform*, 2, 8–27.

INDIA, P. (2011). *Census of India 2011 Provisional Population Totals*. New Delhi: Office of the Registrar General and Census Commissioner.

Kennedy, L. (2007). Regional industrial policies driving peri-urban dynamics in Hyderabad, India. *Cities*, 24(2), 95–109.

Knack, S. (2001). *Trust, Assocational Life, and Economic Performance*. MPRA Paper No. 27247, posted 06 Dec 2010.

Kundu, A. (2003). Urbanisation and urban governance: Search for a perspective beyond neo-liberalism. *Economic and Political Weekly*, 3079–3087.

Kuznets, S., & Murphy, J. T. (1966). *Modern Economic Growth: Rate, Structure, and Spread* (Vol. 2). New Haven: Yale University Press.

Locke, A., & Henley, G. (2016). *Urbanisation, Land and Property Rights*. Report. Shaping policy for development, odi.org

Martin-Brelot, H., Grossetti, M., Eckert, D., Gritsai, O., & Kovacs, Z. (2010). The spatial mobility of the 'creative class': A European perspective. *International Journal of Urban and Regional Research*, 34(4), 854–870.

Massey, D. S., Arango, J., Hugo, G., Kouaouci, A., Pellegrino, A., & Taylor, J. E. (1993). Theories of international migration: A review and appraisal. *Population and Development Review*, 19(3), 431–466.

Moore, L. A. (1970). *U.S. Patent No. 3,503,369*. Washington, DC: U.S. Patent and Trademark Office.

Morton, J., Solecki, W., Dasgupta, P., Dodman, D., & Rivera-Ferre, M. G. (2014). *Cross-Chapter Box on Urban–Rural Interactions–Context for Climate Change Vulnerability, Impacts, and Adaptation* (pp. 153-155). Cambridge and New York, NY: Cambridge University Press.

Narain, V. (2009). Growing city, shrinking hinterland: Land acquisition, transition and conflict in peri-urban Gurgaon, India. *Environment and Urbanization*, 21(2), 501–512.

Nilsson, K., Pauleit, S., Bell, S., Aalbers, C., & Nielsen, T. A. S. (Eds.). (2013). *Peri-Urban Futures: Scenarios and Models for Land Use Change in Europe*. Springer Science & Business Media.

Niosi, J., & Zhegu, M. (2005). Aerospace clusters: Local or global knowledge spillovers? *Industry & Innovation*, 12(1), 5–29.

Nuhu, S. (2019, March). Peri-urban land governance in developing countries: Understanding the role, interaction and power relation among actors in Tanzania. In *Urban Forum* (Vol. 30, No. 1, pp. 1–16). Springer Netherlands.

Piorr, A. (Ed.). (2011). *Peri-Urbanisation in Europe: Towards European Policies to Sustain Urban-Rural Futures; Synthesis Report; PLUREL [Sixth Framework Programme]*. Forest & Landscape, University of Copenhagen.

Porter, M. E., & Takeuchi, H. (2013). *Aerospace Cluster in the Toulouse region*. Harvard Business School.

Pryor, R. J. (1968). Defining the rural-urban fringe. *Social Forces*, 47(2), 202–215.

Ravetz, J., Fertner, C., & Nielsen, T. S. (2013). The dynamics of peri-urbanization. In Nilsson, K., Pauleit, S., Bell, S., Aalbers, C., & Thomas S. Nielsen (eds), *Peri-Urban Futures: Scenarios and Models for Land Use Change in Europe* (pp. 13–44). Berlin, Heidelberg: Springer.

Ramachandra, T. V., & Bharath, H. A. (2012). Spatio-temporal pattern of landscape dynamics in Shimoga, Tier II City, Karnataka State, India. *International Journal of Emerging Technology and Advanced Engineering*, 2(9), 563–576.

Rothwell, A., Ridoutt, B., Page, G., & Bellotti, W. (2015). Feeding and housing the urban population: Environmental impacts at the peri-urban interface under different land-use scenarios. *Land Use Policy*, 48, 377–388.

Roy, A. (2009). The 21st-century metropolis: New geographies of theory. *Regional Studies*, 43(6), 819–830.

Salvati, L., Ciommi, M. T., Serra, P., & Chelli, F. M. (2019). Exploring the spatial structure of housing prices under economic expansion and stagnation: The role of socio-demographic factors in metropolitan Rome, Italy. *Land Use Policy*, 81, 143–152.

Schenk, H. and Rohilla, S. K. (2004). Role of groundwater in urban development case study of Delhi and its peri-urban areas. Unpublished paper presented at Association of American Geographers Centennial conference, Philadelphia (March 2004).

Simon, D. (2008). Urban environments: Issues on the peri-urban fringe. *Annual Review of Environment and Resources*, 33(1), 167–185.

Stark, O., & Bloom, D. E. (1985). The new economics of labor migration. *The American Economic Review*, 75(2), 173–178.

Surge, G. (2015). A Typology of Urban Green Spaces. Ecosystem provisioning services and demands. Seventh Framework Programme, http://greensurge.eu/working-packages/wp3/files D, 3.

Tacoli, C. (1998). Rural-urban interactions: A guide to the literature. *Environment and Urbanization*, 10(1), 147–166.

Theobald, D. M. (2001). Land-use dynamics beyond the American urban fringe. *Geographical Review*, 91(3), 544–564.

Tjallingii, S. (2003). Green and red: Enemies or allies? The Utrecht experience with green structure planning. *Built Environment*, 29(2), 107–116.

Woltjer, J. (2014). A global review on peri-urban development and planning. *Journal Perencanaan Wilayah dan Kota*, 25 (1), 1.

2 Theorisation of Peri-Urban and Land Use Changes – Elucidation through LU/LC Mapping

Conceptualisation

The term peri-urban is used in different ways such as "Urban Fringe", "Peri-Urban Interface" by various authors. Peri-Urban Interface is a place where urban and rural uses of the land were blended, shaping together a change zone among city and countryside (Johnson, 1974). The historical dichotomy of urban and rural space started to blur in Europe with the formation of nation-states, industrialisation and the advancement of the economy in the nineteenth century (Nilson et al., 2013). In the newly urbanised cities of Europe, the term peri-urban interface is common (Ravetz et al., 2013). The rural-urban fringe is the zone of transition in land use, social and demographic characteristics, lying between continuously built-up urban and suburban areas of the central city and the rural hinterland, characterised by the almost complete absence of non-farm dwelling, occupations and land use, and of urban and rural social orientation (Pryor, 1968). He considered the rural-urban fringe areas as residential zones lying between the two extremities of the rural and the urban with transition encountered. Maconachie (2016) in his article "the Rural-Urban Fringe" defined the region as the area of transition between well-recognized urban land uses and an area devoted to agriculture. Tali & Nusrath (2014) defined urban fringe as the "active expansion sector of the compact economic city and to the periphery of this urban fringe is the rural-urban fringe". Due to its location between the two extremes, the peri-urban is of a unique character which is neither truly urban nor totally rural.

Urban fringe as "the interstitial area which lies between an urban unit and its outlying rural-farm areas" (Rodehever's, 1946). In the European perspective, peri-urban areas are often understood to be mixed areas under an urban influence but with a rural morphology (Caruso, 2001). The peri-urban is something between neither urban nor rural. Geographic definitions of the Peri-Urban are used in the PLUREL[1] project. The basic spatial types Rural-Urban Region (RUR) include: Urban core, Suburban area, Urban Fringe, Urban periphery, Rural hinterland. Sarkar and Bandyopadhyay

DOI: 10.4324/9781003362333-2

Table 2.1 Peri-urban concepts; literature review

Author	Peri-Urban Concept	Findings
R J Pryor (1968)	Rural urban fringe, process and pattern of peri-urbanisation	Urban fringe is the zone of transition between land, social and demographics between urban/rural areas.
German Adell (1999)	Theories and models of the peri-urban interface/case studies of Bangkok, Jakarta, Santiago	Different conceptualisations of the rural-urban interface emerging in the development planning discourse has been analysed.
Iaquinta and Drescher (2000)	Defining peri-urban understanding rural-urban linkages.	Conceptual peri-urban typology including its relationships to rural and urban form.
Ravetz (2013)	The dynamics of peri-urbanisation – European trends – theoretical concepts.	Urbanisation is unevenly distributed in Europe. The peri-urban agenda is a challenge for the global urban system. Areas closer to cities are faced with high development pressures linked to an increasing per capita consumption of urban land.
Fiona Marshall et al. (2009)	Perspectives of peri-urban dynamics-conceptualisation and theorisation.	Conceptualisations of the peri-urban as transitional, place placed flows oriented as urban or as rural have major implications for peri-urban planning and policy process
Cecilia Tacoli (1998)	Rural-urban interactions	Rural-urban interactions are that population and activities either as rural or urban, are more closely linked to both space and sectors. Flows of people, goods and wastes and the related flows of information and money act as linkages across space between cities and countryside.
N. R. Wills (2007)	The rural-urban fringe: some agricultural characteristics with specific reference to Sydney.	Physical resources of rural-urban fringe are under transition. Agricultural activities in the city centre remain overlooked.
Marshal et al. (2009)	On the edge of sustainability: perspective of peri-urban dynamics	The way in which peri-urban has been theorised; the implications for a normative research agenda towards improved environmental and social justice.

(Continued)

Author	Peri-Urban Concept	Findings
Browder et al. (1995)	Patterns of development on the metropolitan fringe	Socio-economic composition and structure of such urban fringe settlements using three sets of household surveys in respect of Bangkok, Jakarta and Santiago 1990.
Morton John (2014)	Urban-rural interactions – context for climate change vulnerability, impacts and adaptation	Rural areas and urban areas have always been interconnected and interdependent, but recent decades have seen new forms of these interconnections: a tendency for rural–urban boundaries to become less well-defined, and new types of land use and economic activity around those boundaries.
Veronique Dupont (2005)	Peri-urban dynamics: population, habitat and environment on the peripheries of large Indian metropolises	Specific forms of urbanisation are evolving on the peripheries of the large metropolises like Chennai and Jaipur. Peri-urban is the "mixed spaces" midway between urban centres and rural spaces – transitional spaces subject to rapid and multiple transformations.
Naraian et al. (2013)	A review of literature and evidence in Indian context Chennai, Ahmedabad, Patna, Guwahati, Chandigarh. Contested natural resource use, rural–urban links, socio-economic drivers of land use change	PUI creates important changes in livelihoods, affecting the scale and pattern of agricultural activities and practices; sustainability is often challenged by other uses.
Annapurna Shaw (2005)	Peri-urban interface of Indian cities	The outward expansion of larger metros, gradual changes in land uses and occupations have transformed the rural hinterland into semi-urban or peri-urban areas.
Manita Saxena (2015)	Review of problems and resolutions of peri-urban	Peri-urban is the cheap land and the place for population under migration. Densification of peri-urban area may lead to chocking of the core city.
Dinesh Singh (2015)	Planning strategies for the development of peri-urban area Indore	There is a rapid physical development process operating in the rural-urban fringe area outside Indore.

Source: Compilation by the author.

(2013) refers to these as "complex mosaics of juxtaposed activities previously regarded as incompatible" the concept of "Kotedesatie", meaning city villagisation, has emerged from this though which is used for areas where the urban and rural activities take place together. What's more, it is considered place where urban and rural areas meet. The peri-urban evolution not only consists of flows of people, but of capital, labour, commodities and information leave the central urban context for a periphery (Adell, 1999) (Table 2.1).

In Indian context, rural-urban fringe is designated as starting from the point "where agriculture land use uses appear near the city and extends up to the point where villages have distinct urban land uses" (Datta, 2004). He attempted to trace the origins and the phenomenon of the rural-urban fringe in India (Fazal, 2012); the rural-urban fringe is an area that is a blend of rural and urban populations and land uses. Preceding the industrialisation studies in land use in urban and peri-urban had less significance; nevertheless, the modern cities of the eighteenth, nineteenth and twentieth centuries spread to the countryside, bringing about the structural changes because of the demands of urban dwellers. The peri-urban areas show a close relationship between the city and the periphery.

Theorisation of Peri-Urban

Theoretical framework suggests that various strategies for depiction, models related to the economic divergence, land use and land value are debated at the context of changing periphery. The obscuring of the urban-rural boundary motivated research into the idea of an urban-rural continuum. Bryant et al. (1982) showed this by a model where the urban-rural region ranges from core city through inner and outer fringe; notwithstanding, truly, this model works in general. This is the case paying little mind to the way that the idea of the continuum includes several dimensions of urbanisation in the urban-rural space, which can bring about complex spatial patterns. Friedberg (2001) has contended that the peri-urban is fundamentally integrated into urban contexts. As such, peri-urban areas occupy "unique space, in that they are simultaneously sustained and imperilled by the dynamics of the urban economy" (Marshall et al., 2009).

The peri-urban should thus be conceived as a zone of complementariness. The association between natural resources, agriculture and urban processes in peri-urban spaces suggests that complementarities don't exist in detachment from contestation. The interrelated idea of social, economic and environmental frameworks (Moffat & Finnis, 2005) further makes difficult theorisation. People's perceptions of the peri-urban have been largely disregarded in the theorisation of the peri-urban. Iaquinta and Drescher (2000) point out "the reality of peri-urban, underestimates the prevalence of social change and misclassifies the experiences of numerous people and communities in the real world". Theoretical framework throws light on the relevant model of regional divergence.

Regional Economic Divergence – Growth Pole Theory

Growth pole theory demonstrates the spillover effect of growth to the periphery. This theoretical angle is known as territorial development theories. According to the growth pole theory, governments of developing countries can induce economic growth and welfare by investing heavily in capital-intensive industries in large urban centres or regional capitals. This growth is supposed to spread to the rural areas in a process of regional development (Winoto & Schultink, 1996). The growth pole theory states that "free market forces" provide conditions for development through the existence of the so-called trickle-down effect that is meant to put together various economic forces, creating a virtuous cycle that spreads economic growth from urban to rural areas (Adell, 1999). Economic growth and modernisation required a surplus transfer from the agricultural sector to the industry by the appropriation of resources, capital and labour by cities. A contradictory model based on spatial polarisation and core-periphery relations was formulated. The benefits to the core were at the expense of the periphery, rural-urban linkages being part of a global chain of power that perpetuated rural conditions of poverty and underdevelopment. This pattern started the main policy response to the problem: the creation of growth poles, actuating urbanisation into the periphery. From 1970s, development policies based on the central place theory, proposed to promote market towns to fill the gap between the "evil city" and the countryside (Douglass & Friedmann, 1998).

Theoretical debate is enhanced by further empirical evidence. The fast-growing economies of the Southeast Asian "miracle" indicate that fast urbanisation processes featuring a synergetic mix of agricultural and industrial activities are creating economic growth though it is expanding social imbalances, environmental problems (Firman & Dharmapatni, 1994). Evidence from China with special reference to Pearl River Delta, etc., reinforce this phenomenon. There is a delineation from physical definition of the fringe as discussed by Pahl (1965). He defined it as being the result of particular social processes, mainly the migration of mobile middle-class families oriented to the city and dominated by urban lifestyles: a new population is invading local communities, bringing in national values and class consciousness at the same time that a new type of community, associated with dispersed living is emerging.

According to Rondinelli (1985) and Unwin (1989), the growth pole theory is based on the conviction that governments of developing countries can induce economic growth and welfare by investing greatly in capital-intensive industries in large urban or regional capitals. This growth is expected to spread to the rural areas in a process of transition. The growth pole theory is reinforcing "free market forces" which provide conditions for development, further leads to the so-called trickle-down effect results in external demand and innovation impulses, heavily invests in "high technology" urban industrial development (Stöhr & Taylor, 1981). This strategy has not only allowed experiences in capitalist countries but tempted socialist planners as well. This debate is a matter of great importance today, as the cities grew to the countryside by setting up of capital-intensive industries in Asia where IT industries lead to a rapid transition. Certain authors have shown evidence demonstrating that growth pole-oriented policies are still widely in use in Less Developing Countries, contributing to the maintenance of a conceptual division between the city and the fringe.

There exists a divide in planning as the consequences of this rural-urban conceptual dichotomy (Douglass & Friedmann, 1998) and the policies have a decisive "urban bias" (Lipton, 1977). The rural -urban areas are not clearly demarcated; therefore, the policy adopted by the two administrative department is also different. The urban policies have a "rural bias", with "little or no interest in investigating how cities might be better brought into rural planning frameworks". However, for a rural household, daily life includes both rural and urban elements (Douglass & Friedmann, 1998). He points out the rural-urban divide acting as the backdrop of growth pole theories in development planning, contending that economic growth and modernisation required a surplus transfer from the agricultural sector to industry, thus defending the appropriation of rural resources, capital and labour by cities. The dispersal of growth on the peripheries of the fringes is a phenomenon in the industrialised and developing countries (Ingram, 1998).

According to Ingram (1998), these movement towards the fringe as follows a dispersal process from the centre to the periphery of both population and employment, with the largest metropolitan areas converging to decentralised and multiple sub-centred areas (cities in developing countries tend to have higher population densities, but, the difference is narrowing); highly decentralised manufacturing employment and emerging specialisation of the central business district in service employment; increased reliance on road-based transport for both passengers and freight, industrial countries have experienced decreases in transit level as automobile ownership rises; developing countries have higher transit-ridership levels and a mix of options in terms of vehicle sizes and levels of services. Another significant development is the real estate, land-markets are strong determinants of this outward movement, land rents being closely related to development densities in the periphery. Ingram states that population growth in large cities usually promotes densification of less developed areas and expansion at the urban fringe, largely following either price constraints or preferences of households acting within the housing market (Fazal, 2001). Thus, the spillover effects of the growth pole as in the case of Silicon Valley of the world is visible in the major metropolitan cities around the globe.

The central idea of economic development or growth is not uniform over an entire region but takes place in a specific cluster or pole as we see in South East Bengaluru. Propulsive pole is a business unit, or a set of these units and these units are the main force of economic development by Perroux, (1949). According to Perroux, governments of developing countries can induce economic growth and welfare by investing heavily in capital-intensive industries. Capital-intensive industries are located in the fringe areas of the city. Therefore, growth is supposed to spread to the rural areas in a process of regional development (Rondinelli, 1985; Unwin, 1989). Perroux identified the dominant region where poles of development are concentrated, which develops more economic activities. Further, Jacques Boudeville gave a regional dimension to the growth pole. According to him, growth pole is a set of expanding industries in urban area spilling over benefits to the surrounding area. The area where propulsive industries are located becomes the pole of the region and agglomeration takes place. A typical example of such growth pole effect is found in the Silicon Valley in San Jose, California. The Information Technology (IT) industry grew at a faster rate in the 1990s, but the economic stimulus was not restricted to the state of California or the United States but to Asian countries as well. Same phenomenon is evident in Bengaluru, the major hub of IT industries of India, and it is known as the Silicon Valley of India – a comparative reference to the original Silicon Valley has the highest number of IT job in Asia and growth pole led to the spread effects to the entire periphery leading to spatial expansion.

The theory talks of the creation of growth poles, inducing urbanisation into the periphery; the 1970s development policies, based also on the central place theory, which proposed to promote market towns to fill the gap between the "evil city" and the countryside (Douglass & Friedmann, 1998). The growth pole theory states that "free market forces" that spreads economic growth from urban to rural areas. Growth poles theory documents the polarisation to the development poles and identifies four basic types of polarisation (Adamcik, 2002).[2] They include (i) Technological Polarisation – concentration of technology in the growth pole, (ii) Income Polarisation – growth poles leading to concentration and growth of income, (iii) Psychological Polarisation – leading to optimistic anticipation of demand in the propelled region, (iv) Geographical Polarisation – leading to concentration of economic activity in a geographical space. The regional economic divergence theory illustrates the dynamics of rural-urban transition in the context of economic growth and urbanisation.

Theory of Land Use

Population as a driving force of land use change has been unique in its plausibility and ease of quantification (Meyer & Turner, 1992). With the increase in food requirements because of growing population, the first reaction of farming communities in developing countries is conversion of land (Jolly & Torrey, 1993). Thomas Malthus, David Ricardo and Ester Boserup have described the land use changes. In the neo-Malthusian position, population growth is accordance with most land use change, including both field expansion and increased land use intensity, in the view of the resources essential to sustain the population. Hardaway (1997) contended that agro-ecological zones have a certain population carrying capacity which must not be exceeded. As per Malthusian view, a finite stock of suitable land is, thus, assumed to lead to a strict competition between land uses and, eventually, to a shortage of productive land, with negative welfare impacts which is a main barrier to agricultural growth.

In the work of Esther Boserup (1975), a static view of carrying capacity is questioned. Rather, agricultural development, including its technological base, is attributed to the pressures on production that mount from a growing population. Population growth results in land use changes, but it may also result in environmental degradation. Friis and Nielsen (2014) have displayed a land-use transition model that depicts a sequence of land-use stages, beginning with 100% of the landscape with natural ecosystems, subsistence agriculture and small-scale farming, and finally, the intensive stage, characterised by expanded urban areas, intensive agriculture and expanded protected and recreational lands, leaving small proportions of the landscape covered by either natural ecosystems or agriculture. This clearly shows the decline in the extent of agriculture.

Von Thunen Model

The Von Thunen model of agricultural land use also known as location theory was shaped by the German farmer, landowner and economist Johann Heinrich Von Thunen et al. (1966). Like any other scientific research, it is based on a series of assumptions that Von Thunen sums up in his concept of an "Isolated State". He was concerned about the ways people tend to use and would use the land around a city if the conditions were laboratory-like, as in his Isolated State. He introduced the concentric ring model consisting of "Four Rings". Von Thunen theorised that a pattern of rings across the city would expand based on land cost and transportation cost. According to him as the distance from the city centre increases the cost of land goes down.

Most of land use models that have incorporated economic theory in its framework have its origins in the family of spatial interaction models.

Employing the micro-economic theory of consumer behaviour, the optimal allocation to destinations is obtained by postulating a utility function which reflects the relative preferences of people at the origin zones for the attributes of the destination zones (Koomen & Buurman, 2002). This approach is based on the description of individual choice behaviour and subsequent aggregation to the level of a market segment.

The same utility maximisation framework was applied by Alonso (1964) to describe the urban land market. He built his model on an idea whose essence is based on land uses installation in the city as a reflection of differences in land uses rents. These uses are just a translation of land prices and rents variation. This means that several activities that constitute structure vary according to intensive competition between land prices and rents. His model of the land market inspired many land use models (Ogawa & Fujita, 1980) that, applied to mono-centric cities, provide a well-known concentric land use patterns. The above-mentioned models that apply utility maximisation all have a micro-economic focus on the behaviour of individuals. A more general, macro-economic approach is used in the equilibrium models that consider the balancing of supply and demand. Models that concentrate on more than one market (housing and agriculture) and more than one region are referred to as spatial general equilibrium models.

Land Value Model

Agent-based Land Markets (ALMA) are explicit models that show micro-scale interactions between buyers and sellers of spatial goods and macro-scale feedbacks of market transactions. The main agents in the ALMA model are land users operating in an urban area (households, that buy land, and farmers, who sell land). The main good they exchange via market mechanisms is a spatial good, which can be viewed as a plot of land or a house. The ALMA model was customised in Net Logo (Filatova et al., 2009). The land market structure indicates the existing research on spatial economics. Nonetheless, differences are there in the implementation of a spatially explicit setup, and direct modelling of price formation and market transactions.

The land market in ALMA is represented as a two-side matching market (Alonso, 1964). According to his bid-rent theory, households choose locations at a certain distance from the central business district by means of maximising utility they get from the joint consumption of a spatial good and a composite good under their budget constraints. Applying market-clearing conditions assuming that demands derived from the consumer's first-order conditions are equal to supply at equilibrium and assuming that utility is equal for all agents in the city, one derives the equilibrium land rent $R^*(d, u)$. In this case, equilibrium rent is the maximum rent per unit of land that the representative consumer is willing to pay at distance d, while enjoying a given utility level u

(Filatova et al., 2009). The outcome of the bid–rent model is a set of rent gradients, i.e. land prices at different distances from the city centre.

Land value model is a variant of the classic bid–rent model developed by William Alonso. Analysis of land use by Beckmann (1972) and further refinements to his work by Alonso (1960) are based on basic principles. Market access is a significant factor. The market access is at the centre of population and transportation, and economic agents are willing to pay more for land at the centre of a city. The methodology is closely related to the duality approach of modern microeconomics. Thus, by utilising it, one can develop modern land use theory.

In the backdrop of these theories, the spatial and temporal growth of Bengaluru is traced. In the case of Bengaluru, the Silicon Valley of India as in the case of original Silicon Valley shows the polarisation of growth effects in terms of the transition from rural to urban, the flow of resources, movement of people, growth of real estate resulting changes in the land use and subsequent changes in the land value. Since the study focuses on land use and land value, models of land use and land value are relevant for the current study. The land use model by Von Thunen is relevant; the theory has a micro-economic focus on individuals who are the agents in the land market since the land market survey in this deal with agents in both demand side and supply side. The models used focus more than one market that is both the market for agriculture and non–agriculture. The land value model is an agent-based land market by Alonso which specify the two–sided land market. As the study look at peri-urban in the context of changing land uses, I examine the meaning and definition of Land Use/ Land Cover.

Land Use/Land Cover (LU/LC)

Meaning and Definition

Land

Land alludes to land resource or real estate as opposed to simply land. Land is the essential, fixed and limited natural resource. Land assumes a key role in economic activities of everyday life. Land has five most regular entities such as the landscape, atmosphere, soils, water and forest. All the natural resources are related with the land asset. As per Barlowe, land can be categorised by its utilisation (Anderson, 1976).

FAO characterises land as

> a delineable territory of Earth's earthbound surface, incorporating all qualities of the biosphere promptly above or underneath this surface, including those of the close surface atmosphere, the soil and landscape

shapes, the surface hydrology, the close surface sedimentary layers and related ground water reserve, the plant and animal populaces, the human settlement systems and physical activities of over a wide span of time human action.

Land Use (LU)

Land use is characterised by *the arrangements, activities and inputs people under-take within in a certain land cover type to produce, change or maintain it* (Di Gregorio & Jansen, 2000). Land use concerns the function or purpose for which land is used by the population; it can be defined as "the human activities that are directly related to land, making use of its resources or having an impact on them" (Pelorosso et al., 2009). Meaning of land use along these lines sets up an immediate connection between land cover and the activities of individuals in their condition.

Land Cover (LC)

The definition of land cover is fundamental because in many existing classifications and legends, it is confused with land use. *Land cover is the observed (bio) physical cover on the earth's surface, (Di Gregorio, 2005).* While considering land cover in an exact sense, it ought to be bound to depict vegetation and man-made features. Thus, regions where the surface comprises of rock or bare soil are portraying land itself instead of land cover. There are debates over whether water surfaces are real land covers, scientific authority confirm those as land covers. Land Use/Land Cover (LU/LC) change is a major challenge of peri-urban area.

Land Use Changes in the Peri-Urban

Changes in the (LU/LC) pattern of the locale are the direct implication of peri-urban and sprawl. Land use changes involve fast spatial and temporal pattern change and it is a dynamic change (Quan et al., 2007). Land use (LU) change is a function of biophysical and socio-economic driving factors. Modelling (LU/LC) is a technique for unravelling the complex relationships in the land use changes systems and provides insights into the extent of the land use change (Ganasri & Dwarakish, 2015). The city slowly progresses towards the rural countryside. The peri-urban transition is in the form of usage of land as a resource. The major land use changes include industrial, residential and commercial uses. Land use changes lead to several other changes. The entire economic structure of the region changes. It leads to new occupational changes, extension of roads, construction of industrial and residential complexes and emergence of small business units and thriving real estate activities. This is mainly due to the migration of people to cities in search of jobs and increasing demand for housing facilities. Lack of cheap housing facilities in the core city and increasing demand for real estate developments lead to spatial expansion of the urban areas and there by growth in the fringe areas. Peri-urban land use change is a complex and dynamic process (Quan et al., 2006). Geographic Information System (GIS) is used to assess the dynamic changes and it is an integrating tool in order to capture the spatial and temporal changes of urban growth. To forecast future land use pattern, GIS with the Markov Cellular automata is used (Samat et al., 2011). Land scape metrics is an important tool used for quantification and pattern analysis (Ramachandran et al., 2012).

Urbanisation is a universal socio-economic phenomenon that prompts Land use/Land cover change (LU/LC). It is one of the significant reasons for the declining vegetation cover and conversion of the rural landscape to urban landscape and leading to economic impact. Since the most recent decade, remote sensing has become a significant information gathering device for exploration of these changes. Existing investigations did not analyse spatial and temporal changes of megacities, with an emphasis on peri-urban land use changes are not many and by hardly few researchers (Dekolo & Olayinka, 2013).

Regression-based land use analysis shows the locations of LU/LC change to a set of spatially explicit variables and uses models such as logistic. It is unlikely that agricultural land converted to developed uses will ever become available again for agricultural production (Su et al., 2011). Decline in the total area of agricultural landscape would definitely result in lower self-supply abilities and threat to food security of this region accordingly. These fragmented sets of land are unsuitable for urban development (Dredge, 1995). Under rural agricultural use, the changes in demand for land have contributed to the growth of land markets in Africa (Holden & Ghebru, 2010). On the other hand, studies on land use and urban proximity indicate that increasing demand for land nearer urban centres is mainly a function of population growth, migration, economic development and accessibility to the city.

Most empirical studies on land use change depend on the application of remote sensed data and GIS for analysis (Dekolo, 2013). In recent years, the techniques of satellite remote sensing and GIS have been increasingly used to examine the spatial and temporal patterns of land use and land cover change, especially related to urban growth. The models of LU/LC change process fall into two groups: regression-based and spatial transition-based models (Weng, 2002). The majority of research utilises regression-based approach, which relates the locations of LU/LC change to a set of spatially explicit variables, and uses models such as logistic (Turner, 1987). Changes from one land class to another can be mathematically described as probabilities that a given pixel will remain in the same state or be converted to another state. The analysis focuses on changes in spatial patterns of agricultural land use, driving factors and their implications. Differences in this phenomenon over time can be determined and evaluated visually or using digital techniques such as GIS in most of the metropolitan cities of India.

The conversion of land from agricultural production to urban and industrial development is one of the critical processes of change in the developing economies undergoing industrialisation and urbanisation. The supply of urban land is limited while the demand for industrial, commercial as well as residential land is growing. As country develops economically, more land will be utilised for non-agricultural uses in various metropolitan cities. There are frequent land use changes in the peri-urban areas and land use change is a major challenge at global and local level. In order to meet the growing demands of urbanisation, the fringe areas are converted into industrial residential and commercial establishments. City developments curb the fringe areas and lead to uncontrolled spatial expansion. Within the last decade, the built-up area doubled. Land-use has enormous effects through fragmentation of natural habits. Though Bengaluru the international technological hub known for its industrial and IT growth, growth has led to the deterioration of the green cover and reduced the environmental quality, such changes attributed to land-use change. Various studies throw light on land use changes and spatial expansion of Bengaluru over the past decades. LU/LC change in Bengaluru has resulted in the loss of green cover, agricultural land, increase in the land value and variability in temperature. With an increasing urbanisation and population, people migrate from other states to Bengaluru city, causing an urban sprawl. The other significant factors affecting the growth include IT industries, industrial and commercial establishments. The LU/LC change shows the extent and pattern of peri-urban locales.

Selected Peri-Urban Villages for the Land Use/Land Cover (LU/LC) Analysis

A sample of two peri-urban villages was taken from both East and South peripheries for the analysis. Peri-urban villages of Hoskote Taluk, Eastern periphery are known for industrial development, mixed development and real estate growth, especially places like Samethanahalli, Chokkahalli and Bhaktharahalli. Places like Tavarekere and Devanagundi are known for its manufacturing units and industrial establishments, especially in the fringe areas (Table 2.2).

Table 2.2 Selected peri-urban villages for LU/LC analysis-relevant information

Peri-Village	Geographic Area (Hectare)	Distance from Taluk Headquarter, City	Population	No of Households	Significant Developments
Devanagundi	578	15 km, 33 km	2,004	–	Railway station, oil refineries
Tavarekere	356	20 km, 25 km	2,481	–	Manufacturing units
Harohalli	1675	24 km, 41 km	13,044	3,121	Industrial
Sathanur	596	35 km, 64 km	4,966	1,162	Mixed development

Source: Author's compilation using Census data, village directory.

Selection of sample villages was based on the above village statistics, land expert opinion and availability of Land Use /Land Cover statistics. Some of the peri-urban villages were eliminated from the LU/LC change detection in view of an insufficient availability of Land Use/ Land Cover data for relevant years.

Peri-Urban Villages – Hoskote Taluk

i) Devanagundi: Devanagundi is in Hoskote City in Karnataka State, India. Devanagundi village is located in Hoskote Tehsil of Bengaluru Rural district in Karnataka, India. It is situated 17 km away from sub-district headquarter Hoskote and 30 km away from district headquarter Bengaluru Rural. As per 2009 statistics, Devanagundi is the gram panchayat of Devanagundi village. The total geographical area of village is 629.33 hectares. Devanagundi has a total population of 2,004 people. There are about 472 houses in Devanagundi village. Hoskote is the nearest town to Devanagundi which is approximately 15 km away.

ii) Tavarekere: Tavarekere Village Hoskote is situated in Bengaluru Rural District. This village has a very proud history. Agriculture is the main profession of this village. Still this village is waiting for industrial development. Education, drinking water, Road and Electricity are the main concern of this village. If banks and finance institutions proved loan and other financial support to the villagers, this village will see the real development. Medical and health services have to be improved.[3]

Peri-Urban Villages – Kanakapura Taluk

i) Harohalli: Harohalli is a Village in Kanakapura Taluk in Ramanagara District of Karnataka State, India. It is located 20 km towards East from District headquarters Ramanagara, 24 km from Kanakapura and 41 km from State capital Bengaluru. Harohalli is surrounded by Kanakapura Taluk towards South, Channapatna Taluk towards west, Thally Taluk towards East, Bengaluru Taluk towards North, Ramanagaram, Bengaluru, Magadi, Maddur are the nearby cities to Harohalli. The vast agricultural land in Harohalli and surrounding villages has already caught the attention of real estate developers, with some apartment complexes coming up in the periphery of the village. KIADB also has plans industrial development in Sathanur and Solur to have more industrial estates. There are 7,000 industries here and KIADB has recently notified 1,000 acres in Harohalli Phase III in Kanakapura.

ii) Sathanur: Sathanur is a Village in Kanakapura Taluk in Ramanagara District of Karnataka State, India. It is located 35 Km towards South from District headquarters Ramanagara and 64 Km from State capital Bengaluru. Sathanur is surrounded by Thally Taluk towards East, Channapatna Taluk towards west, Ramanagara Taluk towards North, Malavalli Taluk towards west, Ramanagaram, Malavalli, Maddur, Bengaluru are the nearby Cities to Sathanur.[4]

Methodology

A selection of multispectral and multi-temporal images is used for the study. This adopting a time interval of five years suggested by experts and a spatial resolution of 30 m, the investigation is carried out. In this study, ERDAS[5] software is used at different stage for analysis and map production. A supervised classification is used to facilitate land use change detection. The time period for the analysis is 2000–17 in Hoskote and Kanakapura. In order to facilitate land use change detection in this research, five classes of land uses were generated Habitation, Waterbody, Agriculture, Vegetation and Others which include Fallow Land or Waste Land. Level 1 of classes will be used to generate change statistics (Table 2.3).

The LU/LC map of the study area, i.e. Hoskote Taluk and Kanakapura Taluk and its fringe area, has been prepared by the data acquired from the above source of Landsat series. To identify the characteristics of the two peri-urban cluster data collected from sources like Bengaluru Metropolitan Development Authority, Town and Country Planning Organisation, Karnataka Remote Sensing Application Centre and Census of India. The study area is formed by an outer fringe which is a contiguous area outside boundary of Bruhat Bengaluru Mahanagara Palike (BBMP). Based on the above-mentioned land use classes, the maps are produced using ERDAS[6] software. LU/LC maps are generated for the two peripheral clusters and the two villages each from two peripheral clusters. Using LU/LC statistics, further statistical analysis is conducted to understand the extent and pattern in the land use cover of the periphery. Time series plot is used to analyse the structural transition in the Land Use/Land Cover pattern. The structural break in the land covers is identified using dummy variable technique.

Table 2.3 Data used and sources

Acquisition Date	Satellite Number	Sensor Type	WRS Path/Row	UTM Zone	Datum	Spatial Resolution (m)
26/10/2000	Landsat 7	ETM	144/051	43 N	WGS84	30
17/01/2005	Landsat 5	TM	144/051	43 N	WGS84	30
31/01/2010	Landsat 5	TM	144/051	43 N	WGS84	30
23/03/2017	Landsat 8	OLI	144/051	43 N	WGS84	30

Source: Compilation by the author.

Land Use/Land Cover (LU/LC) Changes in East and South Taluk

Most empirical studies on land use change have depended on the application of remote sensing data and GIS for analysis to the study area chosen. Several change detection techniques have been identified in the literature; the commonly used techniques include principal component analysis vegetative indices, clustering and post-classification comparison (Dekolo et al., 2017). Markov chain models are used to identify changes in land use and land cover at a variety of spatial scales. These models focus on a much larger spatial scale and involve both urban and non-urban covers (Drewett, 1969). These studies use the first-order Markov chain models (Weng, 2001). In this study, change detection is done using LU/LC data from 2000 to 2017. In order to facilitate land use change detection, five classes of land use were generated, Water Body, Agriculture, Vegetation, Built-up and Others which include Fallow Land or Waste Land. Level 1 classes were used for generating change detection statistics. ERDAS Software is used at different stages for analysis and map production. For the land use change detection, a supervised classification is used. The change detection is analysed in every five-year starting from 2000 to 2005, 2005 to 2010, 2010 to 2017 (to the recent period where the data collection is done). This is based on expert's opinion. There are not many changes in the Land Use/Land Cover year on year. Therefore, initially change detection is observed for the five intervals, and later, it is extended to the recent period. The change detection shows the changes in the LU/LC pattern[7] in the Taluk from 2000 to 2017.

Hoskote is a peripheral area located on the eastern side of Bengaluru which has close proximity to Whitefield is a major IT hub of the city. There is a surge in demand of residential units; nearby there is a continuous spree of development to feed the rising demand from Whitefield. Consequently, there is rapid changes in the LU/LC of Hoskote. Initially, a Taluk-wise analysis of LU/LC is conducted. Next, LU/LC of peri-urban village is conducted to understand extent of transition in land covers in the village level (Figure 2.1 and Table 2.4).

The LU/LC map depicted shows a visible change in the various land covers taken for the analysis. The map shows a noticeable change in the agriculture, built-up land and other category of land by 2017. The LU/LC map is based on the data acquired from land sat (refer Table 4.1: LU/LC change detection using LU/LC statistics for Hoskote [2000–2017]). Figure 2.2 shows the changes in various land covers across the years. The change detection of land covers is conducted, and the extent of change is depicted.

Figure 2.3 shows five land classifications in graphs starting from Waterbody (I), the % in share area of waterbody to total hectares of land area. In the year 2000, the extent of water body is of 2.56% of the total hectares of land area; in 2005, it is 6.44%; in 2010, 5.74%; and in 2017, 3.4%. From 2000 to

Table 2.4 LU/LC change detection of Hoskote Taluk for the year 2000–17 (area in hectares)

LU/LC	2000		2005		2010		2017		2000–05	2005–10	2010–17
	Area	%	Area	%	Area	%	Area	%	%	%	%
Water body	1,408	2.56	3535.79	6.44	3111.48	5.74	1868.85	3.40	3.88	-0.7	-2.34
Agriculture	32,580	59.34	35978.91	65.58	29060	53.61	25064	45.69	6.24	-11.97	-7.92
Vegetation	3,444	6.27	3556	6.48	3111.48	5.74	3444	6.27	0.21	-0.74	0.53
Built Up	1,524	2.77	1400.41	2.55	2834.86	5.23	3153.95	5.74	-2.77	2.68	0.51
Others	15,901	28.96	10385.89	18.93	16739.18	29.67	21326.2	38.87	-10.	10.74	9.2
Total	54,857	100	54,857	100	54,857	100	54,857	100	0	0	0

Source: Author's calculation using Landsat data.

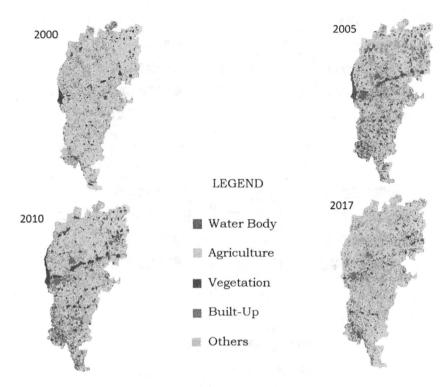

Figure 2.1 LU/LC Map of Hoskote for the period 2000–17. Author's compilation using Landsat data.

2005, there is 3.88% increase in water body. However, waterbody declined to 0.70% in the period 2005–10. Further waterbody has come down 2.34% in the seven-year period 2010–17.

Graph II shows the percentage share in area of agriculture to total hectares of land area. Agricultural land has major share among total land covers in Hoskote. In the year 2000, the extent of agriculture is of 59.34% of the to-tal hectares of land area; in 2005, it is 65.58%; in 2010, 53.61% and in 2017, 45.69%. From 2000 to 2005, there is 6.2% increase in agriculture. However, agriculture declined to −12% for the period 2005–10. Further agriculture has come down −7.9% in the seven-year period 2010–17. Hoskote Taluk faces drastic changes and water scarcity is a major problem in this area.

Graph III shows the percentage share in area of vegetation to total hectares of land area. In the year 2000, the extent of vegetation is of 6.27% of the total hectares of land area; in 2005, it is 6.48%; in 2010, it is 5.74% and in 2017, it is 6.27%. From 2000 to 2005, there is 0.2% increase in vegetation. However, vegetation declined to −0.7% in the period 2005–10. Further vegetation has increased to 0.5% in the seven-year period 2010–17.

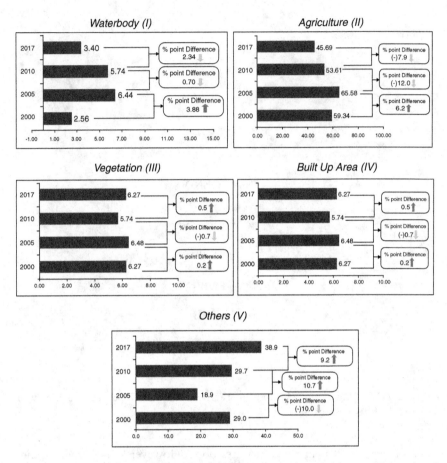

Figure 2.2 Share (in % area) of various land uses in Hoskote to the total hectares of land area and Percentage change detection (in % point difference) of hectares in various land uses. Author's compilation using LU/LC data.

Graph IV shows the percentage share in area of built-up to total hectares of land area. Built-up land has second major share among total land covers in Hoskote. In the year 2000, the extent of built-up is of 2.77% of the total hectares of land area; in 2005, it is 2.55%; in 2010, 5.23% and in 2017, 5.74%. From 2000 to 2005, there is −0.2% decline in built-up land. Further, built-up increased to 2.7% in the period 2005–10, 0.5% for the seven-year period 2010–17. From 2005 to 2010, there is a huge decline in agriculture in Hoskote.

Graph IV shows the percentage share in area of other land to total hectares of land area. Other land has third major share among total land covers in Hoskote. In the year 2000, the extent of other land category is of 29% of the

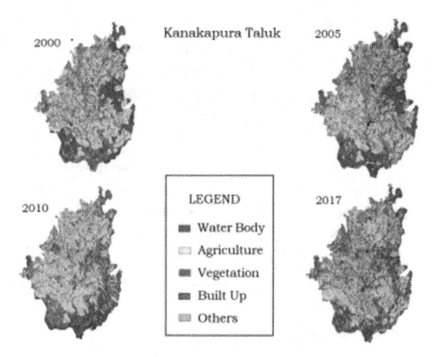

Figure 2.3 LU/LC Map of Kanakapura for the period from 2000 to 2017. Compilation by the author.

total hectares of land area; in 2005, it is 18.9%; in 2010, 29.7% and in 2017, 38.9%. From 2000 to 2005, there is −10.0% decline in other land. However, it increased to 10.7% in the period 2005–10. Further, it has come increased to 9.2% in the seven-year period 2010–17 (Figure 2.4 and Table 2.5).

LU/LC change detection shows changes in the pattern of Kanakapura Taluk from 2000 to 2017. Kanakapura Taluk has 159,426 hectares of land. Major portion of Kanakapura is farmlands. It is 73,916 ha for the year 2000. The LU/LC map shows a gradual change in 17 years. The change detection shows the changes in LU/LC from 2000 to 2017.

The changes in the five-land classification in five graphs starting from Waterbody (I) which shows the changes in share in % area of waterbody to total hectares of land area in Kanakapura. In the year 2000, the extent of water body is of 0.424% to the total hectares of water body; in 2005, it is 1.2%; in 2010, 1.27% and in 2017, 1.14%. From, 2000 to 2005, there is only 0.78% increase in water body. Increase in waterbody is just 0.07% in the period 2005–10. Further, it has declined to −1.13% in the seven-year period 2010–17.

Graph II shows the percentage share in area of agricultural land to total hectares of land area in Kanakapura. In the year 2000, the extent of agriculture is of 46.36% of the total hectares of land. In 2005, it is 43.68%; in 2010,

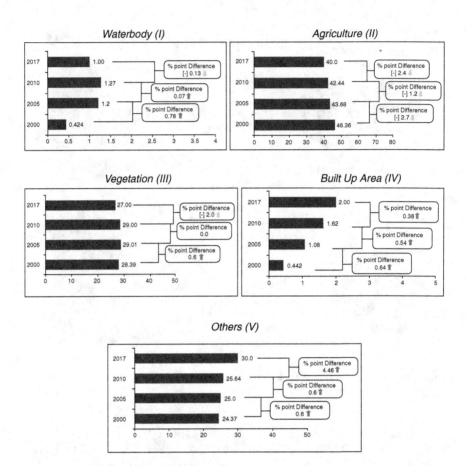

Figure 2.4 Share (in % area) of various land uses in Kanakapura to the total hectares of land area and Percentage change detection (in % point difference) of hectares in various land uses.

it is 42.44% and in 2017, it is 40%. From 2000 to 2005, there is only −2.7% decrease in agriculture. Decrease in agriculture is just −1.2% in the period 2005–10. Further, it has come declined to −2.67% in the seven-year period 2010–17. Kanakapura has more farmlands. However, the farmlands have not declined much over a period of 17 years.

Graph III shows the percentage share in area of vegetation to total hectares of land area in Kanakapura. In the year 2000, the extent of vegetation is of 28.39% of the total hectares; in 2005, it is 29.05%; in 2010, it is 27% and in 2017, it is 26.5%. From 2000 to 2005, there is only 0.6% increase in vegetation. Increase in vegetation is just −0.01% in the period 2005–10. Further, it has come declined to −2.5% in the seven-year period 2010–17.

Graph IV shows the percentage share in area of built-up land to total hectares of land area in Kanakapura. In the year 2000, the extent of other

Table 2.5 LU/LC change detection of Kanakapura for the years 2000–17 (area in hectares)

LU/LC	2000		2005		2010		2017		2000–05	2005–10	2010–17
	Area	%	Area	%	Area	%	Area	%	%	%	%
Water body	676.26	0.424	1925.84	1.2	2,039	1.27	1818.8	1	0.776	0.07	−0.13
Agriculture	73,916	46.36	69652.34	43.68	67,661	42.44	62,237	40	−2.67	−1.22	−2.44
Vegetation	45,263	28.39	46263	29.01	46,263	29	4,6263	27	0.61	−0.01	−2.5
Built Up	704.74	0.442	1724.82	1.08	2,585	1.62	2,674	2	0.63	0.54	0.38
Others	38,866	24.37	39,858	25	40,878	25.64	46433.2	30	0.63	0.64	4.46
Total	159,426	100	159,426	100	159,426	100	159,426	100	0	0	0

Source: Author's calculation using Landsat data.

built-up is of 0.442% of the total hectares of land. In 2005, it is 1.08%; in 2010, 1.62% and in 2017, 1.67%. From 2000 to 2005, there is only 0.64% increase in water body. Increase in waterbody is just 0.54% in the period 2005–10. Further, it has come just increased to 0.05% in the seven-year period 2010–17.

Graph V shows the percentage share in the area of other land[8] to total hectares of land area. Others land has third major share among total land covers in Kanakapura. In the year 2000, the extent of other land category is of 24.37% of the total hectares of land area; in 2005, it is 25%; in 2010, 25.64% and in 2017, it is 30%. From 2000 to 2005, there is 0.6 increase in other land. It just does not have much change in the period 2005–10. Further, it has just increased to 4.46% in the seven-year period 2010–17.

Trends in Land Use/Land Cover (LU/LC) Changes in Peri-Urban Locales

Two villages from Hoskote periphery were selected, they are Devanagundi and Tavarekere. Peripheral villages are known for mixed developments and significant industrial developments. Both villages are neither urban nor rural. They subject to a peri-urban transition (Tables 2.6 and 2.7).

Figures 2.5 and 2.6 show the LU/LC changes in the peri-urban villages, Hoskote Taluk. Statistics shows the LU/LC changes in Devanagundi peri-urban village. In Hoskote, there is a rapid transition due to the growth of industrial units in the past decades. The extent of agricultural land has got reduced with a change in the built-up land from 4.72% in 2000 to 8% in

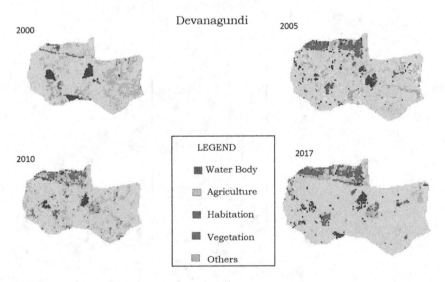

Figure 2.5 LU/LC map of Devanagundi peri-urban village. Compilation by the author.

Table 2.6 LU/LC statistics for Devanagundi (2000–17), and change detection (area in hectare)

LU/LC	2000		2005		2010		2017		2000–05	2005–10	2010–17
	Area	%	Area	%	Area	%	Area	%	%	%	%
Water body	32.16	5.56	28.36	4.9	22.2	3.84	16.2	2.8	−0.66	−1.06	−1.04
Agriculture	486.81	84.22	485.75	84	480.16	83	475.34	82.23	−0.22	−0.03	−0.77
Vegetation	2.6	0.44	2.4	0.41	2.23	.38	2.15	0.37	−0.03	−0.17	−0.01
Built Up	27.33	4.72	30.2	5.22	41.31	7.14	47.39	8.19	2.87	1.92	1.05
Others	29.1	5.03	31.29	5.41	32.1	5.55	36.92	6.38	2.19	0.14	0.83
Total	578	100	578	100	578	100	578	100	0	0	0

Source: Author's calculation using Landsat data.

Table 2.7 LU/LC statistics for Tavarekere (2000–17), and change detection (area in hectare)

LU/LC	2000		2005		2010		2017		2000–05	2005–10	2010–17
	Area	%	Area	%	Area	%	Area	%	%	%	%
Water body	7.6	2.13	6.73	1.89	6	1.68	5.9	1.65	−0.87	−0.21	−0.1
Agriculture	318.87	89.57	317.07	89	311.43	87.48	306.32	86	−0.57	−1.52	−1.48
Vegetation	3.46	0.97	3.2	.89	2.9	0.81	2.9	.81	−0.08	−0.08	0
Built Up	12.6	3.53	13	3.65	13.3	3.73	15.2	4.26	0.4	0.08	1.9
Others	13.47	3.78	16	4.49	23.37	6.56	25.68	7.21	0.71	2	0.64
Total	356	100	356	100	356	100	356	100	0	0	0

Source: Author's calculation using Landsat data.

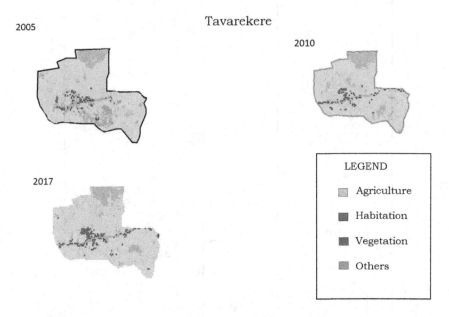

Figure 2.6 LU/LC map of Taverekere peri-urban village. Compilation by the author.

2017, and there is an increase in the wasteland or fallow land belonging to the other category, 5% to 6.38% in 2017. Tavarekere village has undergone transition mainly because of the industrial growth and manufacturing units. The agricultural land in Taverekere is 89.57% in 2000, and it has reduced to 86% in 2017. There are not many changes in the water bodies and vegetation in the area in past two decades. There is a change in the built-up area, while the land under the other category shows an increase to the extent of around 4% increase as compared to Tavarekere village; Devanagundi village has experienced more significant changes in the land use/land cover pattern. The following tables and maps show the LU/LC change of Harohalli and Sathanur. These are two growth nodes of Kanakapura (Figures 2.7 and 2.8; Table 2.9).

Among the villages selected for the study from South Bengaluru, Harohalli has undergone discernible land use changes in the recent decades. The peri-urban growth is attributed to Bengaluru city. There are mixed land use developments observed in Sathanur. The LU/LC change detection analysis shows that agricultural land has reduced considerably with the built up and other land increasing 2% and 5–9% respectively. Peri-urban villages are in a state of transition; among the four peri-urban villages considered for the analysis, Harohalli village shows significant changes in its LU/LC pattern. Therefore, in the further analysis, the significance of land cover is checked only for Harohalli Peri-Urban Village.

Table 2.8 LU/LC statistics for Harohalli (2000–17), and change detection (area in hectare)

LU/LC	2000		2005		2010		2017		2000–05	2005–10	2010–17
	Area	*%*	*Area*	*%*	*Area*	*%*	*Area*	*%*	*%*	*%*	*%*
Water body	17.01	1.01	32.43	1.93	38.07	2.26	27.99	1.67	0.93	0.33	-0.59
Agriculture	1221.18	72.9	1309.79	78.19	1306.51	78	1183.68	70.66	5.29	-0.19	-7.4
Vegetation	3.92	0.23	3.32	0.19	3.2	0.19	2.7	0.16	-0.04	0	-0.13
Built Up	36.51	2.17	53.07	3.16	65.40	3.9	105.94	6.32	0.99	0.74	2.42
Others	396.18	23.65	276.39	16.5	261.82	15.63	354.69	21.17	-7.15	-0.87	5.54
Total	1675	100	1675	100	1675	100	1675	100	0	0	0

Source: Author's calculation using Landsat data.

Table 2.9 LU/LC statistics for Sathanur (2000–17), and change detection (area in hectares)

LU/LC	2000		2005		2010		2017		2000–05	2005–10	2010–17
	Area	*%*	*Area*	*%*	*Area*	*%*	*Area*	*%*	*%*	*%*	*%*
Water body	9.6	1.6	9.4	1.57	8.8	1.48	9.2	1.54	-0.03	-1.43	1.4
Agriculture	508.02	85.23	490.63	82.32	481.1	80.72	470.78	78.98	-2.91	-1.6	-0.74
Vegetation	9.0	1.51	8.6	1.44	9.2	1.54	8.9	1.49	-0.07	0.1	-0.05
Built Up	38.3	6.42	41.1	6.89	46.6	7.81	53.1	8.90	2.8	0.92	1.09
Others	31.08	5.21	46.27	7.76	54	9.06	54.02	9.06	2.55	0	3.72
Total	596	100	596	100	596	100	596	100	0	0	0

Source: Author's calculation using Landsat data.

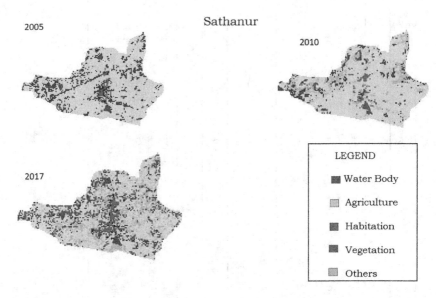

Figure 2.7 LU/LC map of Sathanur peri-urban village. Compilation by the author.

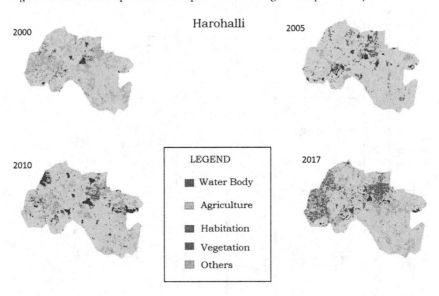

Figure 2.8 LU/LC map of Harohalli peri-urban village. Compilation by the author.

Summary

There is a noticeable change in Land Use/Land Cover (LU/LC) in the periphery from 2000 to 2017 and decrease in the agricultural land and increase in built up and fallow land. The increase in the fallow land is more than the increase in the built-up land. There are visible topographical changes in Hoskote. Agriculture and built-up show visible changes in Harohalli peripheral village of Kanakapura Taluk and Hoskote Taluk. The major reason for this significant change Hoskote is the connectivity and accessibility to IT centres. The growth of Harohalli village is due to the industrial establishments of KIADB. Establishment and growth of KIADB industries during this period up to 2010. In the recent years, visible changes in the land uses are due to the development of metro line and the growth of real estate. The good reason for the growth of Hoskote is its proximity to Whitefield IT park; Whitefield is exhausted due to substantial demand of the people in the previous year up to 2010. There is land conversion in Hoskote for commercial, industrial and residential purposes. Among the four peripheral villages for LU/LC analysis, Harohalli village from Kanakapura periphery shows considerable changes in the land covers.

Notes

1 *PLUREL* is an integrated *project* funded within the sixth Research Framework Programme of the European Union.
2 https://is.mendelu.cz/eknihovna/opory/zobraz_cast.pl?cast=62146
3 https://villageinfo.in/karnataka/bangalore-rural.html
4 https://villageinfo.in/karnataka/bangalore/bangalore/south.html
5 Analysed using ERDAS with the help of expertise from KSRSAC, Bengaluru.
6 Earth Resources Data Analysis System.
7 An adaptive methodology of ground truth data collection increased the accuracy and precision of the final maps. Ground truth (GT) has been conducted through land cover observations and spectral measurements of various land features of interest, using ERDAS.
8 Note: In 2018, fallow land for India was 26,182 thousand hectares. Though India fallow land fluctuated substantially in recent years, it tended to increase through 2004–18 period ending at 26,182 thousand hectares in 2018.Fallow land, which was six around 11 lakh ha, increased to 13.50 lakh ha after mid-nineties in Karnataka. Fallow land area fluctuates from year to year; in certain years (like 1998–99, 1990–2000, 2001–02, 2006–07 and 2008–09), the percentage reached above 10% of the total (190.50 lakh ha) geographical area of the state. This was mainly because of deficient rainfall and the inability of the government to provide irrigation facilities in those years (Agricultural profile of Karnataka state M J Bhende).

References

Adell, G. (1999). *Theories and Models of the Peri-Urban Interface: A Changing Conceptual Landscape.* Draft, discovery.ucl.ac.uk.
Alonso, W. (1960). A theory of the urban land market. *Papers in Regional Science*, 6(1), 149–157.
Alonso, W. (1964). *Location and Land Use. Toward a General Theory of Land Rent.* Harvard University Press, Reprint edition 2013 ed. (February 5, 1964).
Anderson, J. R. (1976). *A Land Use and Land Cover Classification System for Use with Remote Sensor Data* (Vol. 964). Washington: US Government Printing Office.

Beckmann, M. J. (1972). Von Thünen revisited: A neoclassical land use model. *The Swedish Journal of Economics*, 94, 1–7.

Boserup, E. (1975). The impact of population growth on agricultural output. *The Quarterly Journal of Economics*, 89, 257–270.

Browder, J. O., Bohland, J. R., & Scarpaci, J. L. (1995). Patterns of development on the metropolitan fringe: Urban fringe expansion in Bangkok, Jakarta, and Santiago. *Journal of the American Planning Association*, 61(3), 310–327.

Bryant, C. R., Russwurm, L. J., & McLellan, A. G. (1982). *The City's Countryside. Land and Its Management in the Rural-Urban Fringe*. London, UK: Longman.

Caruso, G. (2001). *Peri-Urbanisation, the Situation in Europe: A Bibliographical Note and Survey of Studies in the Netherlands, Belgium, Great Britain, Germany, Italy and the Nordic Countries*.

Datta, R. (2004, September). Territorial integration: An approach to address urbanising villages in the planning for Delhi metropolitan area, India. In *Proceedings of the Territorial Integration of Urbanising Villages 40th ISoCaRP Congress, Geneva, Switzerland* (Vol. 22).

Di Gregorio, A. (2005). *Land Cover Classification System: Classification Concepts and User Manual: LCCS* (Vol. 2). Rome: Food & Agriculture Org., 1998.

Di Gregorio, A., & Jansen, L. J. M. (2000). *Land Cover Classification System, Concepts and User Manual*. GCP/RAF, 287. Rome, 1998.

Douglass, M., & Friedmann, J. (1998). *Cities for Citizens: Planning and the Rise of Civil Society in a Global Age*. London: John Wiley & Son Ltd.

Dredge, D. (1995). Sustainable rapid urban expansion: The case of Xalapa, Mexico. *Habitat International*, 19(3), 317–329.

Drewett, J. R. (1969). A stochastic model of the land conversion process: An interim report. *Regional Studies*, 3(3), 269–280.

Dekolo, S. O., & Olayinka, D. N. (2013). Monitoring peri-urban land use change with multi-temporal Landsat imagery. In Claire Ellul, Sisi Zlatanova, Massimo Rumor, and Robert Laurini, eds., *Urban and Regional Data Management*, 145–159.

Dupont, V. (2005). Peri-urban dynamics: Population, habitat and environment on the peripheries of large Indian metropolises. A review of concepts and general issues. CSH occasional paper, (14).

Fazal, S. (2012). *Land Use Dynamics in a Developing Economy: Regional Perspectives from India*. London: Springer Science & Business Media.

Filatova, T., Parker, D., & Van der Veen, A. (2009). Agent-based urban land markets: Agent's pricing behavior, land prices and urban land use change. *Journal of Artificial Societies and Social Simulation*, 12(1), 3.

Firman, T., & Dharmapatni, I. A. I. (1994). The challenges to sustainable development in Jakarta metropolitan region. *Habitat International*, 18(3), 79–94.

Friedberg, R. M. (2001). The impact of mass migration on the Israeli labor market. *The Quarterly Journal of Economics*, 116(4), 1373–1408, USA.

Friis, C., & Nielsen, J. (2014). *Exploring the Potential of the Telecoupling Framework for Understanding Land Change*. Berlin.

Ganasri, B. P., & Dwarakish, G. S. (2015). Study of land use/land cover dynamics through classification algorithms for Harangi catchment area, Karnataka State, INDIA. *Aquatic Procedia*, 4, 1413–1420.

Hardaway, R. M. (1997). Environmental malthusianism: Integrating population and environmental policy. *Environmental Law*, 27, 1209.

Holden, S. T., & Ghebru, H., (2010). Factor market imperfections and rural land rental markets in Northern Ethiopian Highlands. In *The Emergence of Land Markets in Africa* (pp. 87–105). New York: Routledge.

Iaquinta, D. L., & Drescher, A. W. (2000). Defining the peri-urban: Rural-urban linkages and institutional connections. *Land Reform*, 2, 8–27.

Ingram, G. K. (1998). Patterns of metropolitan development: What have we learned? *Urban Studies*, 35(7), 1019–1035.

Jolly, C. L., Torrey, B. B., & National Research Council. (1993). *Population and Land Use in Developing Countries: Report of a Workshop* (p. 158). Washington, DC: National Academy Press.

Koomen, E., & Buurman, J. (2002, April). Economic theory and land prices in land use modeling. In *5th AGILE Conference on Geographic Information Science, Palma* (Balearic Islands Spain) April 25th-27th (Vol. 7).

Lipton, M. (1977). *Why Poor People Stay Poor: A Study of Urban Bias in World Development*. Temple Smith; Canberra: Australian National University Press.

Maconachie, R. (2016). *Urban Growth and Land Degradation in Developing Cities: Change and Challenges in Kano Nigeria*. London: Routledge.

Marshall, F., Waldman, L., MacGregor, H., Mehta, L., & Randhawa, P. (2009). *On the Edge of Sustainability: Perspectives on Peri-Urban Dynamics*. STEPS Working Paper 35, Brighton: STEPS Centre.

Meyer, W. B., & Turner, B. L. (1992). Human population growth and global land-use/cover change. *Annual Review of Ecology and Systematics*, 23(1), 39–61.

Moffat, T., & Finnis, E. (2005). Considering social and material resources: The political ecology of a peri-urban squatter community in Nepal. *Habitat International*, 29(3), 453–468.

Morton, J., Solecki, W., Dasgupta, P., Dodman, D., & Rivera-Ferre, M. G. (2014). Cross-chapter box on urban–rural interactions – context for climate change vulnerability, impacts, and adaptation, 153–155.

Narain, V., Anand, P., & Banerjee, P. (2013). Periurbanization in India: A Review of the Literature and Evidence. Report for the Project: Rural to Urban Transitions and the Peri-Urban Interface. *SaciWATERs*. First published in India.

Ogawa, H., & Fujita, M. (1980). Equilibrium land use patterns in a nonmonocentric city. *Journal of Regional Science*, 20(4), 455–475.

Pahl, R. E. (1965). *Urbs in Rure. The Metropolitan Fringe in Hertfordshire, Geographical Paper 2*. London: London School of Economics and Political Science.

Pelorosso, R., Leone, A., & Boccia, L. (2009). Land cover and land use change in the Italian central Apennines: A comparison of assessment methods. *Applied Geography*, 29(1), 35–48.

Pryor, R. J. (1968). Defining the rural-urban fringe. *Social Forces*, 47(2), 202–215.

Perroux, F. (1949). Le Macrodecisioni. *Giornale degli Economisti e Annali di Economia*, 463–490. Anno 8, No 9/10.

Quan, B., He-Jian, Z., Song-Lin, C., Römkens, M. J. M., & Bi-Cheng, L. (2007). Land suitability assessment and land use change in Fujian Province, China. *Pedosphere*, 17(4), 493–504.

Ravetz, J., Fertner, C., & Nielsen, T. S. (2013). The dynamics of peri-urbanization. In K Nilsson, S Pauleit, S Bell, C Aalbers, and TAS Nielsen (eds), *Peri-urban futures: Scenarios and models for land use change in Europe* (pp. 13–44). Berlin, Heidelberg: Springer.

Ramachandran, T. V., Setturu, B., & Aithal, B. H. (2012). Peri-urban to urban landscape patterns elucidation through spatial metrics. *International Journal of Engineering Research and Development*, 2(12), 58–81.

Rodehever, M. W. (1946): The Rural- Urban Fringe: An Interstitial area. Unpublished PhD Dissertation. Department of Geography. University of Wisconsin.

Rondinelli, D. (1991). Asian urban development policies in the 1990s: From growth control to urban diffusion. *World Development*, 19(7), 791–803.

Samat, N., Hasni, R., & Elhadary, Y. A. E. (2011). Modelling land use changes at the peri-urban areas using geographic information systems and cellular automata model. *Journal of Sustainable Development*, 4(6), 72.

Sarkar, S., & Bandyopadhyay, S. (2013). Dynamics of the peri urban interface: Issues and perspectives for management. *Transactions: Journal of the Institute of Indian Geographers*, 35(1), 49–62.

Saxena, M., & Sharma, S. (2015). Periurban area: a review of problems and resolutions. *International Journal of Engineering Research & Technology*, 4(09), 2278-0181.

Singh, D., & Vyas, P. A. (2015). Planning Strategies for the Development of Peri-Urban Area.

Shaw, A. (1999). Emerging patterns of urban growth in India. *Economic and Political Weekly*, 969–978.

Stohr, W. B., & Taylor, F. (1981). *Development from Above or Below? The Dialectics of Regional Planning in Developing Countries*. Vienna: WU Vienna University of Economics and Business.

Su, S., Jiang, Z., Zhang, Q., & Zhang, Y. (2011). Transformation of agricultural landscapes under rapid urbanization: A threat to sustainability in Hang-Jia-Hu region, China. *Applied Geography*, 31(2), 439–449.

Tacoli, C. (1998). Rural-urban interactions: a guide to the literature. *Environment and Urbanization*, 10(1), 147–166.

Tali, J. A., & Nusrath, A. (2014). A literature survey on rural urban fringe. *Journal of International Academic Research for Multidisciplinary*, 2(1), 504–517.

Thunen, J. H. V., Hall, P., & Thünen, J. H. V. (1966). *Von Thunen's Isolated State*. Trans. by Wartenberg, Carla M. ed. by Peter Hall.

Turner, M. G. (1987). Land use changes and net primary production in the Georgia, USA, landscape: 1935–1982. *Environmental Management*, 11(2), 237–247.

Unwin, T. (1989). Urban-rural interaction in developing countries: A theoretical perspective. In Potter and Unwin (eds.), *The Geography of Urban-rural Interaction in Developing Countries: Essays for Alan B. Mountjoy*. London: Routledge.

Weng, Q. (2002). Land use change analysis in the Zhujiang Delta of China using satellite remote sensing, GIS and stochastic modelling. *Journal of environmental management*, 64(3), 273–284.

Winoto, J., & Schultink, G. (1996). *Impacts of urbanization on agricultural sustainability and rural life in West Java, Indonesia*. Research report from the Michigan State University Agricultural Experiment Station, East Lansing.

Willis, A. M. (2007). From peri-urban to unknown territory. *Design Philosophy Papers*, 5(2), 79–90.

3 Econometric Analysis of Land Use Changes

Land Use/Land Cover (LU/LC) Changes in Hoskote

Land use change is a major challenge in the peri-urban environment. Dynamic changes result in persistent loss of forest and agricultural resources in peri-urban areas of large cities (Lawanson et al., 2012). Regression-based land use analysis shows the locations of land use and land cover change to a set of spatially explicit variables and uses models such as logistic. The analysis focuses on changes in spatial patterns of agricultural land use, driving factors and their implications. Differences in this phenomenon over time can be determined and evaluated visually or using digital techniques such as GIS. In this analysis, LU/LC-based data is used for regression analysis and identified the direction of land use changes in the periphery. The analysis of land use changes in Hoskote Taluk from 2000 to 2017 is conducted with the help of LU/LC change initially. There is a change in the land use pattern over 17 years.

Hoskote Taluk has 54,857 hectares of land in 2000. In 2000, major portion of it was farmland, 32,580 ha. That is, 59.34% of the total land use. However, the wasteland or fallow land constituted second, 15901 Ha. It is 28.96% of total land use. But over a period of 17 years, the agrarian land is converted to different other purposes. By the year 2017, farmland was reduced to 25,064 that is 45.69%, whereas the built-up land has increased to 3153.95; it is 5.74% of the total land use and waste land is 21325.2 that is 38.87% of the total land use. There is a small variation in the water body and vegetation from 2000 to 2017. There is a considerable decrease in the agricultural land and increase in built-up and wasteland. The increase in the waste land is more than the increase in the built-up land. It can be concluded that there is a change in the LU/LC pattern in the Hoskote Taluk. LU/LC analysis of the Hoskote Taluk shows a structural break in the year 2009 and decrease in the agricultural land and increase in built-up and wasteland. The increase in the waste land is more than the increase in the built-up land. It can be concluded that there is a change in the land use/land cover pattern in the Hoskote Taluk. Hoskote is a peripheral area located on the eastern side of Bengaluru laying at the intersection of National Highway (NH) 4 and NH 207. Hoskote has close proximity

DOI: 10.4324/9781003362333-3

to Whitefield that is a major IT hub of the city. There exists a surge in demand of residential units; nearby area such as Hoskote is also on the continuous speed of development to feed the rising demand from Whitefield.

Industrial area in Hoskote has the presence of nearly 200 industrial units that are occupied by global automotive brands such as VOLVO and Honda especially in the peri-villages like Tavarekere. Further to this, a slew of manufacturing hubs is being developed in nearby locations such as Narsapura and Budigere. Hoskote has superb connectivity with Whitefield (14 KM), Outer Ring Road and lies on the growth corridors of NH-4 that connects Pune-Bengaluru-Chennai. The location has close proximity to proposed Peripheral Ring Road that will reduce the travel time to nearby areas such as Whitefield, Hoodi and Marathahalli upon completion. According to Square Yards GIC, Hoskote has shown price appreciation of more than 11% in the past one year on the back of better job opportunities, connectivity and a prolific social infrastructure and affordable investment destination.

Land Use/Land Cover (LU/LC) Changes in Kanakapura

The analysis of land use changes in Kanakapura Taluk from 2000 to 2017 shows the change in the land use pattern over 17 years. Kanakapura Taluk has 159,426 hectares of land in the year 2000. In 2000, major portion of it was farmland, 73,916 ha. That is, 46.36% of the total land use. The wasteland or fallow land constituted 38866 ha; it is 24.37% of total land use. But over a period of 17 years the agrarian land is converted to different other purposes. By the year 2017, farmland was reduced to 62,237 ha that is 39%, whereas the built-up land has increased to 2674 ha; it is 1.67% of the total land use and wasteland is 46433.2 ha that is 29.1% of the total land use. There is a small variation in the waterbody and vegetation from 2000 to 2017 and decrease in the agricultural land and increase in built-up and waste land. The increase in the waste land is more than the increase in the built-up land.

There is gradual change in the land use/land cover pattern in the Kanakapura Taluk. Among the four peri-urban villages taken for the analysis, Harohalli village shows a visible change. There is a considerable decrease in the agricultural land and increase in built up and waste land. The increase in the waste land is more than the increase in the built-up land. It can be concluded that there is a change in the land use/land cover pattern in the Kanakapura Taluk. Land use pattern has changed mainly because of significant infrastructural changes, changing industrial commercial and residential land uses.

LU/LC analysis points out significant transformation of the periphery. Hoskote and Kanakapura Taluk have shown substantial growth in their population, land use and land value in the last two decades. Hoskote is a part of East Bengaluru periphery which shows remarkable changes in the land utilisation, demography, transition from agriculture to industrial and service-led growth. This is mainly because of the proximity to the city centre, IT corridors of the East Bengaluru. The increase in the population and extent of migrants and establishment of factories and small-scale industrial units has led to the demand for land in the peripheral regions of Hoskote. In Hoskote, growth is mainly because of industrial and IT developments.

Kanakapura is away from the city centre there is substantial growth of the industries of KIADB since 2006 and a significant change in the land value in the recent past due to the NICE road and metro line, further rapid growth in the land value in the Kanakapura road zone. Hence, there is very high demand for land in the South periphery. Peri-urban growth is because of Bengaluru city influence. There is a remarkable increase in the population growth. Kanakapura is known for its greenery and growth induced by the city influence. Kanakapura has the highest net sown area compared to all other peri-urban clusters. Most of the changes are rapid in this cluster; it is the Southern periphery which is known for farming, industrial growth and affordable housing and connectivity. In Kanakapura, growth is mainly attributed to the city influence. It led to a skyrocketing change in the land value in both the peripheries. The LU/LC analysis showed significant change in the land use pattern in Hoskote periphery and a gradual change in the Kanakapura periphery.

Impact of Land Use Change

Land use changes play a vital role in determining the land prices. Apparently, the decisions of public authorities contribute to the increase in land prices. The change of land use from agricultural to residential, industrial and commercial land use results in the creation of additional land value. The change in the land value is created by a decision of the public authority. However, some of the changes in the land use take place in Bengaluru without the permission of planning authority, illegally leading to distortions in the appropriate policy. Despite several restrictions on the transfer or changes in the land use, the land values in the periphery. There is a rising trend in the peri-urban land. This leads to the tendency of land conversion legally or illegally. Based on the evidence from the field it is concluded: The divergence between the market value and the government value of land is very wide and the quantity of land supplied by the public authority is small; the market prices continue to be at a skyrocketing level. The land use changes in the study areas lead to the following changes.

1. Conversion of agricultural land for non-agricultural purposes.
2. Land purchases for speculative purposes and real estate.

Land degradation in the areas surrounding agricultural land is a major problem in Hoskote. Fringe areas where land use was predominantly agricultural become sites for rapid, unplanned urban development. Land use change is a basic driver of peri-urban transition and with it, emerge changes in access to other natural resources such as water, engendering further socio-economic changes in livelihoods, migration and social composition of the population. Land acquisition for urban expansion has been noted to be a cause of great dissent among peri-urban residents against urban authorities in peri-urban (Kolathur Village Hoskote). There is an encroachment into the peripheral land, and it restructures existing development. Although peri-urban developments have led to considerable developments, it resulted in the reduction of the extent of farmlands and leading to land conversion at a rapid rate. In order to meet the growing demands of urbanisation, the fringe areas are converted into industrial, residential and commercial establishments (Hoskote and Kanakapura Periphery). It leads to haphazard growth and poor city planning, inadequate housing, slums, overcrowding, ill health, social polarisation, traffic congestion, environmental pollution, etc.

Structural Breaks in the Land Covers in Hoskote Taluk

Land use (LU) change is a major driving force underlying global environmental changes. Land use in peri-urban areas has grown with an increasing population and urbanisation process. Peri-urban villages have undergone many changes in the recent decades with an increase in the built-up land and a reduction in farmland. A perusal of these indicates that there was a structural change in land covers around 2010 in the peripheries. The structural breaks in the land covers are tested for Hoskote Taluk and Harohalli peri-urban village of Kanakapura Taluk of Bangalore using dummy variable technique. There exists visible change in land covers in Hoskote Taluk and there is a gradual transition in the Kanakapura Taluk. The structural breaks in agriculture and built-up land are captured in Hoskote. Similarly, among the four peripheral villages used for the change detection shows that Harohalli peripheral village shows a change in the land covers. To check the hypothesis, structural break in the land covers test is conducted for the peri-urban locales and the results are discussed for the areas where is a significant change in the land covers.

Agricultural Land in Hoskote Peri-Urban

To test the break in the land covers, the dummy variable technique is used as shown in model given by

$$lnYt = \propto +\beta_1 t + \beta_2 D + +\beta_3 Dt + \varepsilon \tag{3.1}$$

where

Yt = Agricultural land in Hoskote
D = 0 before 2009
  =1 after 2009
$$\ln Yt = 436.97 + 0.12t + 0.19D - 0.353Dt \tag{3.1.1}$$

(436.97) (2.99) (2.98) (−5.92) figures in the brackets are their respective t statistics

R square = 0.93, DW = 2.2
$d(\ln Y_t)/dt$ = 0.12−0.35
= 0.12 for D = 0 Pre 2009
= 0.12−0.35 for D = 1 Post 2009
= −0.23

If the estimated equations are of a semi-logarithmic form, the regression coefficients can be interpreted as the proportional growth of the relevant dependent variable. The regression coefficients tend to support the change of trend hypothesis as the periods 2000–09 and 2009–17. All the coefficients are significant at 1% level including interactive dummy.

The results show that agricultural land covers have registered a structural break. The structural breaks are visible for agricultural land covers after 2009. This analysis is conducted using LU/LC data for 18 years in two different seasons. Further, it is hypothesised that built-up land covers would show change and the testing of the same is conducted.

Built-Up Land in Hoskote

To evaluate the changes in the LU/LC pattern in the pre- and post-2009, a semi-logarithmic equation has been fitted against log linear built-up land covers with a trend, dummy variable and interaction variable.
  Where

ln Yt = built up land Hoskote
  D = 0, before 2009
    =1, after 2009
ln Yt = 7.966 − 0.090t − 0.45D + 0.97Dt   (3.1.2)

(30.07) (−1.92) (−0.63) (1.46) figures in the brackets are their respective *t* statistics

R squared = 0.53, DW = 1.6
$d(\ln Y_t)/dt$ = −0.090 + 0.97
= −0.090 for D = 0 Pre 2009
= −0.090 + 0.97 for D = 1 Post 2009
= 0.88

The trend coefficient is significant at 10% level. The figures in brackets are "t" values. The dummy variable remained negative, whereas the interaction variable is positive implies that the slope of the growth rate at the post-2009 period is more than the slope of growth in the pre-2009. The role of speculation is understood in this context of increasing built-up land in the periphery and the general sentiment and inclination of people towards land let them to possess land and to get an attractive return from the future sale of land. The structural breaks for the two land covers are tested for Hoskote. The structural breaks in the land covers such as agriculture and built up are evident in the process of peri–urban transformation. The time series plot of land covers supports the above testing of hypothesis (Figure 3.1).

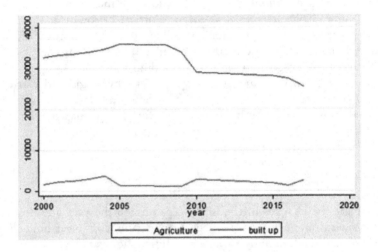

Figure 3.1 Time series plot of agriculture and built up Hoskote Taluk. Compilation by the author.
Note: Log value of area in hectares is used.

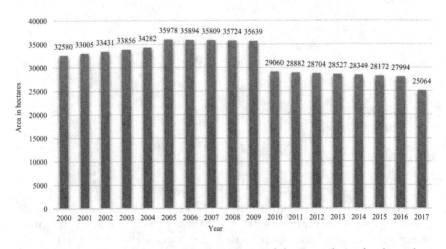

Figure 3.2 Decrease in agricultural land Hoskote Taluk. Compilation by the author.

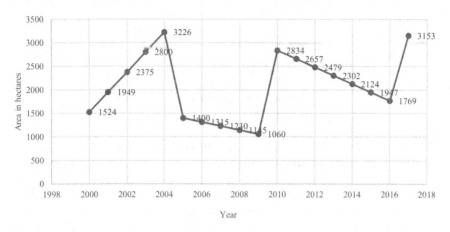

Figure 3.3 Increase in built-up land Hoskote Taluk. Compilation by the author.

As we see in the graph, the structural break is evident in agriculture land and built-up land in Hoskote. The time series plot of the land covers shows that there is a decline in the agriculture land in 2009. The extent of changes in the agricultural land and built-up land is shown in the graph (Figures 3.2 and 3.3).

In the case of Hoskote Taluk, structural changes in land cover in the year 2009. These findings have implications for structural changes and urbanisation especially in the agricultural sector which is more sensitive to land use/land cover change. Comparative examinations of the observatories of Taluk turned out that more remarkable phenomenon is since the structural break was evident in the changing peri-urban.[1] In Hoskote, the influence is mainly as that of ITPL, the changes are visible over a period of time due to the influence of IT parks and consequently, there is a growth in the land market.

Structural Breaks in Land Covers in Harohalli Peri-Urban Village

Agricultural Land in Harohalli Peri-Urban Village

Where

Yt = agricultural land Harohalli
D = 0, before 2010
  = 1, after 2010
$$\ln Yt = 7.11 + 0.007t + 0.217D - 0.021Dt \qquad (3.1.4)$$

(1,176) (8.02) (10.38) (−13.06) figures in the brackets are their respective t statistics

> R square 0.94, DW = 1.5
> $d(\ln Yt)/dt = 0.007 - 0.021$
> $= 0.007$ for D = 0 Pre 2010
> $= 0.007 - 0.021$ for D = 1 Post 2010
> $= -0.014$

The results show that agricultural land covers have shown a structural break. All the coefficients are significant at 1% level including interactive dummy. The structural breaks are visible for agricultural land covers after 2010. There is a decline in the agricultural land after 2010. Further, it is hypothesised that built-up land covers would show change and the testing of the same is conducted.

Built-Up Land in Harohalli

The structural break in the built-up land is captured using the following specification.
   where,

> Yt = built up land Harohalli
> D = 0, before 2010
> D = 1, after 2010
> $\ln Yt = 3.54 + 0.065t - 0.113D + 0.003Dt$ (4.1.5)

(298.96) (34.26) (−2.76) (0.99) figures in the brackets are their respective t statistics

> R square 0.99, DW = 1.6
> $d(\ln Yt)/dt = 0.065 + 0.003$
> $= 0.065$ for D = 0 Pre 2010
> $= 0.065 + 0.003$ for D = 1 Post 2010
> $= 0.068$

The trend coefficient and the coefficient representing dummy variable are significant at 1% level. The figures in brackets are "t" values. The dummy variable remained negative, whereas the interaction variable is positive. The LU/LC analysis and the hypothesis test showed there is a visible change in the land cover pattern Harohalli village as compared to the other peripheral villages. Harohalli Village and its peri-urban growth are attributed to the influence of KIADB. In the first phase in 2005, industrial developments started taking place. These developments accelerated in the second phase in 2008. The State-level Single Window Agency cleared an investment of Rs. 11,203 crores in 2005–06, to Harohalli in Kanakapura taluk for setting up townships of general industries. The phase II started in the year 2008, and since then, there has been a rapid change in the land use and the changes are evident since 2010. And, it is visible in the LU/LC mapping and the test results. The time series graph of land covers is given (Figure 3.4).

The time series plot of agriculture and built-up land shows the changes since 2010. The extent of change in agriculture land and built-up land is visible in the graphs (Figure 3.5).

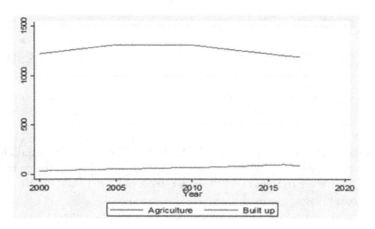

Figure 3.4 Time series plot of agriculture and built-up in Harohalli peri-urban village. Compilation by the author.

Note: Log value of area in hectares marked is used.

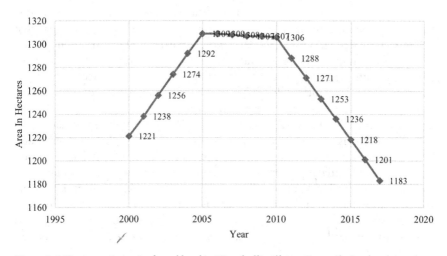

Figure 3.5 Decrease in agricultural land in Harohalli village. Compilation by the author.

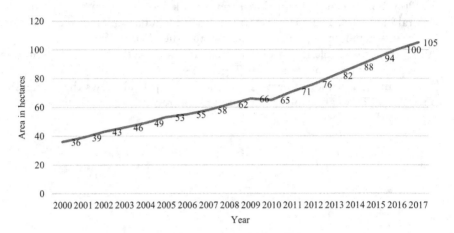

Figure 3.6 Increase in built-up land in Harohalli village. Compilation by the author.

Harohalli industrial belt shows the significant industrial development in the periphery. The investments of KIADB have shown a substantial change in the land use pattern. There is an active conversion of land in this peripheral village. As we see in the graph, there is a decrease in the built-up land in the peri-urban village (Figure 3.6).

The price of land has increased overtime with sufficient real estate developments taking place. This village has undergone many changes in the recent decades with an increase in the built-up land and a reduction in farmland. The built-up area has increased considerably. A perusal of these indicates that there was a structural change in land covers around 2010 in the peri-urban village.

Village or Taluk, it becomes clear that the land cover changed rapidly due to the development in the peri-urban location. By these facts, it is clear that urbanisation factor has influence on land use pattern. There are many future examination subjects, there are various patterns of change and it is guessed that they have a useful piece of information on the difference in land use changes concerning city scales. Thereby, it will be expected that the further knowledge concerning the determinants is required. In this study, structural break is evident in Harohalli[2] village and Hoskote Taluk level that shows the sudden change in land cover pattern is triggered by the residential and industrial growth. Similar structural break is not found in Kanakapura Taluk and the LU/LC analysis supports the same. There were overall changes in the land covers in Hoskote over 17 years. It shows the key drivers determine the land use changes in each periphery is different and also similar pattern in land cover does not happen in another periphery at the same time due to which Hoskote and Kanakapura differ significantly in terms of their land use pattern.

Implications of the Changes in Land Use/Land Covers (LU/LC)

These changing trends in land covers show other issues with respect to the changing land utilisation pattern. As evident from the LU/LC analysis, urbanisation and consequent demand for residential and industrial land use have engulfed agricultural land though it is a phenomenon in growing periphery of the metropolitan cities of India. Indeed, the loss of arable land to urban development has become a nationwide phenomenon. The loss of farm-land due to urban development has implications on agricultural productions and sustainable development of the country. Rapid urbanisation leads to industrial pollutions and lack of air and water quality. Another issue relates to the weakening of urban service delivery and compensation for land acquisition in the selected periphery and the provision of livelihood of the people in the peri-urban villages in the eastern cluster of Hoskote. The lateral expansion of cities without adequate demarcation has led to the increase in unplanned housing in periphery (Shaw, 1999). The reason for inadequate service delivery in these regions is the overlapping administrative boundaries or the absence of any arrangement in function, roles and responsibilities of the institutions resulting in poor accountability (Rathee, 2014). Apart from the socio-economic aspects, there are environmental implications in land-use conversions process. As urbanisation expands, the rapid increase in the built-up area results in depletion of water table and creating more stress on environment due to the excessive drilling of bore wells in the selected periphery of Hoskote as the demand for industrial and residential land use increases in the periphery.

Studies show land use change is a major problem at global and local level. Both population growth and rural-urban migration drive this change (Jedwab & Vollrath, 2015). Urban dynamics and its consequential persistent loss of forest and agricultural resources affects the environment in peri-urban areas of large cities (Lawanson et al., 2012). Regression-based land use analysis shows the locations of LU/LC change to a set of spatially explicit variables and uses models such as logistic. It is unlikely that agricultural land converted to developed uses will ever become available again for agricultural production (Su, 2011). Decline in total area of agricultural land scape would definitely result in lower self-supply abilities and threat to food security of this region accordingly. These fragmented lands are unsuitable for urban development (Dredge, 1995). Under rural agricultural use, the changes in demand for land have contributed to the growth of land markets (Holden & Ghebru, 2010). Land use change is a major challenge in the scenario of peripheral clusters of fast-growing metropolitan cities like Bengaluru.

Land use change is an inevitable process, and it is essential for economic development, but land use changes have an important cost to the society. The LU/LC analysis shows the conversion of agriculture land into non-agricultural land in the periphery. First of all, the conversion of agricultural land reduces the amount of land available for cultivation and reduces agricultural productivity (Lubowski et al., 2006). Second it poses changes to the farmers in periphery as seen in the peripheral Hoskote and Kanakapura which, in turn, leads to the competition for labour from non-agricultural sectors may raise farmers' labour costs, gradually leading to non-viability of agriculture as an occupation; there is a change in the land use pattern in both Kanakapura and Hoskote. The extent of agriculture is reduced more in Hoskote as the LU/LC analysis shows. It reinforces city has limited scope for agriculture.

In this process, urban development reduces the land available for the agriculture which, in turn, affects the lives and livelihoods of peri-urban farmers. This process leads to a surge in land prices in the periphery and there is more scope for the real estate in periphery and increase in the land value is the major implication. The shift in the occupational pattern of the people and the change in livelihoods of the people is a social aspect of the LU/LC change as it was evident in both peripheries. The implications of LU/LC change include loss of farmlands and less productivity, loss of livelihoods, increase in land value and demand for real estate. This is true for a larger context as well as that of a specific context of a peri-urban as it was evident in South East periphery.

Summary

Time series graph and the hypothesis testing showed a structural break in the LU/LC pattern in Harohalli peri-urban in 2010 and structural breaks in land covers of Hoskote Taluk is visible in 2009. There is active land transactions and land conversion in Hoskote for commercial, industrial and residential purposes. I analyse the difference in the land use pattern in Southeast peripheries and discuss why there is significant differences in the land utilisation. Structural breaks are visible in particular years due to the significant developments in the periphery. Structural breaks in the land covers have some important policy implications. Land use change has important consequences for sustainability and agriculture. Protection of farmland is a significant issue of policy implementation. Food security is an important consideration and priority for policy makers. Bangalore is known for vulnerability to drought; it is coincided by the socio-economic factors, land conversion and loss of livelihood for farmers. Policy assistance for sustainable farming and conversation of resources are needed for the sustainable development and planned city development.

Notes

1 Peri-urban areas are different across globally. In Bengaluru itself, peripheral areas of east and south are different. The study tries to bring the divergent nature of peri-urban. Although overall topographical changes are more in Hoskote, the yearly change in the particular land covers was high in Kanakapura and structural break is visible in a particular year in Kanakapura.
2 It is a peri-urban village in Kanakapura Taluk.

References

Dredge, D. (1995). Sustainable rapid urban expansion: The case of Xalapa, Mexico. *Habitat International*, 19(3), 317–329.

Holden, S. T. & Ghebru, H., (2010). Factor market imperfections and rural land rental markets in Northern Ethiopian Highlands. In Stein Holden, Keijiro Otsuka, and Frank Place, eds., *The Emergence of Land Markets in Africa* (pp. 87–105). New York: Routledge.

Jedwab, R., & Vollrath, D. (2015). Urbanization without growth in historical perspective. *Explorations in Economic History*, 58, 1–21.

Lawanson, T., Yadua, O., & Salako, I. (2012). *Environmental Challenges of Peri-Urban Settlements in the Lagos Megacity*. Environmental Science.

Lubowski, R. N., Vesterby, M., Bucholtz, S., Baez, A., & Roberts, M. J. (2006). *Major uses of land in the United States, 2002*. Economic Information Bulletin No. EIB-14.

Rathee, G. (2014). Trends of land-use change in India. In K. S. Sridhar, G. Wan (eds.), *Urbanization in Asia* (pp. 215–238). New Delhi: Springer.

Shaw, A. (1999). Emerging patterns of urban growth in India. *Economic and Political Weekly*, 34(16/17), 969–978.

Su, S., Jiang, Z., Zhang, Q., & Zhang, Y. (2011). Transformation of agricultural landscapes under rapid urbanization: A threat to sustainability in Hang-Jia-Hu region, China. *Applied Geography*, 31(2), 439–449.

4 Land Transactions in Peri-Urban Land Market of Bangalore

Land Transactions in Peri-Urban

Urban areas spread and grow further into the fringes assimilating farmland and open public spaces. It is evident that peri-urban areas are turning out to be the places where a lot of changes and activities are occurring due to urbanisation and population growth (Cotula & Neve, 2007). Land Market is centred around peripheral areas of Bengaluru, mainly residential commercial and industrial transactions are taking place in the periphery. In general, peri-urban zones experience unprecedented levels of land transactions due to potential purchasers and sellers for different land use purposes. Generally, there is less scholarly writing on peri-urban regions. Prominent attention is needed to problematise land transactions in peri-urban areas, and to make sure about the land rights in these areas (Toulmin & Quan, 2000). A remarkable development of edges has brought about dynamic land use changes and incessant land transactions. Peri-urban areas are the focal points of urban developments that range from urban expansion both formally and informally leading to the decline of agricultural land and rural employment opportunities (Allen, 2003).

In peri-urban zones, trends on land transactions are a clear indication of how the systems that regulate access to land are neglecting to adapt with the rapid demand and competition for land (Peters & Kambewa, 2007). Land markets in urban areas are categorised by the concurrence of different modes of supply that originate from the different stages of their development. In the peri-urban land market, land is rapidly being changed from agricultural to residential use (Gough & Yankson, 2000). Peripheral land markets attract builders and investors for various residential, industrial and commercial transactions. Therefore, the presence of peripheral areas along with the associated complexities throws up a debatable research problem in the context of Bengaluru City. The reasons for land transactions are diverse; there is a rapid growth observed in the real estate activities across the peri-urban land market. A rapid development of peri-urban areas promotes the growth of land markets along with a progressive commoditisation of land growing and land ending up being continuously commoditised.

DOI: 10.4324/9781003362333-4

In ordinary usage, price is the quantity of payment given by one party to another in return for goods or service (Omboi, 2011). Price alludes to the quantity of payment requested by a seller of goods or services, rather than the eventual payment amount. This requested amount is often called the asking price or selling price, while the actual payment may be called the transaction price or exchange value (Wales, 2009). Accordingly, land transactions in peri-urban regions have become increasingly frequent with the excess demand leading to the sub-division of land into smaller parcels so as to increase its supply and monetary benefits. Urban expansion and the vivacious competition for land which may result in changes in land use, ownership, property rights regime and land tenure (Wehrmann, 2008). The competition for land as a result of rapid urbanisation increases the importance of peri-urban land even more (Payne, 1997). Studies feature problems of land transactions, strife and natural resource management in peri-urban area (Saruchera & Omoweh, 2004). The extent of land transactions increases in the peri-urban areas, given the limited supply of land at CBD.[1]

Phases of Land Transactions in Peri-Urban Bangalore

A large number of buyers have actively engaged in the land transactions in Bangalore periphery. There are various phases in the growth of the land markets of Bangalore. They are as follows.

1 Early 1980s–90
2 Second phase: 1991–2000
3 Third phase: 2001–10
4 Fast growing phase: From 2010

Early 1980s–90

Several domestic IT firms and multi-national companies began their operations in Bangalore during this period. IT activity was concentrated in CBD; residential activity was restricted to BDA layouts within a 5–8 km radius of the CBD; the development of the IT industry was in its initial stages, with several domestic firms like Infosys, Wipro and others commencing their operation.[2] The impact of the IT sector on the growth of real estate sector was less during this period. BDA was responsible for land acquisition, development and distribution of developed sites. Construction was carried out by individual site owners as according to their assets. Residential land transaction development during 1991–95 was seen mostly in a few places such as BDA layouts of the South like Jayanagar, JP Nagar, Koramangala, Indiranagar and BTM Layout, due to their proximity to Electronics City. Land transactions were minimal during this phase since the impact of the IT sector was limited (Heitzman, 2001).

Second Phase

The second phase (1991–2000) is considered the emerging phase, wherein the IT industry assumed a significant role in the economy of the city. Residential land transactions witnessed a marvellous move during this period. In the period 1996–2000, the Government of Karnataka (GoK) made significant strides that supported the development of the IT industry in Bangalore and implemented three major policy and infrastructure initiatives to advance the IT industry in this stage.

1   Development of International Tech Park ITPL, in Whitefield
2   Announcement of IT policy by GoK in 1997
3   Development of outer ring roads which opened new areas for the residential development in peripheral areas.

All through this period (1991–2000), real estate development in the central and off-central locations was active due to constrained accessibility of land and proximity to economic hubs.[3] By 2001, Bangalore had established itself as a major centre of Technology in Asia. Electronics City, Whitefield and Outer Ring Road were established IT hubs in Bangalore, with an average annual assimilation close to 6–7 million sq. ft. With the development of IT activity in peripheral areas, especially Electronics City, residential activity in the Emerging Phase moved towards the BDA layouts and peripheral areas in the south-east periphery of Bangalore (Vestian, 2012). There is a continuous growth of land transactions during this period.

Third Phase

The period after 2000 is viewed as Growth Phase because this phase saw the transformation of Bangalore's IT sector to an export-oriented offsite software and service production centre from a body shopping on-site production hub. This period saw a phenomenal increase in number of IT jobs as compared to the previous two phases, leading to increased supply and absorption of IT-related office space as well as residential land transactions. The growth phase considered to be of Bangalore as an IT outsourcing hub and the city saw an expansion of about 150% in its average annual absorption of IT space. With about 50,000 employments made in the sector every year, demand for residential transactions expanded to 8,000–10,000 units in this stage from 2,000 to 4,000 units in this period (Vestian, 2012). Active areas of economic development and land transactions include Phase 2 of Electronics City, Whitefield and Outer Ring Road. With the accessibility of huge parcels of land in fringe areas, Electronic city, Whitefield and ORR, South Eastern quadrant kept on seeing a noteworthy level of residential activity. Large number of developers entered the real estate segment in Bangalore; this prompted an expansion in residential land transactions to meet the prerequisites of the growing demand (BDA, 2000).

Fast Growing Phase

The growth period after 2010 is considered the fastest developing stage; this is on the grounds that most IT and industrial units are established in peripheries. This has led to rapid changes in the land markets particularly in the fringe areas. The South Eastern periphery continues to be active in terms of residential transactions, but new micro-locations in the North Eastern periphery are witnessing medium to high levels of activity. The highlight of this phase is the differentiation of product types catering the needs of the people of all income levels in the peri-urban land markets. Most of the peripheral locations are acquired by the builders and developers. Farmers were willing to sell off their land expecting quick returns. There is quick development of real estate in the peripheries during this period.

The most promising residential markets in Bangalore are Sarjapur Road, ORR and Whitefield. Commissioning of Bangalore International Airport (BIA) has led to increase in residential development in Bangalore North.[4] The most encouraging private markets in Bangalore are Sarjapur Road, ORR and Whitefield. Commissioning of BIA has prompted increment in private improvement in Bangalore North. Old Madras Road is a potential site for residential growth due to its proximity to economic hubs Whitefield, ORR, Bangalore International Airport and CBD. Old Madras Road is a potential site for private development because of its closeness to financial centre Whitefield, ORR, Bangalore International Airport and CBD.[5] Development of the Outer Ring Road opened new areas for development in peripheral areas. Advancement of the Outer Ring Road opened new zones for improvement in fringe areas. This led to the development of the South Eastern quadrant with Electronics City to the south, Whitefield to the east and the stretch of Outer Ring Road connecting these two IT hubs as the "IT corridor" in Bangalore.[6] This resulted in improvement of the South Eastern quadrant with Electronics City towards the south, Whitefield towards the east and the stretch of Outer Ring Road interfacing these two IT centre points as the "IT hall" in Bangalore.

The land transactions in the peripheral locations started by 2000; it became frequent from 2010 in the peripheral locations where the IT firms and industries are located in Sarjapur, White field and Hebbal. The land transactions in the fringe areas began by 2000; it increased from 2010 in the fringe areas where the IT firms and enterprises are situated in Sarjapur, White field and Hebbal. Places like White field are exhausted after 2014 and IT professionals consider Hoskote as a place of moderate speculation. And the residential land market in East periphery is flourishing due to the proximity to IT centres and its connectivity via ORR. South Periphery shows progressive changes; transition is due to industrial developments by KIADB, connectivity of Bangalore city via Nandi Infrastructure Corridor Enterprises (NICE) Road and so on. The residential land transactions are frequent in the Kanakapura Road (BDA, 2000).

Agents in the Land Market

Buyers and sellers play a crucial role in the land markets. A statistical analysis has been used for estimating land sale pattern and land purchase. All the selected villages are located on the periphery of Bengaluru and have been subjected to land transactions in recent years. The land transactions include agricultural, residential, industrial and commercial transactions. Agents in the land market are buyers and sellers. Buyers and sellers create land prices; therefore, it is the behaviour of these buyers and sellers which needs to be modelled. To analyse the land transactions, regression equation is used. There are two "markets" for land, agriculture and non-agriculture. However, these markets are rarely in equilibrium, in that within either market there may be land offered for sale which is not purchased or there may be too little land available for all prospective buyers. In either case, a land market is then out of equilibrium. The amount of land moving from one "market" to the other in order to take advantage of differing demand and supply conditions may play a role in the pricing land. Land transfers from agriculture to non-agriculture use have been clearly visible in the selected peri-urban villages of Hoskote and Kanakapura Taluk.

For the collection of primary data on the land transactions for the study, a survey was conducted in two peripheries, Hoskote and Kanakapura, during 2018–19. Five villages from each periphery were taken for the land transaction survey. Although the survey was carried out in the recent period, what emerged was that the sample farmers/landlords had sold their land at different period time, beginning from 2001 to 2002. Furthermore, it emerged that not all the individuals had transacted (selling of their lands) at two different time periods. As collected data on land transactions over a period of 18 years (from 2001–02 to 2018–19) involving number of transactions carried out by different sample farmers under the study. I had a situation where the target respondents were randomly sampled from cross-sections of individuals at different points of time. List of villages is as per the given list of villages given in the appendix.

The fringe area is located outside the 198 wards of BBMP boundary. The peri-urban zone is very large to be covered by survey. Therefore, ten sample villages whose boundary is clearly identified by the BMRDA are selected. Sampling and selection of study sites are given utmost care as the representativeness of the selected sites and the peri-urban respondents determine the quality of the outcome of the research. The peripheral villages are selected based on the criteria of distance from NH from a distance of 0–10 km. The relationship between distance and from NH and transactions are discussed in this chapter.[7] The ten villages are from a distance closer to NH which is between 0 and 10 kilometres where there are active land transactions.[8] Distance is taken as criteria of selection of villages because distance plays an important role in the determination of land prices. As the distance from the NH increases, land value decreases.

Table 4.1 Category of farmers

I.	Marginal	1. Below 0.5
		2. 0.5–1.0
II.	Small	3. 1.0–2.0
III.	Semi-medium	4. 2.0–3.0
		5. 3.0–4.0
IV.	Medium	6. 4.0–5.0
		7. 5.0–7.5
		8. 7.5–10.0
V.	Large	9. 10.0–20.0
		10. 20.0 and above

Source: Agricultural census.

Table 4.2 Number of transactions by the respondents

Sellers (250)	Buyers(250)
Marginal	Real estate agent
Small	Farmers
Semi medium	Individual Buyer (peri-urban resident)
Medium	Individual buyer (Business purpose
Large	

Source: Compilation by the author.

There are 500 respondents in this survey from both the periphery. It includes 250 buyer[9] respondents and 250 seller[10] respondents. Buyers and sellers are interviewed by two different structured questionnaires in 2018. Sellers are farmers. They belong to category of Marginal, Small, Semi-Medium, Medium and Large farmers – as per agriculture census classification. Buyers include the four categories such as farmers, real estate agent and individual buyers who are peri-urban residents and individual buyer for business purposes. However, the sample size of the buyer category is not uniform.[11] For identifying the land purchase, door to door survey was conducted among farmers and individuals' buyers who are peri-urban residents and individuals who buy land for business purposes.

Sellers belong to the Table 4.1 category. In peripheral areas, there is less scope for agriculture; the number of farmers who belong to large farmer category who has land above 25 acres is less in the study area. Majority of them are farmers with nearly 2.5 acres of land. Therefore, practically, it was difficult to get large farmer respondents who have large size holding. Hence, the number of farmers with large size holding is less in the study.

The data are collected cross sectionally and with respect to a time period from 2000 to 2018, but not all individuals have land transactions in all 18 years. And the total number of land transaction is 500[12] (Table 4.2). The number of transactions by each category is given in the appendix. In general case, the respondents have multiple transactions, but not all 500 respondents have not showed multiple transactions across 2000–18 years.[13]

Von Thunen Theory – Relationship between Distance and Land Price

There are only a few studies which used the principles and method developed by Von Thunen (1826). At the same time, Von Thunen theory has been subjected to various interpretations. The writers who advocate the relevance of Von Thunen principles are such as Chisholm (1968), Horvath (1969), Found (1971), Katzman (1974) and Thiele (1984). Using the traditional assumptions of the Von Thunen model, Quinn et al. (1997) observed that the land use as a function of distance from Sydney, which is the primate city, has a tendency toward concentric zonation. I seek the empirical evidence of Von Thunen theory in the study of distance and land prices in the Bengaluru periphery (Figure 4.1).

The figure shows how villages are selected in the periphery using the distance from National Highway. The land uses are different at various distances from the city, farther away from the city the greenery is more. But at a distance closer to National Highway less than 1 km–5 km, there is more of built-up land and developments. The land uses differ as the distance from the National Highway increases.

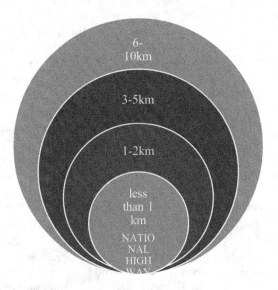

Figure 4.1 Distance from National Highway. Compilation by the author.

Relationship between Distance and Land Transactions in the Periphery

There exists active land transactions in the periphery. As Figure 4.2 indicates, as the distance increases, the number of land transactions decreases. At a distance less than 1 km from the national highway, the number of land transactions is more and vice versa. At a distance closer to national highway with less than 1 km, majority of land transactions are taken place, 226 land transactions (out of total 500) are very close to the highway and farther from the city centre the land transactions are less.

As the distance from the national highway increases, the agricultural land transactions are more as we see in Figure 4.3. Similarly, the land price decreases as the distance from the city increases. As the distance increases, the number of agricultural transactions increased to 17 and land price reduced to Rs. 665. The residential land transactions are so high in the periphery where land is very closer to the National Highway at a distance less than 1 km. Similarly, the land prices are comparatively more in the distance less than 1 km and it is Rs.905 at a distance less than 1 km, but at a distance between 6 and 10 km, the land price is just Rs. 595. Distance plays an important role in the determination of land prices. Villages like Sathanur are away from city centre where there is more of farming. According to the Von Thunen model, the patterns of farming and production are the result of competitive bidding among various rural land uses for access to a given parcel. Therefore, the type of production that can give the maximum return for a specified parcel of land will bring the highest bid for the use of that plot. Land uses that cannot pay enough to get the highest price land will settle on less expensive land.

Commercial and industrial land transactions are more at the periphery. At a distance closer to national highway less than 1 km, the number of

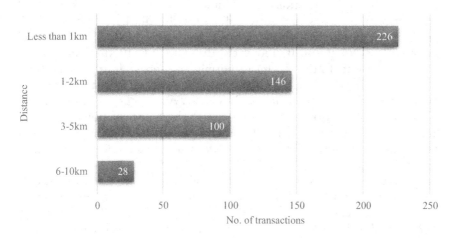

Figure 4.2 Land transactions and distance. Compilation by the author.

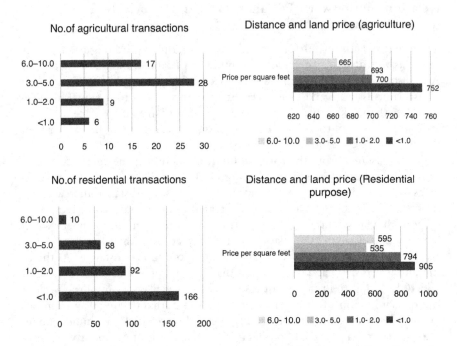

Figure 4.3 Agricultural-Residential land transactions and distance. Compilation by the author.

Note: Distance from NH is marked in y axis in Panel, and x axis shows the number of transactions and the Price per square feet corresponding to the land transaction.

commercial land transactions is 33, but as the distance increases, the land transaction reduces as in Figure 4.4. Similarly, the land price also decreased; at a distance closer to national highway less than 1 km, the land price is Rs. 1267 per sq ft, and at the distance of 6–10 km, land price is Rs. 599 per sq ft. In the south east periphery, more industrial land transactions are very closer to the peripheral villages like Harohalli where the land is very closer to the National Highway. As it is shown in the figure, the number of industrial land transactions is high near National Highway at a distance less than 1 km and the land price is Rs. 1331 per sq ft, and as the distance increased to 6–10 km, the land price reduced to Rs. 1169 per sq ft.

As Figure 4.1 shows the agricultural land uses are away at a distance of 6–10 km from NH and the price is Rs. 665 per square feet, whereas residential, industrial, commercial land uses are closer to the NH less than 1 km, 1–2 km and 3–5 km in the peripheral villages. At a distance less than 1 km from national highway, the residential land price is Rs. 905 per sq feet; for commercial use, it is Rs. 1267 per sq ft and for the industrial use, it is Rs. 1331 per sq ft. Land price is highest for the industrial land uses and for commercial second highest, in the periphery land, prices are affordable.

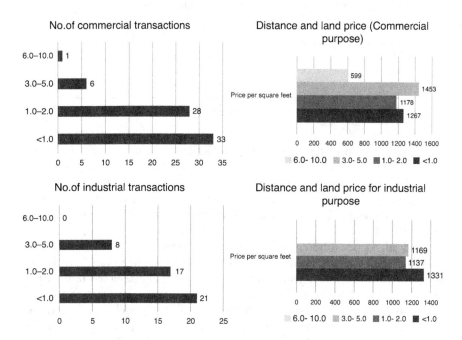

Figure 4.4 Commercial-Industrial land transactions and distance. Calculation by the author using primary data.
Note: Distance from NH is marked in y axis in Panel, and x axis shows the number of transactions and the Price per square feet corresponding to the land transaction.

Demand for and Supply of Land in Periphery

It is important to look at the percentage of farmers in different categories as per the survey. The category of farmers in the sample size varies as per the accessibility of the respondents and also their willingness to share the information. In this survey, majority are marginal farmers (Table 4.3). This is because there were more respondents who had land less than five acres of land. As the size holdings increase, there are fewer respondents available for the survey in the selected periphery. The Total Land Transacted by seller and buyers in sample villages is given in Table 4.4.

Table 4.3 Category of farmers considered in Hoskote and Kanakapura peri-urban area

Famer Category	N	%
Marginal	152	60.8
Small	26	10.4
Semi-medium	31	12.4
Medium	35	14.0
Large	6	2.4
Total	250	100

Source: Calculation by the author using primary data.

Table 4.4 Total land transacted by seller and buyers in sample villages

	N	Total Land Transacted (in ha)
Sellers	250	123.94
Buyers	250	112.76
Total	500	236.70

Calculation by the author using primary data.

I take into consideration of land transactions of both buyers and sellers from 2000 to 2018 across ten peripheral villages with respect to the various categories of buyer and seller. Hence, the total size of land transacted by 250 sellers is 123.94 hectares and total size of land transacted by 250 sellers is 112.76 hectares. I have analysed the trend in the land sale pattern and purchase.

Land sale as per different seller category is shown in Tables 4.5 and 4.5a. Marginal farmers sold their land for the residential purposes; there is 122 residential land transactions by marginal farmers in the selected ten peripheral villages of Hoskote and Kanakapura in the 250 respondents of farmers. This shows active residential land transactions in the periphery. Land transfers from agriculture to non-agriculture use have been clearly visible in the studied peri-villages in Hoskote and Kanakapura Taluk.[14] High prices of land followed by sale and purchase of land for earning more profit or money have been found the main governing factors for buying or selling of land. Small and medium farmer have higher number of sales for residential transaction. Six large farmers sold land for residential, commercial and industrial purposes. Small and Marginal farmers sell their land to meet their emergency requirements of education, marriage and loan repayment. They have sold land mainly to meet the basic economic needs. A high demand for land by IT employees, urban middle class and salaried people are the major reasons for a considerable increase in the price of land over time. Large and medium households sold their land from business point of view and to transfer their farming assets into more advantageous resource, while marginal and small farmers sold their land for meeting the basic needs of the household, social ceremonies, loan repayment and education purposes. Some of the medium farmers are found to have started construction of flats to earn rental incomes, while large farmers have entered into joint ventures expecting good returns. The distribution of sellers by size group and reasons for the sale of land is important.

The distribution of sellers by size group of holdings and the reasons for land sale are shown in Table 4.6. The average size of the land transacted for distress sale amounts to 15.82 hectares, while the average price of the total land sold to Rs. 11.02 crore per ha. The average size of the land transacted for

Table 4.5 Land sale for agricultural and non-agricultural uses by different *farmers' category* in sample villages belonging to Hoskote and Kanakapura peri-urban area

Category	Agricultural Purpose				Residential (Housing)				Commercial				Industrial			
	Average				Average				Average				Average			
	No	Size of Land Holding (in ha)	Land Transacted (in ha)	Price* Received (in Rs) (per Sq.ft)	No.	Size of Land Holding (in ha)	Land Transacted (in ha)	Price* Received (in Rs) (per Sq.ft)	No	Size of Land Holding (in ha)	Land Transacted (in ha)	Price* received (in Rs) (per Sq.ft)	No.	Size of Land Holding (in ha)	Land Transacted (in ha)	Price* Received (in Rs) (per Sq.ft)
Marginal	30	0.79	0.32	960	122	0.61	0.29	842	–	–	–	–	–	–	–	–
Small	7	1.50	1.05	886	18	1.38	1.29	670	1	1.62	1.62	1337	–	–	–	–
Semi-medium	1	2.83	1.83	1179	7	2.06	1.43	1039	14	0.84	0.22	1334	9	0.69	0.25	991
Medium	2	4.60	1.07	537	14	4.49	1.16	682	8	0.99	0.29	1268	11	1.06	0.24	1296
Large	0	–	–	–	4	5.79	1.15	691	1	6.09	1.05	599	1	8.09	1.05	1179

Source: Calculation by the author using primary data.
N = 250. (Marginal – Less than 1.0 ha, Small – 1.0 to 2.0 ha, Semi-medium – 2.0 to 4.0 ha, Medium – 4.0 to 10.0 ha, Large – 10.0 ha and above) * Deflated Real Price value. Note: As much as 67% of India's farmland is held by the marginal farmers with holdings below one hectare, against less than 1% in large holdings of 10 hectares and above (latest Agriculture Census); https://www.business-standard.com/article/news-ians/nearly-70-percent-of-indian-farms-are-very-small-census-shows-115120901080_1.html

Table 4.5a Price (in crores) for one hectare of land across agricultural and non-agricultural uses by different farmers' category (value in crore)

Category	Agricultural Purpose			Residential (Housing)			Commercial			Industrial		
	No	Average Price Received (in Rs) (per Sq.ft)	Price (Rs in Crores) (per hectare)	No.	Average Price Received (in Rs) (per Sq.ft)	Price (Rs in Crores) (per hectare)	No	Average Price Received (in Rs) (per Sq.ft)	Price (Rs in Crores) (per hectare)	No.	Average Price Received (in Rs) (per Sq.ft)	Price (Rs in Crores) (per hectare)
	(1)	(2)	(3)	(1)	(2)	(3)	(1)	(2)	(3)	(1)	(2)	(3)
Marginal	30	960	10.33	122	842	9.06	–	–	9.06	–	–	–
Small	7	886	9.54	18	670	7.21	1	1337	14.39	–	–	–
Semi-medium	1	1179	12.69	7	1039	11.18	14	1334	14.36	9	991	10.67
Medium	2	537	5.78	14	682	7.34	8	1268	13.65	11	1296	13.95
Large	0	–	–	4	691	7.44	1	599	6.45	1	1179	12.69

Source: Calculation by the author using primary data.
Note: 1 ha = 1,07,640 Square feet. This value is multiplied by the average price [col (2)] for one sq.ft to obtain the price for one hectare [col (3)] across each famer category.

Table 4.6 Distribution of sellers by size group and reasons for sale of land by the farmers in peri-urban in sample villages

Reason for Sale	Type of Farmers (in Numbers)						Total Land Transacted (in ha)	Average Price Received (Per Sq.ft)	Average Price Received (Rs in crores /per hectare)
	Marginal	Small	Semi-Medium	Medium	Large	Total			
Distress sale	20	8	4	6	1	39 (15.6)	15.82	1,024	11.02
High market value of land	101	10	23	26	5	165 (66.0)	82.18	1,113	11.98
Low income and productivity	31	8	4	3	–	42 (18.4)	25.94	1,116	12.01
Total	152	26	31	35	6	250 (100)			

Source: Calculation by the author using primary data.

Note: **Distress Sale** – A sale held for the purpose of raising money to meet emergency expenses (marriage/education) or selling asset under adverse conditions (sale of land adverse climate)

Low income and Productivity: Degradation of soil resources leading to less productivity and water crisis is adding more problem to the crisis. It further leads to lack of farm income to the farmers.

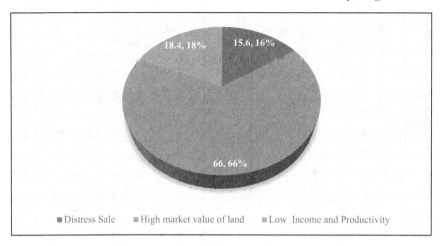

Figure 4.5 Reasons for Land Sale. Compilation by the author.

high demand amounts to 82.18 hectares, while the average price of the total land sold to Rs. 11.98 crore per ha. The average size of the land transacted for low productivity amounts to 25.94 hectares, while the average price of the total land sold to Rs. 12.01 crore per ha. The reasons for land sale is given in Figure 4.5.

Gradually, farmlands are being converted into non-agricultural purpose in the periphery. There is a high market value for land in the periphery because of its proximity to the city, commercial and IT centres, and hence, land value shows an increase in the periphery. Increase in the market value of land leads to 66% of sales in periphery and land sale is frequent in the periphery as it offers a very feasible solution to the farmers. Peripheral areas of Hoskote and Kanakapura are suitable for vegetables, flower farming and ragi cultivation. The income earned by the households in the periphery from this is very less compared to the income earned by the rental income and the real estate activities. Farmers are always faced with water shortage in the summer season, lack of continuous supply of labour's and lack of good pricing during the off season; gradually, there is a shift in these occupations of the villagers as the real estate offered attractive income. The income earned from rental, residential, commercial and industrial transactions is very high compared to the income earned from the peri-urban farming. Nearly, 18.4% of sales recorded is due to low income and productivity and 15.6% is distress sale by the marginal farmers. People sold their land for meeting various household requirements such as education and marriage, while some others have sold their lands expecting an attractive rental income and profit from joint ventures with builders (Tables 4.7 and 4.7a).

Table 4.7 Land purchases for agricultural and non-agricultural uses by different categories of *buyers* in sample villages belonging to Hoskote and Kanakapura peri-urban area

Buyers' Group	Agricultural Purpose Average			Residential (Housing) Average			Commercial Average			Industrial Average		
	No.	Land Transacted (Purchased) (in ha)	Price** (in Rs) of Land (per Sq.ft)	No.	Land Transacted (purchased) (in ha)	Price (in Rs) of Land (per Sq.ft)	No.	Land Transacted (Purchased) (in ha)	Price (in Rs) of Land (per Sq.ft)	No.	Land Transacted (Purchased) (in ha)	Price (in Rs) of Land (per Sq.ft)
Builder (real estate)	–	–	–	44	0.32	1276	29	0.87	599	15	1.14	1001
Farmers	20	0.490	838	–	–	–	–	–	–	–	–	–
Individual (peri-urban resident)	–	–	–	84	0.45	753	–	–	–	–	–	–
Individual business purpose*	–	–	–	–	–	–	35	0.41	1276	23	0.52	1317

N = 250. *Individual business investors that are used for industrial activities. ** Deflated Real Price value.

Table 4.7a Land purchases for agricultural and non-agricultural uses by different categories of *buyers* in sample villages (value in crores)

Buyers' Group	Agricultural Purpose Average			Residential (Housing) Average			Commercial Average			Industrial Average		
	No.	Land Transacted (Purchased) (in ha)	Price (Rs in Crores) (per hectare)	No.	Land Transacted (Purchased) (in ha)	Price (Rs in Crores) (per hectare)	No.	Land Transacted (Purchased) (in ha)	Price (Rs in Crores) (per hectare)	No.	Land Transacted (Purchased) (in ha)	Price (Rs in Crores) (per hectare)
Builder (real estate)	–	–	–	44	0.32	13.73	29	0.87	6.45	15	1.14	10.77
Farmers	20	0.490	9.02	–	–	–	–	–	–	–	–	–
Individual (peri-urban resident)	–	–	–	84	0.45	8.11	–	–	–	–	–	–
Individual business purpose*	–	–	–	–	–	–	35	0.41	13.73	23	0.52	14.18

Note: 1 ha = 1,07,640 Square feet. This value is multiplied by the average price [col (2)] for one sq.ft to obtain the price for one hectare [col (3)] across each famer category.

Land Purchase for Agriculture and Non-Agriculture

The buyer category consists of Real Estate Agent, Farmer, Individual Buyer who is a peri-urban resident and Individual Buyer who buy land either for small-scale industry or the purpose of commercial purpose such as office space, construction of hotel and building (Tables 4.7 and 4.7a). The land bought by peri-urban farmer is only for agricultural purpose. Real estate agent bought land for residential purposes mainly. It is emerged from peri-urban land market survey that there is a huge demand for residential land transactions (128) in the periphery. This is mainly by the individual buyers who seek residential space in the periphery because of the comparatively cheaper land in periphery and the accessibility to work and commercial centre is possible. The next category of buyer whose land transaction was high is individual buyer for business purposes-(58).

Overall, peri-urban area is a thriving land market for Residential land transactions. It was evident in both the periphery. The transaction by individual buyer for commercial and industrial purposes shows the transition of periphery into the commercial and industrial outgrowths. Land is bought for both agricultural and non-agricultural purposes. The average size of land purchased by farmer for agriculture is 0.490 hectares. The real estate agent purchase land mainly for non-agricultural purposes. Their average of land is bought by real estate agent for the residential purposes is 0.32 hectares. More residential land transactions are by the individual buyer; the average size of land transacted is 0.45 hectares. The average size of the land transacted for commercial and industrial purposes is 0.41 and 0.52 hectares, respectively.

Table 4.8 and 4.8a show the land transaction as per the distance from National Highway. It is observed in the periphery that the land adjacent to highway has huge demand by the residential, industrial and commercial purposes. Nearly, 166 residential land transactions were done in a distance which is less than 1 km from National Highway. Similarly, commercial (33) and industrial (21) land transaction is high in the land very close to NH which is less than 1 km. And as the distance increases, there is less demand for the land by the buyers. Distance is a significant factor affecting the land price. In 3–5 km distance, land is bought for agricultural (28) and residential purposes (58). As the distance increases, price decreases; therefore, it is convenient for the people to buy farmland in the periphery and also to get cheap residential accommodation in the periphery. In 5–10 km, land is bought for both agricultural (17) and residential purposes (10). There is a demand for land in the periphery where majority of the new peri-urban residents and real estate agent buy the land.

Location of land transactions has been an important factor for non-agricultural use vis-à-vis than agricultural purpose. Total owned land of sellers and price of land have been the two important determinants in the land sale. Similarly, the total owned land of buyers and their non-farm income have been the major determinants of demand for agricultural land. Also, distance from National Highway and sold land under distress has been

Table 4.8 Land purchases for agricultural and non-agricultural uses in sample villages by location (distance from National Highway) – Hoskote and Kanakapura peri-urban area

	Agricultural Purpose			Residential (Housing)			Commercial			Industrial		
	Average			Average			Average			Average		
	No.	Land Transacted★ (in ha)	Price (Rs per sq.ft)	No.	Land Transacted (in ha)	Price (Rs per sq.ft)	No.	Land Transacted (in ha)	Price (Rs per sq.ft)	No.	Land Transacted (in ha)	Price (Rs in per sq.ft)
Distance from NH (in km)												
<1.0	6	0.54	752	166	0.47	905	33	0.39	1267	21	0.39	1331
1.0–2.0	9	0.40	700	92	0.48	794	28	0.37	1178	17	0.35	1137
3.0–5.0	28	0.50	693	58	0.60	535	6	0.28	1453	8	0.74	1169
6.0–10.0	17	0.57	665	10	0.29	595	1	1.05	599	–	–	–

N = 500 ★ Total land sold by the farmers (seller) and the total land bought by the buyers (real estate agents/Farmers/individual buyer – peri-urban resident and individual buyer for business purpose) combined.

Table 4.8a Land purchases for agricultural and non-agricultural uses in sample villages by location (value in crore)

	Agricultural Purpose			Residential (Housing)			Commercial			Industrial		
	Average			Average			Average			Average		
	No.	Land Transacted★ (in ha)	Price (Rs in Crores) (per hectare)	No.	Land Transacted (in ha)	Price (Rs in Crores) (per hectare)	No.	Land Transacted (in ha)	Price (Rs in Crores) (per hectare)	No.	Land Transacted (in ha)	Price (Rs in Crores) (per hectare)
<1.0	6	0.54	8.09	166	0.47	9.74	33	0.39	13.64	21	0.39	14.33
1.0–2.0	9	0.40	7.53	92	0.48	8.55	28	0.37	12.68	17	0.35	12.24
3.0–5.0	28	0.50	7.46	58	0.60	5.76	6	0.28	15.64	8	0.74	12.58
5.0–10.0	17	0.57	7.16	10	0.29	6.40	1	1.05	6.45	–	–	–

Calculation by the author using primary data.

Note: 1 ha = 1,07,640 Square feet. This value is multiplied by the average price [col (2)] for one sq.ft to obtain the price for one hectare [col (3)] across each

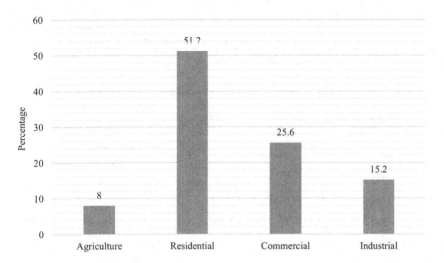

Figure 4.6 Reasons for purchase of land. Compilation by the author.

an important factor. The linear trends in land sale and land prices indicate a steady increase in the area of land for sale over the years as also in the price of land. Most of the land purchased for housing purpose was situated nearby National Highways, whereas the land purchased for cultivation, poultry, industry and dairy was situated outside the villages. The lands situated on or near to the periphery of the villages had more demand for housing, dairy and poultry. Lands purchased for the housing purposes were transacted in 0.00-km to 1.00-km periphery of villages. The lands situated at a distance of 1–2 km from villages and highway are in huge demand.

Major portion of land is bought for residential land uses. It is of 51.2% of the total land uses (Figure 4.6). In peri-urban areas, major industries are located. The second highest amount of land purchased as per the land market survey is commercial purposes; it is of 25.6%. Nearly, 15.2% of land is bought for industrial purposes and 8% land is bought for agricultural purposes. The demand for residential land use is highest in the periphery and the second highest requirement is for commercial land uses in peripheries.

Extent of Land Transaction in Peri-Urban Villages

I analyse the trends in the land transactions, both the land sale and land purchase and extent of land transactions in the peri-urban village. Both Kanakapura and Hoskote are known for remarkable land transactions in the periphery. The land transactions of the respondents from 2000 to 2018 for the selected periphery are observed.

The trends in the number of land transactions in the periphery are shown in Figure 4.7. Land transactions are frequent since 2010 in both peripheries. The

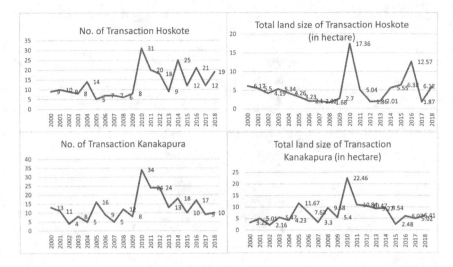

Figure 4.7 Trend in the number of land transaction and total size of land transaction in acres by the sample respondents for the period from 2000–01 to 2017–18, Hoskote and Kanakapura Taluk. Compilation by the author from field survey, Kanakapura.

major reason for the increase in the land transaction in 2010 in Hoskote is the establishment of the factories, office spaces and so on in the study area. There is an active residential land transaction in Hoskote periphery especially after 2010 due to the demand from the individual buyer for residential purposes and individual buyer for business and investment purpose and it has come a preferred investment location of the individuals. The extent and volume of land transactions are high in Kanakapura by 2010, mainly because of the industrial establishments in Kanakapura and the spillover effects of the industrial establishments like KIADB changed the face of Kanakapura and the peripheral villages like Harohalli is developed due to industrial development, and hence, the outgrowths led to the growth of real estate significantly and transition led to more of residential land transactions in Kanakapura is visible. It is a thriving land market of south peripheral area and a favourite residential location.

Determinants of Land Transactions in the Periphery

The primary survey on land transactions was conducted in 2018–19 during which it emerged that sample respondents had sold and bought their lands at different time points beginning from 2001 to 2002, thus resulting in a cross-section data format. Further, it was also learnt that not all the individuals had transacted (selling of their lands) at two different time periods. The land transaction includes both land sale and land purchase. Determinants of land sale and land purchase are captured using the regression equation.[15]

Table 4.9 Description of the variables used in the model

Independent Variables	Description	Source
L_PRICE (SR VALUE)/ per sq ft	The price at which land is sold – a major factor determine the land sale and purchase	Secondary data
L_TOT_LND_HOLD Per sq ft	The extend of land owned before the sale of land which shows the capacity of seller to sell land	Primary data survey
L INCOME (in Rs)	It shows the capacity of the buyer to buy the land	Primary data survey
D_AGRICULTURE	Dummy variable for agri-land use	Primary data survey
D_OTHER LAND USE	Dummy variable for other land use	Primary data survey
DIST_DISTR_DQ (in km)	Distance from District Headquarters	Secondary data
DIST_NAT_HW (in km)	Distance from National Highway	Secondary data
DIST_NEAR_COMM (in km)	Distance from nearest Commercial Centre	Secondary data

Source: Compilation by the author.

Dependent Variables

LQTY SOLD: Quantity sold shows the size of land transacted per sq ft for land sale which denotes the sale of land.

LQTY BOUGHT: Quantity bought shows the size of land transacted per sq ft for purchase which denotes the purchase for land. Description of the variables used in the model is given in Table 4.9.

Determinants of Land Sale in the Periphery

The following specification is used to identify the land sale. The log-log regression model is given by

$$log Y = \propto +\beta_1 log X_1 + \beta_2 X_2 + +\beta_3 X_3 + \beta_4 X_4 + \beta_5 X_5 + \varepsilon$$
$$log(land\_sold) = \propto +\beta_1 log(SR\ Value) + \beta_2 log(LAND\_HOLDINGS)$$
$$+\beta_3(DIST\_DISRT\_HQ) +\beta_4(DIST\_NAT\_HW)$$
$$+\beta_5(DIST\_NEAR\_COMM) + \varepsilon$$

Where
   Y = LAND_ Sold (log transformed)
and
   X_1 = PRICE (SR VALUE) (log transformed)
   X_2 = LAND_HOLDINGS (log transformed)
   X_3 = DIST_DISRT_HQ (Distance to the District Head Quarters)
   X_4 = DIST_NAT_HW (Distance to the National Highway)
   X_5 = DIST_NEAR_COMM (Distance from the Nearest Commercial Centre)

Now, the estimated log-log regression model is given in Table 4.10.

The regression coefficient of PRICE (SR VALUE) is 0.146 (Table 4.10). The p-value for PRICE is less than the significance level alpha of 0.05. Thus, we could conclude that PRICE is a significant determinant of land sale.[16] Similarly, the size of the land holdings and distance is the significant determinants of land sale. The elasticity coefficient of size of land holdings is 0.701 which shows the farmers are willing to sell their land in the periphery. The major reason is that farmers are not able to cultivate the land due to various problems like water scarcity in the peripheral locations of Hoskote, and the income from agriculture is meagre; therefore, they seek alternative options of income generation and they have sold the land for high land prices and most of them are engaged in the alternative occupations after land sale.

Finally, it is observed that DIST_DISRT_HQ and DIST_NAT_HW are statistically significant. The Distance from National Highway is also showing a very significant determinant ($t = -2.70$, $p < 0.05$) of the PRICE. In essence, it could be inferred that as one moves from a closer proximity to the District headquarters, National Highway the price would be lesser. Distance is a significant predictor of the land transaction and it has an inverse relationship with the land price, and it shows the empirical evidence to the Von Thunen model. In the periphery, the land transactions are high due to the accessibility via Metro. These two peripheral locations in the study are the strategic locations, and it is known for its connectivity to the employment hub. This led to more residential land transactions in the periphery.

From Table 4.11, the chi-square value is 0.010 and p-value is 0.9316 for the determinants of land sale. As the p-value is greater than the significance alpha level of 0.05, we accept H_0. In essence, there is no problem of heteroscedasticity, and the error term is homoscedastic in nature and has constant variance.

Table 4.10 Log-log ordinary linear regression result

Independent Variables	Coefficient	t value
LG_PRICE	0.146 (0.672)**	2.22
LG_LAND_HOLDINGS	0.701 (0.194)***	3.62
DIST_DISRT_HQ	−0.133 (0.028)**	−2.11
DIST_NAT_HW	−0.443 (0.164)**	−2.70
DIST_NEAR_COMM	−0.015 (0.019)	−0.77
CONSTANT	1.260 (5.43)	0.23

Observation: 72
R-squared: 0.68
F statistic: 12.71
Pro>F 0.000

Source: Author's Estimation.
Note: *** $p < 0.01$, ** $p < 0.05$, * $p < 0.1$, the value in the parenthesis is standard error. Though, survey collected land transaction details from 2000, for the purpose of analysis only recent years data is used as the information provided by the respondent is mainly influenced by various limitations.

Table 4.11 Breusch–Pagan/Cook–Weisberg test for heteroscedasticity for land sale

Ho: *Constant variance*
Variables: fitted values of LG_TOT_QTY_TRANS
chi2(1) = 0.01
Prob > chi2 = 0.9316

Source: Author's Estimation.

Determinants of Land Purchase in the Periphery

The determinants of land purchase are captured using the log-log regression model using the following specification.

$$logY = \propto +\beta_1 logX_1 + \beta_2 X_2 + +\beta_3 X_3 + \beta_3 D_2 + \beta_4 D_3 + \beta_5 X_5 + \beta_6 X_6 + \beta_7 X_7 + \varepsilon$$
$$log(land\_bought) = \propto +\beta_1 log(SR\ value) + \beta_2 log(INCOME)$$
$$+\beta_3(D_2\ \star\ Land\_use) + \beta_4(D_3\ \star\ Land\_use)$$
$$+\beta_5(DIST\_DISRT\_HQ) +\beta_6(DIST\_NAT\_HW)$$
$$+\beta_7(DIST\_NEAR\_COMM) + \varepsilon$$

Where

Y = LAND_BOUGHT (log transformed)

and

X_1 = PRICE (SR VALUE) (log transformed)
X_2 = INCOME OF THE BUYER (log transformed)
X_3 = LAND_USE is classified as dummies where
D_1 = 1 if the land use is for *Residential purpose*
     = 0 otherwise (i.e., for Other Purpose of land use)
X_4 = DIST_DISRT_HQ (Distance to the District Head Quarters)
X_5 = DIST_NAT_HW (Distance to the National Highway)
X_6 = DIST_NEAR_COMM (Distance from the Nearest Commercial Centre)

Now, the estimated log-log regression model is given in Table 4.12.

Table 4.12 Log-log ordinary linear regression result

Independent Variables	Coefficient	t value
a) LG_PRICE	−0.127 (0.938)★★	−2.20
LG_INCOME	0.131 (0.103)★★	2.27
D1 (RESIDENTIAL)	1.062 (0.350)★★	−3.03
DIST_DISRT_HQ	−0.166 (0.037)★★	2.45
DIST_NAT_HW	−0.025 (0.218)	−0.12
DIST_NEAR_COMM	−0.059 (0.032)★	−1.82
CONSTANT	12.39 (7.28)★	1.70
Observation: 81		
R-squared: 0.4		
F statistic: 2.28		

Source: Author's Estimation.
Note: ★★★$p < 0.01$, ★★$p < 0.05$, ★$p < 0.1$, the value in the parenthesis is standard error.

Table 4.13 Breusch-Pagan/Cook-Weisberg test for heteroscedasticity for land
            purchase

Ho: *Constant variance*
Variables: *fitted values of* LG_TOT_QTY_TRANS
chi2(1) = 0.75
Prob > chi2 = 0.3861

Source: Author's Estimation.

The regression coefficient $_1$ of PRICE (SR VALUE) is −0.127. Thus, I could conclude that PRICE is a significant determinant of demand (purchase) for land. Since it is a log-log transformation, the unit considered is the percentage change.[17] With respect to interpretation of the LAND_USE, OTHER *(Agriculture, Commercial and industrial combined)* is considered the reference category. It is observed from the above table that dummy D1 is statistically significant at 5% (since the p-value is less than 0.05). It could be inferred that as compared to *OTHER category of usage of land*, one would expect the Demand for RESIDENTIAL purpose would be higher in peri-urban areas. Similarly, distance is a significant predictor of land use. As the distance increases, the demand for land decreases.

From Table 4.13, the chi-square value is 0.750 and p-value is 0.3861 for the above model. As the p-value is greater than the significance alpha level of 0.05, we accept H_0. In essence, there is no problem of heteroscedasticity, and the error term is homoscedastic in nature and has constant variance.

Empirical Evidence of the Von Thunen Model

In the study of Bengaluru periphery, the empirical evidence shows that the theory (Von Thunen) holds true. The analysis of the determinants of land transactions shows that distance is a significant variable affects the land price, Figures 4.3 and 4.4, and the regression results from Table 4.12 shows the Von Thunen theory holds true. I conclude that *Distance to National highway and Distance of District Headquarters* are significant determinants of land transaction. The hypothesis is tested, and the distance is a significant predictor of the land transaction and it has an inverse relationship with the land price, and it shows the empirical evidence to the Von Thunen model. In South periphery, Kanakapura, the land transactions are high due to the accessibility via Metro. These two peripheral locations in the study are the strategic locations, and it is known for its connectivity to the employment hub. This led to more residential land transactions in the periphery. The significant relationship between land use and land value is identified. The interpretation of the land use variable shows that it is a significant predictor of land transaction. OTHER LAND_USE is considered the reference category. It could be inferred that statistically there is an evident to conclude that land transaction (from the perceptive of buyers) is determined on whether the land can use for residential purpose keeping other land use purpose as the reference category.

It could be inferred that as compared to other uses *of land*, one would expect the land bought for RESIDENTIAL would be higher by 1.06 (approximately one time) times. The field insights in both Kanakapura and Hoskote show that there is active land transactions in both peripheries; therefore, with the empirical results, it concluded that land use is a significant predictor of land transaction in the periphery and distance plays a significant role in the land price. There is an inverse relationship between distance and the land prices.

Summary

In the attempt of exploring the land transactions in the peripheral areas of Bengaluru City, land transactions of both land sale and land purchase analysed. The average size of land sold by marginal farmers works out to 0.32 ha. The key reason for increased land sale is the high market value for land in the periphery with 66% land of sold due to the high demand. The high demand for land is for residential purposes, constituting 51.2% in the study area. Substantial land purchase takes place with an active participation of people belonging to category such as real estate agents, individuals who are peri-urban residents and those who buy land with business purpose. The extent of land transactions, volume of land transactions, market value and the year-on-year growth in the land prices have also been examined. The extent of land transactions increased in 2010 in Hoskote and Kanakapura. The price of land varies from year to year; there is an increase in the land price in both peripheries in 2010. This is largely due to the growth of IT corridors and industrial clusters. More land transactions have taken place in Kanakapura Taluk from the establishment of Industries by KIADB (2008 – Harohalli third phase). The regression results show that SR value, distance, income and land uses are the significant determinants of land transaction. The empirical evidence of Von Thunen model is sought; there exists a significant relationship between distance and land prices.

Notes

1 Central Business District.
2 1990a. Electronics City Bangalore. Bangalore: Karnataka State Electronics Development Corporation Limited.
3 City Profile of Bangalore, 1999.
4 https://www.moneycontrol.com
5 https://www.fortiusinfra.com/old-madras-road-linking-bangalore-future·
6 ITP. 1997. International Tech Park – Bangalore. Bangalore: Tata Technology Park Marketing Services.
7 The list of villages based on distance criteria is mentioned in the table, appendix.
8 There is high demand for land closer to the highway.
9 Real estate agent, farmers, individual buyers who are peri-urban residents and individual buyer with business purpose. With respect to the buyer, category respondents are restricted into these four categories. Here considering the practical difficulty in collecting data buyers are identified only as four relevant group from whom information is accessible.

10 Seller category is as per agricultural Census; therefore, the category of seller respondents were only farmers who has the capacity to sell land. However, considering any other seller category respondent avoided due to the practical difficulty in collecting data and getting respondents from them. Land transaction survey is a tedious process of collecting data with respect to land market variables from various respondents. There are 250 land sale transactions.

11 Overall, there are 250 land purchase transaction is used here. However, the sample size of the buyer is not uniform across the villages due to the practical difficulty of getting equal respondents from all sample villages. Therefore, the sample size of buyers is different across villages.

12 The number of transactions by each respondent is given in the appendix.

13 In that case, the latest transaction by the respondent is used in this study.

14 In this study among the 250 sellers, majority who did the land transaction is marginal farmers. The sample size of farmers is not uniform. Seeking information related to land transaction of the individuals is sensitive. Majority of them were reluctant to provide information. In that case it was difficult to get a uniform sample size across seller category.

15 Though, survey collected land transaction details from 2000, for the purpose of analysis only recent years data is used as the price information provided by the respondent is mainly influenced by various limitations.

16 Thus, a 10% change in the PRICE (independent variable) corresponds to (approximately) 0.6% increase in LAND SUPPLY (sq ft). Now, for a 10% change (increase) in PRICE (X_1), the expected (approximate) increase in LAND SUPPLY (Y) would be $(e^{0.146 \times \log(1.10)} - 1) \times 100 \approx 0.60\%$ per square feet.

   Note: For the purpose of analysis land transactions for the recent years are used.

17 Now, for a 10% change (increase) in PRICE (X_1), the expected (approximate) decline in land purchase (Y) would be $(e^{-0.127 X \log(1.10)} - 1) \times 100 \approx -0.53\%$. Thus, a 10% change in PRICE corresponds to (approximately) a 0.53% decline in land (in sq ft) demand in the market.

References

Allen, A. (2003). Environmental planning and management of the peri–urban interface: Perspectives on an emerging field. *Environment and Urbanization,* 15(1), 135–148.

BDA. (2000). *Bangalore 2011 A.D. Comprehensive Development Plan.* Bangalore: Bangalore Development Authority.

Chisholm, M. (1969). *The Relevance of von Thünen.* Annals commentary. *Annals of the Association of American Geographers,* 59(2).

Cotula, L., & Neve, B. (2007). The Drivers of change. In Cotula, L. (ed.), *Changes in Customary Land Tenure Systems in Africa.* Hertfordshire: Russell Press.

Found, W. C. (1971). *A Theoretical Approach to Rural Land-Use Patterns.* London: Edward Arnold.

Gough, K. V., & Yankson, P. W. (2000). Land markets in African cities: The case of peri–urban Accra, Ghana. *Urban Studies,* 37(13), 2485–2500.

Heitzman, J. (2001). Becoming Silicon Valley. In *SEMINAR-NEW DELHI* (pp. 40–48). MALYIKA SINGH.

Horvath, R. J. (1969). Von Thünen's isolated state and the area around Addis Ababa, Ethiopia. *Annals of the Association of American Geographers,* 59(2), 308–323.

Omboi, B. M. (2011). Factors Influencing Real Estate Property Prices a Survey of Real Estates in Meru Municipality, Kenya. *Journal of Economics and Sustainable Development*, ISSN 2222-1700 (Paper) ISSN 2222-2855 (Online), 2(4).

Payne, G. (1997). *Urban Land Tenure and Property Rights in Developing Countries: A Review*. London: IT Publications/ODA.

Peters, P. E., & Kambewa, D. (2007). Whose security? Deepening social conflict over 'customary' land in the shadow of land tenure reform in Malawi. *Journal of Modern African Studies*, 45(3), 447–472.

Quinn, J. M., Cooper, A. B., Davies-Colley, R. J., Rutherford, J. C., & Williamson, R. B. (1997). Land use effects on habitat, water quality, periphyton, and benthic invertebrates in Waikato, New Zealand, hill-country streams. *New Zealand Journal of Marine and Freshwater Research*, 31(5), 579–597.

Saruchera, M., & Omoweh, D. A. (2004). *Nepad, Land and Resource Rights*. PLAAS Policy Brief. Debating land reform and rural development, No 10.

Thiele, G. (1984). Location and enterprise choice: A Tanzanian case study. *Journal of Agricultural Economics*, 35(2), 257–264.

Toulmin, C., & Quan, J. (2000). *Evolving Land Rights, Policy and Tenure in Africa*. DFID/IIED/NRI.

Wehrmann, B. (2008). *Land Conflicts: A Practical Guide to Dealing with Land Disputes*. Eschborn: GTZ.

5 Dynamics of Peri-Urban Land Transaction and Impact on Land Prices

Land Price

Price is a parameter for estimating the value of an article or a property. Price, conveyed in real money terms, is by and large recognised as an instrument to analyse values in a market. The price of land is demonstrated by Walters (1983) to "the estimation of responsibility for rights in unendingness and is equivalent to the evaluated present estimation of the normal future appointments of rents". It is, likewise, influenced by vulnerabilities associated with net rent, interest rate and inflation. There is an essential differentiation between price and value. Market price relegates what a property might be sold for at a specific period in time; value allocates a property's genuine worth in association with other relative properties (Wyatt, 1997). This distinction among "price" and "value" comes from the reason that there are huge varieties in insight, information and readiness that go into the way toward setting up the price when contrasted with value. For decision-making with respect to land, the significant idea is not the price rather it is the opportunity cost of land.

Land is spatially associated with an explicit area. In spite of the fact that land is more precious at the centre of a city, it is hard to produce more of it, and to deliver a greater amount of it either. As per FAO (2003), the opportunity cost of land is more important than its intrinsic production value. According to Walters, the price of land isn't determined by its production value, but by the services, it provides. The land supply may also be compelled by zoning constraints. Such restrictive frameworks ensure that any urban land that is marketed demands a more significant price than in a free market (Verheye, 2007).

There is an extreme interest for land with escalating urban land prices in rapidly growing metropolitan cities. The land price is diverse across various regions of a city. The estimation of land value in the city centre is not exactly equivalent to that of the land value in peripheral zones. Land prices and investment are main impetus behind the wide-ranging impact of land-price dynamics on the macro economy (Liu et al., 2013). Various studies explore the importance of determinants of urban land values or agricultural land values (Chicoine, 1981). The question of what decides land price has engaged the domain of land over two century's years also and has been a

DOI: 10.4324/9781003362333-5

critical research problem in the land market. There exist few studies that have investigated the pattern of land price in the peripheral areas. What define the choice of an individual when he selects property in a particular residential area? Unquestionably, land price is a significant factor that determines land value. Land and price are mostly being a major debate in development. Land is a fixed resources and supply of land cannot be extended. The price of land increases every year due to the high demand of land. This creates major concerns to the development process especially in the context of growth corridors; the implementation of planning measures can be hampered because of the price and limited area.

Land value continuously rose with changing land-use and the real estate prices increased in metropolitan regions further fuelled the lateral expansion. The land value changes are drastic in periphery. The land value is determined by the economic principle of highest and best use of land, which produces the highest net return in any term, over time. Literature review shows that the question of what decides land price related to the domain of real estate for over 200 years has been a critical research question. Economists like Ricardo, Von Thunen and Lloyd have given an insight regarding the land value. Value, in economics, is something which is held or can be traded under current economic situations. There are two types of values, one with direct monetary benefit and the one with exchange value. Land belongs to the second category. As per Ricardo, "value relates to proper equivalent in cash, products and for which something sold or traded; the value of a thing in cash pretty much attractive, useful and significant (Verheye, 2009)". As the amount of land is limited, and due to population pressure and a high demand for land is high, land is getting to be a scarce resource. Value in general economic theory often refers to that of market value. The proper basis of valuation is always market value.

Land value is a complex phenomenon that differs greatly from place to place. Peri-urban growth also alters the pattern of land use and land value. Growth pattern thus involves the twin processes of internal reorganisation and outward expansion. Property value refers to the market value of a particular interest in landed property, i.e. the amount of money which can be obtained for the interest at a particular time from persons able and willing to purchase it. In other words, it means the worth of an interest in land and buildings assessed by the use of appropriate valuation methods. As indicated by Lichfield (1956), values are made and changed by similar factors that change the land use. According to Northam (1975), land value is debated in two contexts. One is the market value, which is the price of a land parcel negotiated at the time of sale of plots, and the other is the assessed value, which is the estimated worth of a parcel made by a competent private or public assessor. Studies show that the first attempt on urban land value was done. He utilised the standards given by Ricardo for farming area to the urban field. Northam indicates theory of urban land values based on the concept of "bid-rent". On account of urban land, different land users have different capacities to pay. It depends upon the size of a city, the particular land use, individual preferences and the land stock accessible in a specific city. According to Clark and Harvey (1965), land value depends on both the present and future use which, in turn, is influenced by the physical and economic characteristics of the site and the social control of land use.

The value of urban land is determined by adding the location factor to the agricultural land value. Various researchers have pointed out that a rapid economic development stimulates the use of lands in urban and peri-urban areas leading to the generation of employment opportunities, external economies, increase in land prices and economic growth in the long run. There is more demand for residential land uses; therefore, the user of residential land competes on a different basis than other land users. Therefore, the value of urban residential land is determined by bid rent. It is a known fact that the land values at a distance from the city centre are less and those locations are desirable for residential land uses. The location with highest value is referred to as the "hundred per cent location". It is logically concluded that the land values of all other locations would be less than that of 100% location. The economic factors underlying demand and supply of land play a major role in this process of land use pattern. The person who is willing to pay the largest sum for a plot will be able to compete it away from other potential users. By this process, sites in urban locales tend to be used for that purpose from which the user makes the greatest net gain through alternative uses of a given site. This would result in the highest and best use land. The scenario above becomes a continuous process on one user giving way to a higher valued user. This is a typical situation that has been observed in city like Bengaluru. The land value is often very high in the core area of the city since it is the centre of economic activities. Therefore, people tend to move towards peripheral areas where the land value is comparatively less. Peripheral areas are initially used for agricultural purposes; however, since there is a high demand for housing, the peri-urban local communities sell their land for various other purposes. In course of time, city expands, there arises more demand and consequently both land uses and land value changes in the peripheries. Various other factors that affect these property values are location, accessibility, physical terrain, water availability and neighbourhood quality.

The fundamental debate related to value refers to the difference in two terms Value and Price when it comes to the land market. Land or property, in general, has value because it gives rise to a stream of future tangible or intangible earnings; those define its exchange value in a functional market. Value, in economics, is the esteem in which something is held or can be exchanged under current market conditions.

Market Value

Market value is determined by the forces of the market at a particular point of time; there can only be one value at one time. This term has different meanings among the real estate valuators. In modern societies, the exchange value is usually associated with price, and the exchange is operated through a money transfer. "Price is thus a parameter to express the (exchange) value of an object or property, and in this respect, it is the generally accepted means to compare values in a market" (Verheye, 2009). According to Walters (1983), the price of land corresponds to the value of ownership of stipulated rights in perpetuity and is equal to the estimated present value of the expected future appropriations of rents. It designates what a property might be sold for at a specific period in time; value designates a property's actual worth in relation to other similar properties.

This difference between "price" and "value" stems from the premise that there are significant variations in intelligence, knowledge and willingness that enter into the process of establishing price as compared to value, and that value has to be based on consideration of much wider basic income or money returns than enter into the day-to-day deliberations that establish market price (Verheye, 2009). Market value is essentially the amount that a current buyer is willing to pay and what a current seller is willing to sell their property for, based on overall real estate market conditions (i.e. supply and demand). Market value is collected via primary data survey as there are no published sources of market prices; thus it simply refers to the price of land.

Guidance Value (Sub-Registrar Value)

The land value used in the discussion of the peripheral land market includes Guidance Value or Sub Registrar value. The guidance value is the minimum rate at which a property can be registered on its sale. It is the value set by the State government and it is the reference price of a property at a particular point in time as per the state government. SR value used is the value set by the Karnataka State Government. Different terms can be used to describe the guidance value. In some states, it is referred to as the circle rate. Guidance value is the minimum price at which a property is to be registered in the office of the registrar, and stamp duty is to be paid by the buyer. The buyer of a property cannot register it at any amount below this price. The guidance value may comprise composite value which will include the land value as well as the value of the buildings on it. In case the guidance value is more than the market value, the property needs to be registered at the guidance value. In case the market value is more than the guidance value, it may be registered at any amount over and above the guidance value. As per the discussion with the officials and examining the data acquired, it was revealed that the Guidance value is revised in every three to four years based on the market value. The SR value is used throughout the study to refer the Guidance value. The average of market value and SR value (Guidance Value) of the selected peripheral villages is used to study the objective of identifying the spatial and temporal variations in the land value and for the identification of the determinants. The market value and SR value used in this research from 2000 to 2017 and there exist a deviation in the values over a period of 17 years and therefore the deflated price is used. The nominal price and the real price are used while analysing the trend.

Nominal Price

Nominal price is the price at which land is bought and sold. The nominal price of both SR value and market value is used.

Real Price

In order to take into consideration of inflation and the variation of the price across various years, the market value and SR value are deflated using the CPI Index, and thus, the real market value and SR value are used here. In the attempt of identifying the spatial and temporal changes in the land value and to identifying the determinants of land value, I examine the various factors influencing the land prices with the evidence from existing literature.

Studies indicate that land value depends on the structural attributes, land price, land use and the location of land and also land use regulations have a positive effect on land value. Land values are influenced by location, urbanisation, land use control shortage of serviced land, financial resources. These studies on urban land market and land value show the trend in the land transactions. Studies carried out on urban land market display a unique pattern of spatial advancement; the populace in its effectively thick downtown area continues to grow, while at the same time, the metropolitan grows in a low thickness design on the outskirts. The growing metropolitan cities expand in their peripheries in the recent past.

Studies provide insights into the land prices; there is a dearth of studies that explore the mutual interactive influences of land transactions. Some studies on peri-urban land transactions are at the global level while others in the Indian context for estimating the extent of land transactions and land prices. For urban land, markets are accomplished to serve the economic and social needs of urban inhabitants and enterprise is one of the most problems that need to be addressed in urban communities all through the Third World (UNCHS–HABITAT, 1996). In the peri-urban zones, there is a rising interest of land for non-rural or urban land uses. Peri-urban regions include a great deal of changes and exercises are occurring because of fast urbanisation and populace development (Wehrmann, 2008). An unprecedented growth of urban population has led to speedy increase in the demand for urban land. The rising interest for urban land, in this manner, will, in general, be met basically by changing over peri-urban rural land at the fringe of the built-up area (Toulmin, 2008). In the effort to understand the peri-urban land market, a trend in the land prices is analysed.

Table 5.1 Determinants of land value

Author	Determinants	Methodology	Determinants
Eugene F Brigham (1965)	Determinants of land values in urban area	Ordinary least square method	Determinants are accessibility index, amenity level, topography.
Raymond B Palmquist (1984)	Estimating the demand for the characteristics of housing	Hedonic regression	The price elasticity of demand for living space is unitary and the demand for other characteristics is more inelastic.
William K Jaeger (2006)	Effect of land use regulations of property values	Analytical review	Land use regulations have a positive effect on land value.
Eric Koomen & Joost Buurman (2002)	Economic theories on land prices	Economics-based land use model	High land values in urban fringes.
Chan Sophal & Sarthi Acharya (2001)	Land Transactions in Cambodia	Descriptive analysis	Land is a unique commodity. Land prices can vary greatly from one location to another without any apparent difference in its productive value.
Bongjoon Kim & Taeyoung Kim (2016)	Land value using spatial statistics	OLS and spatial regression	Land prices determined by environmental conditions, features of neighbourhood and attributes such as distance.
Ping Ai (2005)	Residential land value modelling	Ordinary least square method	Major factors contributing to the land value include location, transportation and environment.
Lichfield (1956)	Economics of planned development	Theoretical	Values are created and changed by the same forces that create and change land uses.
Homer Hoyt (1960)	Dynamic factors in land values	Theoretical	Changing land value pattern
Darin Drabkin H (1977)	Urban land policy and urban growth	Theoretical	Land policy on urban growth explores the relationship between urban growth pattern, land prices and land policies in countries with market economies.
Rabindra (1996)	Land policy	Trend analysis	Land Values are influenced by location, urbanisation, land use control shortage of serviced land, financial resources.

(*Continued*)

Author	Determinants	Methodology	Determinants
Bharagava (2003)	Urban problems and urban perspectives	Theoretical	Major Problems in urban land markets are concentration in few hands, extravagant use, unearned increments, frequent transfers and so on
K.M Patil and Dinesh K Marothia (2009)	Chhattisgarh (1986–2000)	Simultaneous equation modelling	Provides a picture of agricultural land transactions and suggests effective legislations and institutional measures.
Sanjay Chakravarthy (2013)	Singur, Nandigram, Niyamgiri and Maha Mumbai,	Price of land	Issues related to the price of land: acquisition, conflict and consequence.

Source: Compilation by the author.

Table 5.2 Year-on-Year (YoY) growth rate and Annual Average Growth (AAG) rate from (2001–02 to 2017–18) in the Land value transactions – of the sample villages in Hoskote Taluk and Kanakapura Taluk

Year	Average Price per Sq ft Hoskote		Average Price per Sq ft Kanakapura		YoY Growth Rate (in %) Hoskote		YoY Growth Rate (in %)K	
	Nominal	Real Price[a]	Nominal	Real Price	Nominal	Real	Nominal	Real
2000	200	200.0	100	100.0	–	–	–	–
2001	270	270.0	150	150.0	35.0	35.0	50.0	50.0
2002	300	190.0	175	167.0	11.1	−29.6	16.7	11.3
2003	325	298.0	200	190.0	8.3	56.8	14.3	13.8
2004	350	310.0	250	221.0	7.7	4.0	25.0	16.3
2005	380	325.0	300	256.0	8.6	4.8	20.0	15.8
2006	400	328.0	500	410.0	5.3	0.9	66.7	60.2
2007	500	388.0	600	465.0	25.0	18.3	20.0	13.4
2008	600	438.0	650	474.0	20.0	12.9	8.3	1.9
2009	900	608.0	750	507.0	50.0	38.8	15.4	7.0
2010	1,000	599.0	1,000	599.0	11.1	−1.5	33.3	18.1
2011	1,100	1179.0	1,100	1179.0	10.0	96.8	10.0	96.8
2012	1,200	1171.0	1,300	1268.0	9.1	−0.8	18.2	7.5
2013	1,200	1069.0	1,500	1337.0	0.0	−8.6	15.4	5.4
2014	1,375	1156.0	1,600	1346.0	14.6	8.1	6.7	0.7
2015	1,750	1403.0	1,700	1363.0	27.3	21.4	6.3	1.3
2016	2,250	1727.0	2,000	1535.0	28.6	23.1	17.6	12.6
2017	2,250	1667.0	2,200	1630.0	0.0	−3.5	10.0	6.2
2018	2,500	1791.0	2,500	1791.0	11.1	7.4	13.6	9.9
CAG	14.22	12.23	18.46	16.40				

The consumer price index (CPI) is considered for conversion from nominal to real value.
Data source for CPI index, Consumer Price Index – Annual Average, RBI, m.rbi.org. in.
Source:https://economictimes.indiatimes.com/wealth/personal-finance-news/cost-inflation-index.
Source: Field Survey conducted by the author for 500 land transactions across ten villages.
[a]Author's Estimation.

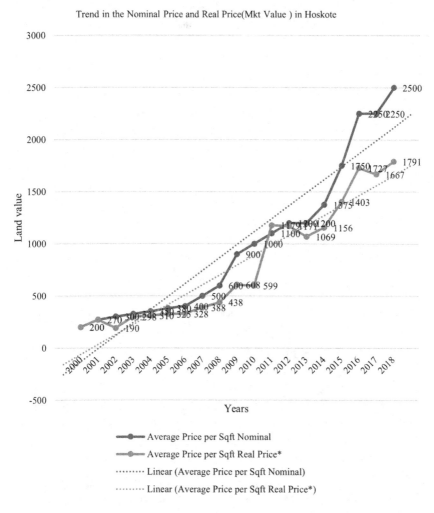

Figure 5.1 Trend in the market value (from 2001–02 to 2017–18) in the land value transactions – of the sample villages in Hoskote Taluk. Compilation by the author from field survey Hoskote periphery.

Trends in the Market Value

Figure 5.1 shows the trend in the real and nominal market value in Hoskote Taluk. The average price of market value per sq ft for the year 2000 is Rs. 200 per sq ft; average price of market value is Rs. 2,500 per sq ft in 2018. The average real market price increased from Rs. 599 per sq ft to Rs. 1,179 per sq ft from 2009 to 2010. The increase in the real market value is the highest for the year 2010. The real market price is Rs. 1,791 per sq ft for the year 2018.

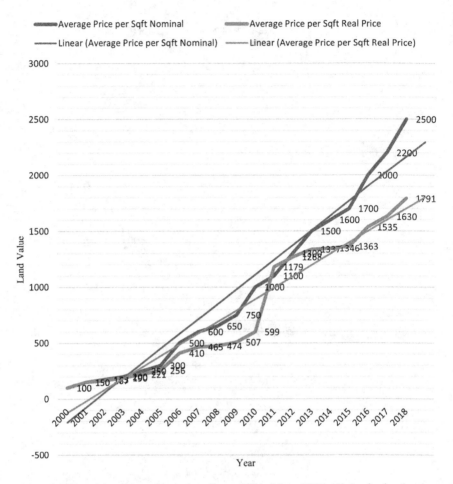

Figure 5.2 Trend in the market value (from 2001–02 to 2017–18) in the land value
transactions – of the sample villages in Kanakapura Taluk. Compilation
by the author from field survey Kanakapura periphery.

Figure 5.2 shows the trend in the real and nominal market value in
Kanakapura Taluk. The average price of market value per sq ft for the year
2000 is 100 and average price of market value is Rs. 2,500 per sq ft in 2018.
The increase in the real market value is highest for the year 2010. Although
Kanakapura has less land prices since 2000, there is an increase in the land
price in Kanakapura in the recent decade especially since 2010.

Trends in the Sub-Registrar Value

Land transfers from agriculture to non-agriculture use are clearly visible in
the studied peri-urban villages. I have analysed the trend in the Sub-Registrar
Value of the periphery.

Figure 5.3 shows the trend in the SR value in the selected five peripheral villages of Hoskote. SR value of Hoskote periphery is from 2000 to 2017. The average of SR value is Rs. 28 per sq ft for the year 2000–01 and Rs 732 per sq ft for the year 2016–17. The SR value shows moderate growth in all the selected peripheral villages of Hoskote from 2000–01 to 2016–17.

Figure 5.4 shows the trend in the SR value in the selected five peripheral villages of Kanakapura. SR value of Kanakapura Taluk is available only from 2005 to 2006. The SR value is highest in the Somanahalli village (Rs. 890 per sq ft for the year 2000 and Rs. 1,690 per sq ft for the year 2016–17) and the least in Sathanur (40 per sq ft for the year 2000 and Rs. 938 per sq ft for the year 2016–17). Kanakapura has higher SR value compared to Hoskote periphery. The average SR value in Kanakapura is Rs. 487 per sq ft for the year 2005–06 and Rs. 1,260 per sq ft for the year 2016–17.

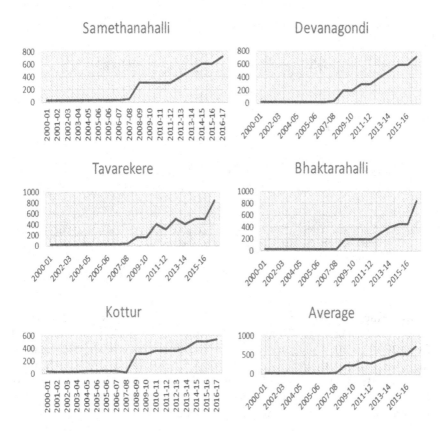

Figure 5.3 Year wise Average SR value per sq ft across selected villages under Hoskote peripheral area. Compilation by the author from SRO reports Hoskote Periphery.

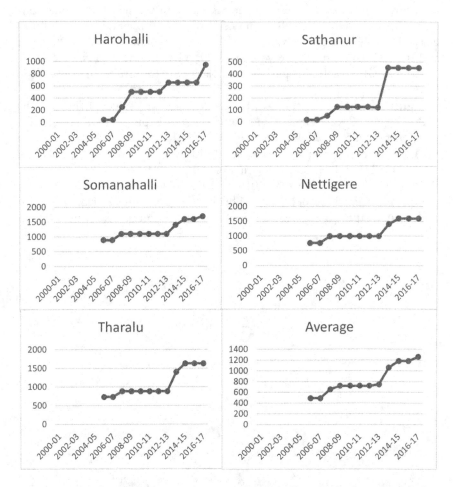

Figure 5.4 Year wise Average SR value per sq ft across selected villages under Kanaka-
       pura peripheral area. Compilation by the author from SRO reports Hoskote
       Periphery.

SR value analysis of villages belonging to Hoskote Taluk (Bengaluru
East) and Kanakapura (Bengaluru South) for the period for the period
from 2000 to 2017 suggests that there is a divergence in the SR value in
the East and South Periphery (Figure 5.5). SR values are significantly
high for Bengaluru South Kanakapura as compared to Bengaluru East
Hoskote Region. There is a significant increase observed in the SR values
in Bengaluru South zone Kanakapura as compared to Hoskote Bengaluru
East Taluk.

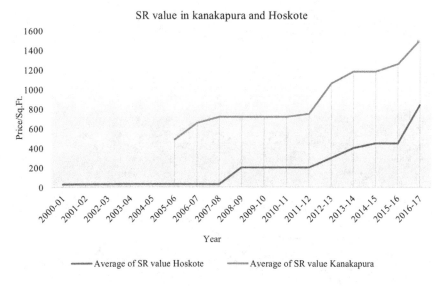

Figure 5.5 Trend in the average SR value for the time period 2000 to 2017 in the selected periphery.

Comparison of SR Value and Market Value in Respect of Periphery

A comparison of SR value and market value trend for the period 2000–01 to 2016–17 is captured and high market value is visible in both peripheries.

In Figure 5.6, the average market value is higher than the average SR value in the study area. The average market value[1] is Rs.200 sq ft for the year 2000–01, whereas the average SR[2] value is just Rs. 28 per sq ft in Hoskote. The average market value for the peripheral village is Rs. 2,250 per sq ft for the year 2016–17, whereas the average SR value is Rs. 732 per sq ft. In 17 years, there is an increase in both SR value and market value.[3] The major reason for the escalation of land prices in the peripheral villages of Hoskote is their accessibility to IT centre. The IT industry's concentration along the Whitefield area has increased the demand for land with an active supply in the area. Further, the completion of infrastructure projects in this area has led to an enhanced activity in the plotted developments along this locality. Infrastructure-related activities have been undertaken which include the upgradation of the road from Marathahalli to Whitefield, Kadugodi Flyover for commuters heading towards Hoskote, further extension of the Metro Phase II up to Whitefield and a new Metro line running up to Nagavara, and the improved connectivity to the ORR are further fuelling the growth in the region. As regards, to the land value in Bengaluru East, especially connectivity, industrial growth,

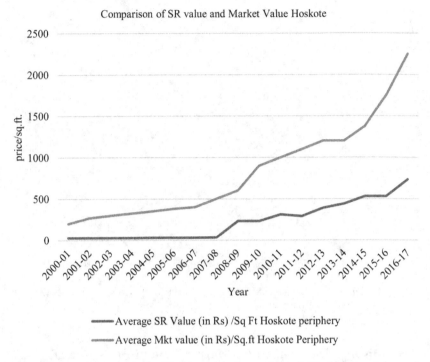

Comparison of SR value and Market Value Hoskote

——Average SR Value (in Rs) /Sq Ft Hoskote periphery

——Average Mkt value (in Rs)/Sq.ft Hoskote Periphery

Figure 5.6 Trend in the SR value and market value of Hoskote periphery for 2000–01 to 2016–17. Compilation by the author from SRO reports Hoskote and Primary survey.

accessibility to the city centre and IT corridors have led to high land values in the East periphery. East Bengaluru has been a growth engine for two decades. Setting up of manufacturing units and concentration of IT/ITeS companies and increase in residential, retail and hospitality demand have triggered the need for social infrastructure. The drive into the city from the airport in Deva-nahalli pushed the growth up to East Bengaluru and Hoskote up to Whitefield. The area's advantageous proximity to the IT growth corridor is also a con-tributing factor. Planned infrastructure developments such as Peripheral Ring Road, high-speed rail link and the Metro are further augmenting connectivity along with residential and commercial development in East periphery.

Figure 5.7 shows the difference between SR value and market value of Kanakapura. Kanakapura has high SR value and market value from 2000–01 to 2016–17. The average market value[4] is Rs. 100 sq ft for the year 2000–01.[5] The average SR value is Rs. 487 per sq ft in the peripheral village, whereas the average market value is Rs. 410 per sq ft for the year 2005–06. The aver-age market value for the peripheral villages is Rs. 2,000 per sq ft for the year 2006–17, whereas the average SR value is Rs. 1503 per sq ft. The Outer Ring Road and Electronics City have led to the expansion of South Bengaluru into new areas and the development of Sarjapur Road and Bannerghatta

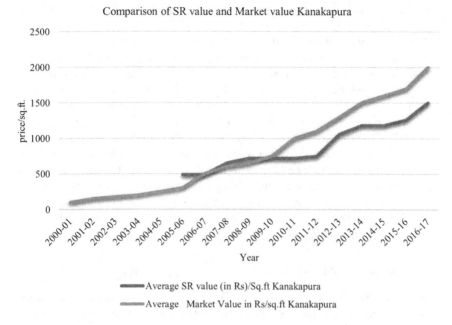

Comparison of SR value and Market value Kanakapura

Figure 5.7 Trend in the SR value and market value of Kanakapura periphery for the period 2000–01 to 2016–17. Compilation by the author from SRO reports Hoskote.

Note: Year in the x axis, Price/sq. ft in y axis.

Note: Price per sq ft varies within a given village. It is not uniform across land within the village. It varies across survey number. The guidance value of survey numbers close to highway is much higher as compared to those survey numbers which are far away from State/National highway Road.

Road on the one hand, and the growth of places like Banashankari metro, Konanakunte up to Uttarahalli zone on the other. The demand for affordable housing comes from price-sensitive buyers, and hence, such projects are developed in the peripheral areas where land acquisition cost is low. These concepts have gained popularity due to the presence of a few graded builders like Shriram Properties, Golden Gate Properties, Ozone Group, Brigade Group, Nitesh Estate and Purvankara, who are predominantly focused on the affordable customer section from Konanakunte to Kaggalipura–Harohalli region. There is a constant demand for budget houses on the outskirts of the city and the availability of land at lower prices has led to an increase in the launch of new projects. Areas such as Banashankari metro have witnessed a high demand. Due to land acquisition and construction activities, there is a substantial rise in the capital values, and therefore, the developers have redesigned their projects to cater the demand of target buyers in South Bengaluru. Both the SR value and market value show a high growth trajectory in Bengaluru South Peripheral zone. South Bengaluru is the most preferred location as most of the affordable and mid-housing, income segment projects are available here. The major driving factors behind the booming demand for these locations are improved metro connectivity, proximate civic facilities that add value to these locations.

The major stimulation for the realty sector comes from the presence of IT companies along the key infrastructure projects. According to the 99acres Insite Report, South Bengaluru and East Bengaluru are offering most affordable residential properties that are equipped with all modern amenities. East and South Bengaluru have entrenched themselves as the cost-effective housing hubs with respective shares standing at 25% and 41% of the total budget, respectively. A trend analysis of South and East periphery shows a significant growth in the land prices. The SR value and market value trend for Bengaluru South periphery shows a rapid growth in the land value after 2010–11. In the case of Hoskote, there is a gradual change observed in the land values, while the peripheral villages have shown a significant change in land prices after 2009. Market prices were low initially in the case of Kanakapura, it has high land prices compared to Hoskote periphery in course of time.

Determinants of Land Value in Peri-Urban Villages

Land value stems from the fact that land is essential for construction, and buildings are necessary for most kinds of production of goods or services such as residential and other land use such as commercial or industrial uses. Land originates its value from the fact that is a vital input, or a factor of production. The nineteenth-century intellectual works of David Ricardo and Johann Heinrich Von Thünen both offered the initial theories on land use and land value. Although the two theories are on opposing sides, most of the later theories on land use and land value were based on them. While Ricardo's economic theory focused on relative productivity of agricultural land, the geographical theory of Von Thünen harped more on the locational qualities of land in terms of its use and value. Alonso developed one of urban economics' critical analytical tools. This study conducted a review of previous research works regarding land use and land values and it was found that the real estate value of land thus comes from what is known as derived demand: people are willing to pay for land not because of its inherent value. Like most economic transactions, factors of demand and supply, ceteris paribus, are expected to determine the value of land in city and the periphery. The factors determining land market value of land in the context of Bengaluru periphery are analysed using the following specification.

The log-log regression model is given by

$$logY = \propto + \beta_1 logX_1 + \beta_2 X_2 + \beta_3 D_2 + \beta_4 D_3 + + \varepsilon$$

$$log(MARKET\ VALUE)_{it} = \propto + \beta_1 log(SR\ VALUE) + \beta_2(DIST\_DISRT\_HQ)$$
$$+ \beta_3(DIST\_NAT\_HW)$$
$$+ \beta_4(DIST\_NEAR\_COMM) + \varepsilon$$

where
   Y = MARKET VALUE (log transformed)
and
   X_1 = SUB REGISTRAR (SR) VALUE (log transformed)
   X_2 = DIST_NEAR_COMM (Distance from the Nearest Commercial Centre)
   X_3 = DIST_NAT_HW (Distance to the National Highway)
   X_4 = DIST_DISRT_HQ (Distance to the District Head Quarters)

The determinants of land use and property values fall within the classification of structural, locational and neighbourhood attributes. The determinants of market value are looked at with respect to the relationship between the sub-registrar value of land and distance is considered major determinant of land value in the periphery. The estimated log-log regression model[6] for peri-urban area is given in Table 5.4.

The regression coefficient $_1$ of PRICE (SR VALUE) is 0.458. The t-value for SR VALUE is 13.56. Thus, I could conclude that PRICE (SR VALUE) is a significant determinant of market value. Since it is a log-log transformation, the unit considered is the percentage change. The change in SR value leads to a visible change in the market value. Similarly, the *Distance from National Highway, District Headquarters and Nearest Commercial Centre* is showing a very significant determinant of the market value.

From Table 5.5, the chi-square value is 0.13 and p-value is 0.422 for the model. As the p-value is greater than the significance alpha level of 0.05, we accept H_0. In essence, there is no problem of heteroscedasticity, and the error term is homoscedastic in nature and has constant variance.

Table 5.3 Description of the variables used in the model

Variables	Description	Source
SR value (Sq. ft) (Rs)	The land value fixed by the sub-registrar office	Secondary data
Real market value (Sq. ft) (Rs)	The real price at which land is bought and sold	Primary data survey
Distance to District Headquarters (in Km)	Distance to TQ is an important parameter of land value	Secondary data
Distance to Nearest Commercial Centre (in Km)	Distance to nearest CC is also an important determinant of land value	Secondary data
Distance to the National Highway (in Km)	Distance to NH is a major determinant of land price	Secondary data

Table 5.4 Log-log ordinary linear regression result

Independent Variables	Coefficient	t value
LG_PRICE (SR VALUE)	0.458 (0.033)★★★	13.56
DIST_DISRT_HQ	−0.68 (0.00)★★★	−5.14
DIST_NAT_HW	−0.45 (0.008)★★★	−5.64
DIST_NEAR_COMM	−0.40 (0.001)★★★	−3.67
CONSTANT	4.307 (0.238)	18.08
Observation: 153		
R-squared: 0.753		
F statistic: 65.01		

Source: Author's Estimation.
★★★ $p < 0.01$, ★★$p < 0.05$, ★$p < 0.1$, the value in the parenthesis is Standard Error.
The land use is not as an explanatory variable in the regression as the land price differs considerably in the case of converted and non-converted land. The above regression is based on primary data survey. In order to identify the determinants of market value, we do not have corresponding land use information from the secondary data source for all ten villages. The determinant of SR value is not captured. SR value is determined by the government.

Table 5.5 Breusch-Pagan/Cook-Weisberg test for heteroscedasticity

Ho: Constant variance
Variables: fitted values of LG_TOT_QTY_TRANS
chi2(1) = 0.13
Prob > chi2 = 0.422

Source: Author's Estimation.

Relationship between Land Use and Land Value

Land use and land value are dependent on each other. Land use is a significant determinant of land value. The relationship between land use and land value is captured using the changes in the market value and the changes land cover.

In Figure 5.8, there is an increase of market value of Kanakapura periphery. It shows a remarkable increase in the land price. As the built-up land increases, market value shows a considerable increase. As the built-up land increases, the land price increases at a faster rate in Kanakapura.

Figure 5.9 shows that the market value increases as built-up land increases in Hoskote. In both peripheries, the increase in the land price is coincided with the visible changes in the land covers. The price is crucial in land and real estate economics (Özdilek, 2010). "market value should rightly be viewed as a social convention whose function is to facilitate transactions between self-interested individuals participating in complex property markets" (Mooya, 2011, p. 2276). Land price depends on land use. It shows a trend of declining farmlands and increasing built up over years and the real market prices have a positive relation with the increase in built-up land and decrease in agriculture in both the peripheries. It is inferred that land use is a major determinant of land value. The other key factors that determine land values within urban areas – accessibility, amenity levels, and topography – were framed almost five decades ago (Brigham, 1965). The effect of non-agricultural income

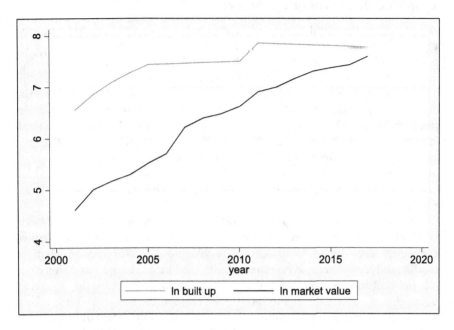

Figure 5.8 Relationship between land use and land value Kanakapura. Compilation
   by the author.

Note: Log value of area in hectares, market value is used for comparison.

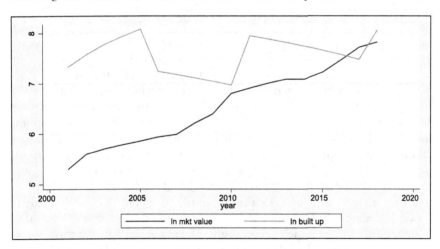

Figure 5.9 Relationship between land use and land value Hoskote. Compilation by
   the author.

Note: Log value of area in hectares, market value is used for comparison.

share is uni-directionally negative, implying that farmers with a lower share
of non-agricultural income tend to sell their land for non-agricultural purposes (Kung, 2002). It leads to the empirical evidence of the land use and land
value variable as mentioned in the theoretical framework.

Empirical Evidence of the Model

According to the Land Use Land value model, the agents try to maximise their utility subject to the budget constraint. Agents are willing to pay more for the land which is closer to the urban centres or the National highway because of the accessibility and amenities. In a very simplified view, households and agents make a trade-off between land price, transportation costs and the amount of land they use. This output in a convex land price curves with the peak land prices close to the city centre. The origin of agricultural and rural land values in the bid rent theory owes more to Von Thunen theory than the work of Alonso. The relationship between distance and land price is tested and structural break in land price in 2010 and the structural breaks in the land covers is visible for the year 2009 and 2010 for peripheral Taluk and Village, respectively.

The coincidence of the land use and land value changes and the relationship between these two are empirically tested. Peri-urban being the focus of the study, more dynamic changes are visible and there are frequent changes in the land use pattern; consequently, the land price changes and therefore the bid rent model is more suitable to understand such a scenario. The land value changes as per the changes in the increase in the non-agricultural land use. In Kanakapura and Hoskote, land use is a major determinant of land value and distance plays a predominant role in the land price. The hypothesis is tested, and the model shows distance impact land price significantly. Land use and land value are related to each other. Several authors pointed out land utilisation changes frequently in the peripheral areas. The valuation model is especially close in its way to the binomial option pricing models of Bartter (1979). Ratcliff R.U (1972) recommends that appraisers decide the future land utilisation. Existing studies suggest that if the government initiates a monetary policy (or any other policy) to stimulate building activity, the policy may actually lead to a decrease in building activity if there is uncertainty about its duration or its effect. But the peripheral villages in this study are known for rapid building activities. There exist complications in this scenario due to the asymmetric information in the land market. Thirkell (1996) remarked inconsistencies in land price determination in informal land market. It is unlikely that farmland converted to developed uses will ever become available again for agricultural production (Su et al., 2011). Decline in total area of agricultural landscape would definitely result in lower self-supply abilities though it increases land price, and it is a threat to food security of this region accordingly. The major challenge at this context is that the fragmented lands are unsuitable for urban development (Dredge, 1995) and it acts as a threat to environmental sustainability at global and local level.

Less empirical analyses of land prices is primarily due to a lack of data on land transactions. Existing studies are limited in scope; for example, Peiser (1987), Kowalski and Paraskevopoulos (1990) used data limited transaction data for the analysis. The survey conducted the land transactions using 500 transaction data and arrived at the findings.

- The analysis on periphery shows South and East are two divergent peripheries. It differs in terms of its land uses, land prices and land transactions. Residential land transactions are common in both the periphery.
- A significant amount of residential land transactions is observed in the periphery. Among the various land transactions 66% is the residential land transactions.
- Land transactions also include industrial commercial and agricultural uses. There is 15.2% industrial land transactions that are noted in the periphery. Land transaction for the commercial space is 25.6%. And the land transaction for the agriculture is the least, it is of 8%. Periphery shows a trend of land conversion from agriculture to non–agricultural transactions. The results of the empirical analysis point to the following key findings.

1 SR value (Guidance Value) is an important determinant of the market value: The OLS estimates of the combined study area show that SR value as a significant predictor of the market value.
2 Distance is a major determinant of land value: Distance from NH and distance from HQ is coming out a significant determinant which influences the land prices.
3 Accessibility to commercial centre is an important determinant of land prices: Another important determinant is accessibility to nearest the commercial centre. Accessibility is a major reason why people purchase land in nearest periphery where they can access all amenities of Commercial centre.
4 Land use and land transaction: There is a relationship between land use and land transaction as we see in the empirical results. Graphical representation of Hoskote based on LU/LC analysis shows all the three land cover changes influences the land prices. Kanakapura shows the more change in the land prices due to the conversion of land for non–agricultural purposes. Graphical representation of land use and land value of both the study areas shows that land price increases due to the conversion of land for the residential and commercial purposes in the study area.

An analysis of the land values resulted in a relevant outcome. The price variation in different periphery proves the theory of Alonso and Von Thunen that the price of land decreases with increasing distance from the city centre. The high land values are due to the increasing tendency towards changing land use for commercial purpose. The land value depends on the land use of the city. As the population expands, spatial extension takes place. The residential buyers purchase the land in peripheries. Another impact of physical expansion is the extensive use of land for high rise buildings. Low-price level in the periphery of the city increases the speculation. Real estate agents purchase land in the peripheral areas with the expectation in future prices. Therefore, the role of government permits the conversion of agricultural land for urban land uses. The distribution of land values affects the land use structure of the city. As the CBD gets congested, it tends to extend to the adjacent periphery. The residential users encroach on farms lands of periphery. The conversion of land for non-agricultural purpose is a manifestation of this phenomenon.

Spatial Distribution of Land Values in the South Periphery

Southern peripheral cluster is known for the active land transactions and high real estate prices in the last decade. Land supply is fixed; land value in an urban community is determined by the demand for space. Demand is a function of the site's accessibility, amenity level, topography, certain historical factors and the value of the land in non-urban uses (Brigham, 1965). The classical Von Thünen hypothesis expresses that agricultural land values or prices are a function of economic rent or profit from agricultural use that is estimated as a function of distance to a commercial centre (Sinclair, 1967). Von Thünen theory provides the basis for agricultural land valuation; Sinclair (1967) demonstrated that industrialisation and increase in urban population can bring about urbanisation and urban sprawl. Likewise, it impacts land use and values even before the expansion of urban infrastructure. That is, a high likelihood of conversion of land use from rural to urban impact land values. The analysis on land values in the south periphery brings forth the following key findings.

- There is a considerable increase in the land value in Kanakapura zone from 2000 to 2018. Average market value is Rs. 100 per sq ft in nominal terms in 2000 and Rs. 100 per sq ft in real terms. There is 96.8% increase in the land price by the year 2010.
- Kanakapura also has a high average SR value for the selected peripheral villages.
- Among the selected peripheral villages Somanahalli, Nettigere and Taralu show high SR value throughout the year compared to Harohalli and Sathanur village. Harohalli and Sathanur had a SR value of Rs. 40 per sq ft and Rs. 17 per sq ft, respectively, for the year 2005–06. However, Nettigere, Somanahalli and Taralu have Rs. 890 per sq ft, Rs. 760 per sq ft and Rs. 730 per sq ft for the year 2005–06. There is a great divergence in the SR value among the selected peripheral villages.
- SR value is highest in Somanahalli Village. It is Rs. 890 per sq ft for the year 2005–06 and Rs. 1690 per sq ft for the year 2016–17. SR value

is the least in Sathanur village i.e. Rs. 40 per sq ft for the year 2000 and Rs. 938 per sq ft for the year 2016–17.

- The average of SR value stands Rs. 487 per sq ft in the year 2005–06 and Rs. 1260 per sq ft for the year 2016–17.
- The influence of Bengaluru and the metro line connectivity increased the real estate prices significantly in the South periphery.
- There is a huge demand for end users for real estate, it is a favourite destination of builders and there is a thriving land market in the south periphery.

Spatial Distribution of Land Values in the East Periphery

The eastern peripheral cluster is known for the moderate transition and the land value analysis shows the key findings.

- There is a considerable increase in the land value in Hoskote zone from 2000 to 2018. Average market value is Rs. 200 per sq ft in nominal terms for the year 2000.
- Hoskote also has a low average prices compared to Kanakapura periphery both in terms of SR value and market value.
- The average of SR value is just Rs. 28 per sq.ft for the year 2000–01 and Rs. 732 per sq ft for the year 2016–17.
- SR value for the selected peripheral villages shows Kottur has least SR value. The other villages like Devangundi, Tavarekere and Baktharahalli show similar SR values in the study period.
- Tavarekere and Baktharahalli have high SR value compared to other three villages; it is of Rs. 40 per sq ft and Rs. 840 per sq ft, respectively.
- The transition of Hoskote as real estate destination is especially after 2006. This is mainly because of the clustering of IT and other industrial clusters. The IT influence is mainly because of ITPL in the Whitefield. Whitefield region gradually exhausted and hence there was more demand for land in the peripheral Hoskote villages; the villages adjacent to the NH have more real estate potential and there is a visible increase in the land prices.

The major reason for the expansion of land prices in the peripheral villages of Hoskote is the accessibility to IT centre. The IT industry's concentration along the Whitefield area pushed demand and, therefore, active supply in the area. The completion of infrastructure projects in this area led to enhanced activity in the plotted developments along this locality. Activities which are infrastructure-related have been undertaken which include upgradation of the road from Marathahalli to Whitefield, the Kadugodi Flyover for commuters heading towards Hoskote, further extension of the Metro Phase II up to Whitefield and a new Metro line running up to Nagavara, and the improved connectivity to the ORR are further fuelling growth in the region. This attributes to the land value in Bengaluru East, especially connectivity, industrial growth, accessibility to the city centre and IT corridors lead to high land values in the East periphery.

East Bengaluru has been a growth engine for two decades. Setting up of manufacturing units and concentration of IT/ITeS companies and increase in residential, retail and hospitality demand have triggered the need for social infrastructure. The drive into the city from the airport in Devanahalli pushed the growth up to East Bengaluru Hoskote up to Whitefield. The area's advantageous proximity to the IT growth corridor will also be a contributing factor. Planned infrastructure developments are also pushing developments such as the Peripheral Ring Road, high-speed rail link and the Metro will further augment connectivity and impact residential and commercial development in East periphery. From the analysis of the price trends of peri-urban land, some challenges are identified.

1 No credible record of land prices is available, the sources from which prices are obtained.
2 Land prices have shown a continuously rising trend in space and time across periphery.
3 Land in commercial areas commands higher value than in residential areas. And there is more residential land transaction in the periphery.
4 Land use changes play a vital role in determining land prices. The change of land use from agricultural to non-agricultural results in creation of additional land value simultaneously. The change in value is created by a decision of the public authority; the additional value is collected by the landowner.
5 Rapid population growth and the expansion of IT centres resulting in an increase in demand for land.
6 Expanding urban sprawl leading to unplanned developments in rural-urban fringe of Bengaluru.
7 Very high land prices in the South periphery.
8 Land policies have paid little demand side of land and concentrated on supply side of land.

Summary

The increasing land prices in the periphery and the determinants of land value are evaluated. The trend in the land prices in the periphery is captured with the help of market value and SR value. Year-wise analysis of average SR value and market value shows a rapid change since the year 2010 in both peripheries. SR value of Hoskote periphery is just Rs. 28 per sq ft in Hoskote for the year 2000–01 and it increased to Rs. 732 for the year 2016–17. The SR value of Kanakapura periphery is Rs. 487 for the year 2005–06 and it increased to Rs. 1503 for the year 2016–17. There is a rapid increase in the land prices in Kanakapura for the selected peripheral villages across the years. The change in the average land prices changes quickly in both peripheries from 2010.

Hoskote has witnessed much more topographical changes as compared to Kanakapura; in the case of land prices, Kanakapura shows a remarkable change. In Kanakapura, there is more of a vertical development than Hoskote, where there is more of a horizontal development. Hoskote has more barren land which is visible in the land use map. The water crisis in this area is a major factor that has forced real estate developers to seek yet other locations. Another reason for an increase in the land price in Kanakapura is the influence of NICE corridor which has increased the land price tremendously. A high price of land in Kanakapura is especially due to a high demand. Further, there is an active growth of real estate and tourism in this place. Government investment in KIADB has also increased speculation significantly. It is a hotspot for the real estate developers such as Godrej, Purvankara, SLV, Provident and Prestige and several other factors affecting land prices are discussed. The market value is a function of Distance from Head Quarters, Distance from National Highway, Distance from nearest commercial centre, SR value; Distance and market value are the significant predictors of land prices.

Notes

1 As per the primary data survey in the peripheral villages.
2 As per the Sub registrar office report of the peripheral villages for the DC converted sites.
3 Here Nominal Market value and SR Value are used.
4 As per the primary data survey in the peripheral villages.
5 SR Value data for Kanakapura selected peripheral villages available from 2005 onwards.
6 Note: Only land transactions for the last three years of survey is used for the analysis, as the information of market value given by the respondents can be affected by memory loss. The deflated market values and SR value are used for the analysis.

References

Ai, P. (2005). Residential land value modelling. *Faculty of Geo-Information Science and Earth Observation of the University of Twente*. 2005. [An electronic resource]. Access mode: https://www. etc. nl/library/papers_2005/msc/upla/ai_ping. pdf (date of publication: December 29, 2017), free. Heading from the screen.

Bartter, B. J. (1979). Two-state option pricing. *Journal of Finance*, 34(5), 1093–1110.

Bhargava, G. (2003). *Urban Problems and Urban Perspectives*. New Delhi, India: Abhinav Publications.

Darin-Drabkin, H. (1977). *Land Policy and Urban Growth* (pp. 256–261). Oxford: Pergamon Press.

Brigham, E. F. (1965). The determinants of residential land values. *Land Economics*, 41(4), 325–334.

Chicoine, D. L. (1981). Farmland values at the urban fringe: An analysis of sale prices. *Land Economics*, 57(3), 353–362.

Clark, W. A., & Harvey, R. O. (1965). The nature and economics of urban sprawl. *Land Economics*, 41(1), 1–9.

Chakravarthy, S. (2013). *Price of Land: Acquisition, Conflict, Consequence*. Oxford University Press.

Dredge, D. (1995). Sustainable rapid urban expansion: The case of Xalapa, Mexico. *Habitat International*, 19(3), 317–329.

Hoyt, H. (1960). *The Urban Real Estate Cycle: Performances and Prospects* (No. 38). Washington, DC: Urban Land Institute.

Jaeger, W. K. (2006). The effects of land-use regulations on property values. *Environmental Law*, 36, 105.

Patil, K. M. & Dinesh, K. Marothia (2009). Agricultural Land Market Transactions in Chhattisgarh: A Case Study. *Agricultural Economics Research Review*, 22, 255–261.

Kim, B., & Kim, T. (2016). A study on estimation of land value using spatial statistics: Focusing on real transaction land prices in Korea. *Sustainability*, 8(3), 203.

Koomen, E., & Buurman, J. (2002, April). Economic theory and land prices in land use modeling. In *5th AGILE Conference on Geographic Information Science*, Palma (Balearic Islands Spain) April 25th–27th (Vol. 7).

Kolowe, P. (2014). The determinants of urban land and property values: The case of Rwanda. *Thesis*, https://repository.usfca.edu/thes

Kung, J. K. S. (2002). Off-farm labor markets and the emergence of land rental markets in rural China. *Journal of Comparative Economics*, 30(2), 395–414.

Lichfield, N. (1956). *Economics of Planned Development*. Estates Gazette, Limited.

Liu, Z., Wang, P., & Zha, T. (2013). Land-price dynamics and macroeconomic fluctuations. *Econometrica*, 81(3), 1147–1184.

Mooya, M. (2011). Of mice and men: Automated valuation models and the valuation profession. *Urban Studies*, 48(11), 2265–2281.

Northam, J. (1975). Ibsen: Romantic, Realist or Symbolist? *Ibsenarbok Oslo*, 3, 155–162.

Özdilek, Ü. (2010). On Price, Cost, and Value. *Appraisal Journal*, 78(1), 70–80.

Ratcliff, R. U. (1972). *Valuation for Real Estate Decisions*. Democrat Press.

Palmquist, R. B. (1984). Estimating the Demand for the Characteristics of Housing. *The Review of Economics and Statistics*, 66, 394–404.

Ravindra, A. (1996) *Urban Land Policy. Study of Metropolitan City*. New Delhi: Concept Publishing Company.

Sinclair, R. (1967). Von Thünen and urban sprawl. *Annals of the Association of American Geographers*, 57(1), 72–87.

Sovannarith, S., Sophal, C., & Acharya, S. (2001). An assessment of land tenure in rural Cambodia. *Cambodian Development Review*, 5(4), 1–5.

Su, S., Jiang, Z., Zhang, Q., & Zhang, Y. (2011). Transformation of agricultural landscapes under rapid urbanization: A threat to sustainability in Hang-Jia-Hu region, China. *Applied Geography*, 31(2), 439–449.

Thirkell, A. J. (1996). Players in urban informal land markets; who wins? who loses? A case study of Cebu City. *Environment and Urbanization*, 8(2), 71–90.

Verheye, W. (2007). *The Value and Price of Land. Land Use, Land Cover and Soil Sciences*. Vol. III - Land Use Planning, UNESCO-EOLSS Publishers.

Verheye, W. H. (Ed.). (2009). *Land Use, Land Cover and Soil Sciences-Volume IV: Land Use Management and Case Studies*. EOLSS Publications.

Walters, L. C. (2013). Land value capture in policy and practice. *Journal of Property Tax Assessment & Administration*, 10(2), 5–21.

Wyatt, P. J. (1997). The development of a GIS-based property information system for real estate valuation. *International Journal of Geographical Information Science*, 11(5), 435–450.

6 What Does Dynamic Forces of Peri-Urban Mean to Land Prices?

Economics of Land Prices

In the backdrop of land transaction survey, I look at the dynamic changes in the periphery and how it affects the land transactions and land prices in the South-East periphery. There is a divergence between these two peripheries; the land use analysis showed structural break in land covers in Hoskote Taluk in 2009 and in Harohalli village in 2010. Kanakapura is known for fast changes in terms of land value and growth of real estate. Though there are less topographical changes in Kanakapura, changes are spontaneous in the recent period, whereas Hoskote changes are not so instinctive at present. The flow of people, goods and services and resources are frequent in the entire stretch of stretch of Kanakapura. The land transaction survey shows the reasons for the transition of periphery are demand and supply factors. I address the dynamic changes in the periphery – what does it mean to the land prices?

Peri-urban transition leads to rapid changes in both peripheries. But land price is a significant factor that shows the economic impact of peri-urban transition. Kanakapura poised to witness a boost in the land transaction with the metro connectivity. It is accessible from several other parts of Bangalore. The extension of Namma Metro to the Anjanapura Township and Kengeri boosted real estate considerably. Kanakapura is known as an attractive segment of affordable housing. There is a rapid increase in demand for homes located along the metro corridors on account of improved accessibility and connectivity. Another hallmark is that the southern region in Bangalore is one of the fastest growing clusters in terms of both residential and commercial properties. It was evident in the land market survey. Kanakapura Road has spurred the development of several real estate projects and shopping centres in this stretch. There are more than 100 developers who have invested in various projects. Top among them are Sobha Developers, Prestige Group, Mantri Developers, Sri Ram Properties and Salarpuria Sattva. Supporting these projects, there are several shopping centres and malls that have come up making the whole region convenient. The rental values in these gated communities are relatively low in comparison to the city centre. With all the facilities and good infrastructure in terms of transport and services, several

DOI: 10.4324/9781003362333-6

families prefer to live in these communities and commute to work is less. It applies both to the formal and informal sector employment. Rapid change in the real estate growth in Kanakapura accelerated with these top builders investing in the area.

Kanakapura Road has become a leading residential hub. Saturation of real estate in the nearby markets of Bannerghatta Road, Banashankari, JP Nagar and Jayanagar has propelled investment in Kanakapura Road. Kanakapura is a budget segment which is affordable to the middle-class segments of the society. Many start-ups and MNCs set up their offices at the heart of the city, demanding the residential space away from the crowded and busy city centre to the nearby affordable residential peripheral township. Majority people of Kanakapura Road stay close to office spaces in Bannerghatta, Silk Board and Electronic City and with the metro, travelling to the centre of the city with the metro connectivity accelerated the demand for real estate in this stretch.

Kanakapura is known for its connectivity. There is a vast population depending on public transport Namma Metro to reach workplace. Kanakapura is well connecting the people to the urban life. Kanakapura also is known for its accessibility to commercial centres like Mantri Mall. Accessibility and connectivity are the major factor driving the land price. The infrastructural facilities lead Kanakapura as a growth corridor after 2010 because of the above-mentioned two factors. Real estate builders attract investment; hence, peri-urban locale is absorbed by the urban growth process in Kanakapura. Thus, peri-urban transition leads to substantial changes and spatial expansion and the economic impact is the increase in the land prices.

For example, price per sq feet in Konanakunte in Kanakapura range between Rs. 215 and Rs. 11,500 and the average price is 10,464.76 per sq feet for apartments; there is 114.5% increase during the period October 2017–January 2018. Kaggalipura is another growth node where the price of residential properties ranges from 10 lakh to 1 crore.[1] On an average, the price of the vacant plot in the selected peripheral villages of Kanakapura showed the land price is just Rs. 100 for the year 2000 and Rs. 599 in 2010. However, by the year 2011, there is a giant leap in the average price of the land in peripheral village. It increased to Rs. 1,179 in 2011. This remarkable growth in price is attributed by the above-mentioned factors.

Distance plays an important role in the fixation of land prices. For example, Prestige Falcon City is an elegant example directing flow of people from apartment complexes to nearby Forum Mall and Metro. Apparently, the top-rated builders are able to set the price high in prime localities due to the accessibility and connectivity, which in turn influence the quality of life of people. This is a region of the city with salubrious weather and there is abundant supply of water and other basic amenities. The price set by the builder is also influenced by the geographic location and forest view surprisingly the quality of an urban life enhanced by the nature's beauty in Kanakapura. The area has an easy access to Cauvery water, thus addressing the biggest need of any household.

Commercial centres, entertainment stretch along the Kanakapura road stretch add more the transformation of the periphery and land prices. Mantri Mall, Forum Mall and other commercial centres are opening up shortly. This accelerates new dynamics in terms of access to city life in the peripheries. Developing green line in South Bangalore with several stations on Kanakapura Road is a distinguishing factor. Besides this, accelerating factors affect growth to be the highest along this road and easy accessibility to other parts of the city and commercial development to pick up in this micro-market. There is a prospect of establishing an IT park to develop the region by IT companies setting up their workplaces along the high talent intensity sites.

An important feature of Kanakapura is the social infrastructure. According to the survey, volume of land transactions is high in Kanakapura belt. Kanakapura has exceptional Social infrastructure. Kanakapura has the well-known educational institutions. Leading among them are Sri Ravishankar Vidya Mandir, Sri Nirvanaswamy Public School, Mother Teresa International School, SSVN Public School, The Valley School, Yashasvi International School and Ekya school. Kanakapura is considered as one of the educational hubs of the city. This is a potential location to set up more educational institutions. Most certainly, the demand for land is on a very high rate in Kanakapura due to the social infrastructure which leads to simultaneous value creation. Kanakapura Road has been one of the most sought-after locations by IT professionals in terms of choice for residences, after Bannerghatta Road. This is because of the presence of social infrastructure and easy accessibility to workplaces. Majority of villa projects and luxury residential projects are concentrated in Bannerghatta Road region. However, this is changing over; with new malls under construction, development of the green metro line and proposed widening of the National Highway, several luxury projects including villa development to take off in this locale.

Art of Living Ashram of Shri Ravishankar Guruji is yet another attraction in the southern periphery. Several residential projects are being built by them and devotee investors from all over the country and abroad invest in these residential complexes. Most of the projects on Kanakapura Road are integrated townships, which are attracting senior citizens as well as young working population. Kanakapura Road has great connectivity to Electronic City, Hosur and Sarjapur. The spurt in the land value of Kanakapura is by the extension plan of Metro Sri Ravi Shankar Swamy's Art of Living Ashram in Udayapura on Kanakapura Road. With the arrival of Metro, it adds more land value as it is the only mean ease of access to commute. This decision to extend the metro line brought a remarkable shift in periphery the necessity to have the residential requirements around the metro line met. Art of living is a very good place for not only people who are looking for some peace and spiritual life but also people who seek some affordable mid-range segment. It is located in Kanakapura Road, midst of greenery and heart of mother's nature. It adds the potential of real estate in this location. The residential real estate activity along Kanakapura Road is expected to rapidly expand with the arrival of Metro Rail network and its extension to Ashram road.

The urban influence of the periphery also changes the face of periphery by providing alternative employment to the people who leave agriculture. The commercial centres, offices, metro, apartments absorb local population for employment. The peri-urban phenomenon substitutes the local population with gainful employment which, in turn, alter the occupational structure of the periphery. The dynamic changes in Kanakapura show the impact on civic society and the cosmopolitan culture. Change makers of Kanakapura road is an umbrella of RWAs & NGOs in wards 184, 185, 186, 194, 195, 196, 197 and 198 spread over on Kanakapura road from Sarakki signal to NICE Road. It is a federation of 37 Resident Welfare Associations (RWAs) and apartments on Kanakapura who indulge in socially committed activities.[2] As the peri-urban transition takes place, there is a shift in people's life, attitude which makes the cosmopolitan culture more inclusive by effectively addressing local issues via twitter and by civic movements. Cycling line Directorate of urban land transport is yet to ring all on cycle track. As the transition takes place, society move towards a sustainable way of living, which, in turn, modify the urban life with a group of socially committed peri-urban residents.

These wide varieties of factors attract the investment in Kanakapura and the change in the land uses and the land values affect the real estate growth trajectory which will add its periphery to the city. Thus, Kanakapura is a growth pole with significant socio-economic transformation of the urban fringe since 2010. This paving the way for skyrocketing real estate growth in south periphery and Kanakapura became a major growth pole spilling over benefits. This makes south periphery an attractive cluster in terms of its growth and dynamic nature. As per the survey, the average price of land is high in Kanakapura compared to Hoskote. The better connectivity, social infrastructure, the luxury and affordable projects and real estate boom increased the land price swiftly in this belt.

Hoskote is the Eastern peripheral cluster that is slowly merging with the city's outer periphery and it is a distinct periphery which is attracting the young population. The industrial areas and the expansion of IT industries located in the Eastern quadrant of the city lead to a significant growth in land prices and volume of land transactions in Hoskote. There are various factors attributed to the growth of Hoskote; the excellent connectivity, affordable land price and there is continued demand for quality IT-related office spaces; there is simultaneous increase in the demand for residential development to cater the needs of the IT sector employees in the area.

Eastern periphery is an excellent residential catchment area for both the industrial as well as IT hubs. Hoskote consists of at least 200 industrial units including automobile, oil refinery, warehousing and logistics. The residential growth location makes Hoskote attractive. The average price of the highly demanded residential plot in Hoskote costs Rs. 1,200 per sq ft by 2017 as per the survey. It is an affordable housing segment. The residential development in this region is mainly mid-segment, in a range of Rs. 30–60 lakhs. By 2001, industrial growth started in Hoskote; by 2010, the residential developments changed the face of Eastern periphery. The structural break in land cover is coincided by rapid changes in land value in 2009 and 2010. A major spurt in real estate is from 2010 and increased the land prices. The growth of Hoskote is attributed by the changes in the land use pattern; here especially, the availability of vacant land parcel is high. Over a period of 17 years, there is a visible change in the land uses. This periphery witnessed an increase in supply of land and the demand for land for non-agricultural purposes also increased. The industrial development in Hoskote has acted as a catalyst to economic growth in East periphery.

ITPL is Bangalore's oldest IT parks and witnessed a transition since the IT boom in 1990s. There is a cluster of offices, along with malls and sporting arenas and luxury hotels, within this tech park. It is, thus, witness to some of the fastest-growing localities around. Places around ITPL currently have nearly 50–60 housing projects under construction and lies near Whitefield and Marathahalli, which have higher property rates. These places are exhausted and the spill over benefits of this led to the growth of the peripheral locations like Hoskote. Real estate market has seen a significant rise in demand due to the proximity to ITPL. Prices have risen swiftly for flats in ITPL and this leads to the next best affordable option of residential requirements in the periphery. There are many leading builders in this stretch from KR Puram to Hoskote including Puravankara, Prestige, K Raheja, Brigade and many others. Some of the landmark housing projects in this area include Puravankara Bougainvillea, Sekhar Hyde Park and Prestige Ozone. This zone is quite a good bet for mid-range housing, whereas neighbouring areas mostly cater to the upper range of the market since the property rates are on the higher side.

Hoskote known for its strategic location. It is well connected to the Whitefield and KR Puram Railway Station, which is 5.3 kilometres away and connected to the rest of Bangalore through the Old Airport Road, which goes via Marathahalli and ITPL Road through Mahadevapura and very near to State Highway 35 through ITPL Road and Varthur Road and nearly kilometres away from the Kempegowda International Airport and BMTC bus services connect it to other parts of the city.

The periphery is known for its proximity to the employment hub. It is adjacent to Whitefield Main Road and Companies present in the tech park – L&T Infotech, Capgemini, Qualcomm, Sharp, Tata Consultancy Services and many others and Manyata Business Park and also closer to Prestige Shanti Niketan. The presence of the International Tech Park ensures employment for 15,000–20,000 professionals and this will always keep the door open for future appreciation and growth. The real estate growth momentum is high due to the propelling growth due to the young population in the Eastern IT Corridor.

Land acquisition by Government in this peripheral area of Hoskote is a significant factor that poised the growth. Government has acquired land for the peripheral ring road in the sample villages like Kolathur used in this study in the year 2017. On an average, villager got amount from 10 lakhs to 2 crores. The lives and livelihood of the people in the sample villages are mainly depending on farming. It does not give an attractive return to the farmers. Hoskote is a less fertile agricultural land compared to Kanakapura. Water crisis aggravated the low productivity in this region; the extent of barren land is 8.5% in 17 years. The local population had already absorbed in the growth process of the city and moved away from agriculture due to lack of regular income and low productivity. But the real estate boom has led to the alternate means of living through rental incomes and joint ventures.

Joint Venture between farmer and builder is a landmark initiative identified in Hoskote sample villages; the profit sharing is 60:40%. There is a change in the livelihood of the people with the growth of real estate in periphery. There is a demand for rental homes with services that led to a new group of residential sectors bound to grow as it caters new and emerging trends. Thus, the livelihood of the local population changes. Now, it is a market for affordable housing with modern amenities. There is a huge demand from buyer price ranging from 17 lakhs to 1.2 crore. Another factor led to the price appreciation is the CREDAI announcement of housing for all by 2020.[3] Now Hoskote KR Puram corridor is with over 80 residential projects at various stages of construction. The top among them is Salarpuria Sattva, Shobha Group and Cosmos. Hoskote is known for its residential and mixed-use developments. Its proximity to Whitefield as well as KR Puram has proved to be the catalysts leading to the increased real estate activity in this belt. Hoskote has at least 200 industrial units, including some of the major auto manufacturers' plants.

As mentioned in the beginning, there is a great divergence in the periphery. It can be found in urban and peri-urban landscape. In the case of South-East peri-urban cluster, there exists a divergence. Both peripheries are in a state of transition, Kanakapura shows more dynamic growth in terms of its development, volume of land transactions, land prices and the real estate growth. It shows a structural break in land cover in 2010. In Eastern periphery, the changes are visible. However, in the case of Hoskote of the peri-urban, growth is not as faster as I can see in Kanakapura. After the 2010, the growth in South periphery is rapid and it has come out significant both practically and statistically.

Land Prices in Divergent Periphery – Why High Land Prices in Kanakapura?

The land price is driven by several factors such as accessibility, amenity, topography, land use in South-East Bangalore periphery. The distinguishing factors lead to a divergence in land prices in the two peripheries and are often questioned. I identified three major factors which determine the significant price difference in the South-East periphery as the pricing strategy, the occupation structure of the people and the infrastructural development in the periphery in the empirical results and from observations in the field.

Pricing Strategy

Field evidence shows that the land prices are high in the South-East periphery year on year. The average land price in Hoskote is Rs. 200 per sq ft for the year 2000, whereas in the Kanakapura, it is just Rs. 100 per sq ft for the year. Although the land price is high in Hoskote initially, there is high land price in Kanakapura in the recent decade. The influence of the IT industries set up in the year 1996 was a key driver of land prices in the East since 2000, but Kanakapura was away from city and the transition in Kanakapura is mainly with the NICE road which is in the recent year. At this context, to understand the economics of land prices in two peripheries the average SR value and the market value is looked at because real estate prices are measured as averages, and they tend to be contingent on a location pattern, the empirical study support theoretical aspect: real estate firms in Kanakapura are more likely to avoid price competition when properties in the vicinity are priced by top rated builders like Brigade group, Salarpuria Sattva, Sobha Limited, Purvankara Limited, Godrej Properties Limited, Provident, Shriram, Mantri Developers and Prestige Group. There are small builders in Kanakapura stretch, but it is dominated by these few large builders. Consequently, real estate agents charge high prices as in the case of oligopolisation. This behaviour of few top builders set a high in Kanakapura; this always make entry to the market difficult as in the case of a cartel; therefore, there exists high land prices in Kanakapura periphery. Therefore, it is concluded that the high price in the South periphery is due to the few large builders and the price strategy adopted by them.

In Hoskote, the land price is not as high as the land price in Kanakapura in all the recent years. The land price in Hoskote is explained from the behaviour of the builders located in the periphery. Hoskote is a location close to ITPL and Whitefield which has already established, and an exhausted region is an old town connected via ring road. And the majority of the builders are medium-range builders like Peramgroup, Jazzy Inc, Ceepiyar, CGr housing India, Rmk Builders and Developers, Anish builders, Brindavana elite, Anciya estate, M1 homes, Souparnika projects Gravity, Shriram, Nisarga and Edifice targeting the working professionals in Whitefield and RMZ infinity providing budget segment houses. There are more than 80 medium level builders in Hoskote. Since they are more in number, they are more likely to compete on price when nearby properties are priced by rivals. Theoretical results indicate that local real estate markets tend to plunge into price competition when nearby properties are priced by rivals in Hoskote. The actual shares of real estate builders are far from the monopoly outcome; our empirical results suggest that oligopolisation in the spatial real estate market appears to induce a price increase in periphery. There is active price competition among medium builders, and the price competition reduces prices in Hoskote periphery. Hence, the price competition among the medium builders tends to arrive at a competitive price strategy.

Occupational Pattern

The occupational pattern of the people is another significant factor responsible for these dynamics. The urban influence of the periphery changes the face of periphery by providing alternative employment to the people who leave agriculture. The commercial centres, offices, metro, apartments absorb local population for employment. The peri-urban phenomenon substitutes the local population with gainful employment which, in turn, alter the occupational structure of the Kanakapura periphery. Kanakapura consists of both affluent and middle-class segment section of the society. Kanakapura is a budget segment which is affordable to the middle-class segments of the society. The nearby markets of Bannerghatta Road, Banashankari, JP Nagar and Jayanagar have already saturated that propelled investment in Kanakapura Road. Many start-ups and MNC set up their offices at the heart of the city and demand the residential space away from the crowded and busy city centre to the nearby affordable residential peripheral township. Majority working-class population of Kanakapura Road to stay close to office spaces in Bannerghatta, Silk Board and Electronic City and with the metro and travelling to the centre of the city with the metro connectivity accelerated the demand for real estate in this stretch. The growth of Kanakapura and the increase in price largely depend on the lives and livelihoods of the people; especially, the occupational structure of the people plays an important role.

The East periphery is known for its IT population. It is adjacent to Whitefield Main Road and Companies present in the tech park – L&T Infotech, Capgemini, Qualcomm, Sharp, Tata Consultancy Services and many others and Manyata Business Park – 27.6 kilometres and also closer to Prestige Shanti Niketan. The presence of the International Tech Park ensures employment for 15,000–20,000 professionals and this will always keep the door open for future appreciation and growth. The real estate growth momentum is high due to the propelling growth due to the young population in the Eastern IT Corridor. The people who work in this stretch are in search of affordable middle segment housing; indeed, a lot of medium builders offer budget houses in Hoskote. The substantial difference in the occupational structure of the periphery leads to a significant change in the prices of the land.

Infrastructural Developments

Infrastructural corridors play a critical role in the appreciation of the land prices in the periphery. The South periphery is known for the dynamic forces of physical infrastructural development and the increase in land price.

Kanakapura Road demands a price of ₹5,000–7,500 per sq. ft among leading developers and ₹3,600–4,200 among the mid-level developers. Metroline, NICE road connectivity and the Metro Cash & Carry together give a boost to property rates.[4]

Another substantial development is the trial run of trains on the first stretch of Phase II Namma Metro.[5] The 6.29 stretch from Yelachenahalli to Anjanapura is in its final stage and is to launch it shortly. There are five major stations of Konanakunte Cross, i.e. Doddakallasandra, Vajrahalli, Thalaghattapura, Anjanapura, and it is a distance of less than 10 km to the study area villages. It will be the first line that will be open under Phase II, the total length of which is 72 km. Mr. M.S. Channappagoudar, General Manager, Land Acquisitions, BMRCL stated that 71,890 square metres were acquired for the stretch and compensation of Rs. 364.52 crores was paid to the respective landowners.

The ridership of the Namma Metro averaged between 3,60,000 and 3,70,000 passengers. The annual ridership in 2015–16 fiscal year was 16.8 million and the daily ridership expanded to 4,10,050 commuters in September 2017, and in 2019, it has reached 4,50,000 daily which is immense. The Green Line works from 6 am to 11 pm with a frequency of 15 minutes and 10 minutes distributing across timings to manage peak hour demand. Each six-coach train has a capacity of 2004 passengers which is largely full; daily ridership is 1,70,685 and 62.3 million in 2018.[6]

Four-lane Expressway works are on towards making it a four-lane highway that is going to impact the land value. Besides, the NICE road junction, a 35 km four-lane expressway, has been sanctioned by the Bangalore Development Authority to widen the road and tie the area to Tumkur Road, Hosur Road, Sarjapur Road, Old Madras Road and Magadi Road, nearly, all the important business districts of the city. The stretch from NICE Road to Kanakapura road is a four-lane road. Kanakapura Road is a vital link to Bangalore with a traffic density of 6,000–8,000 passenger car units per hour. Apart from the metro, there are 20 bus stops across Kanakapura Road. The biggest among that is the Banashankari Bus Stop. This bus stop offers facilitating commute to a lot of areas in South Bangalore like JP Nagar, Bannerghatta Road, Banashankari, Jayanagar along with Mysore Road, IT hub – Electronic City and Majestic Bus Depot, which make connectivity across the city possible. Bus services to International Airport also make the area very favourable to those in IT companies or offices in these areas as well. All these significant developments lead to the rapid change in Kanakapura in the recent past. The influence of the NICE Road is a landmark initiative that led to the giant in the land prices in Kanakapura.

The physical infrastructure plays a critical role in the East periphery, but it is not as much as that of the South periphery. The second phase of the Namma Metro will cover ITPL. The Purple Line from Byappanahalli will be extended to cover the locality. The first face of Namma metro has appreciated the land prices.

Chennai-Bangalore Industrial Corridor extension to trigger realty growth in Hoskote. The Chennai-Bangalore Expressway is a proposed corridor that would start at Hoskote in Bangalore. The proposed road will run parallel to existing to the National Highway-4 which is also the highest traffic carrying corridor of India. The proposed expressway will facilitate high-speed travel on the proposed corridor, which will have a width of 90 metres. It is not only expected to boost commercial development but will also uplift the residential market. Although the project is at its nascent stage, there are some small areas along the stretch that have witnessed traction and some top builders like group started their projects which appreciated the land value. Always the infrastructural corridors lead to rapid transition and the appreciation of land value.

The factors affecting the land sale and purchase are captured in the study; it shows the major determinants of land purchases are change in market values, distance from headquarters of Taluk and the land uses and the major determinants of land sale are market value and the change in total size of land holding. Land transfers from agriculture to non-agriculture use are clearly visible in the studied peri-urban villages and there exist uncertainty in the real estate market. A consequence of this relationship between uncertainty and vacant land values is that expanded vulnerability leads to increase in building activity. Yet, the market for vacant land is unusual, especially within existing urban areas. Land is greatly differentiated; there is a notable lack of information; trading is infrequent, subject to high transaction costs and elaborate "bargaining" (Adams, 1968). Price of land also varies from year to year, with an active growth in the land transactions since 2000–18, and especially the land sales have become frequent since 2010. Land prices are high in urban areas. Yet, we can observe a number of vacant lots and grossly underutilised land in this area (Titman, 1985). Transactions in lands for conversion from agriculture to non–agriculture uses are emerging as a serious problem in the peri–urban locations of Bangalore. Peri–urban villages of East and South Bangalore have witnessed frequent land transactions over the past two decades.

The land market survey shows that residential land transactions are taking place in the peri-urban villages in Hoskote after 2010. There exists high amount of asymmetric information in the property market. Additionally, the development option is an important element embedded in vacant land, which has been argued to increase land values with higher levels of uncertainty in the property market (Titman, 1985). In fact, residential land markets are thriving in the peripheral locations. IT centres and industrial clusters are located in the periphery, and therefore, the peripheral areas are emerging as the drivers of economic growth, with an active growth of land markets. The land market survey concludes that the extent and magnitude of land transactions in the peripheral areas are high since 2010. Speculation increases land prices in the study area.

Drivers of Changing Peri-Urban

i **Population:** Bengaluru population increased over time and spread to the peripheries. From a small figure of 5.1 million in 2001, population has grown to 8.4 Million in 2011. One of the main reasons behind this huge growth is the cosmopolitan nature of the city. Better standard of living and infrastructure are the primary reasons for growth of population in Bengaluru. In spite of various government planning and research, Population is growing at a very fast pace. Bengaluru is currently third most populous city of India after Mumbai and Delhi. The area of the city recorded a significant increase by 92.1% and the population by 37.8% during 1991–2001. The spatial expansion of the urbanised area has increased from 226 sq km in 1995 to 710 sq km. Majority of population have settled in urban areas with urban population of 5.8 million and "population density in Bengaluru city alone is 19,435 persons per sq.km" (Hunse, 2008). It is estimated that the population will rise to 7.74 million by the end of 2015 (Taubenböck et al., 2009). By 2003, it is estimated that the build-up area is approximately 23–24%, compared to 16% in 2000 (Sudhira et al., 2003). The livelihood is better in Bengaluru with the rapid pace of urbanisation. The expected real income in urban areas is larger than that in rural areas, especially as people are more likely to find a job in the city. Additionally, better educational environment and business prospects also drive people to move to city (Datta, 2006).[7]

ii **Urbanisation:** Bengaluru is rapidly urbanising at a pace of 4.6%. Greater Bengaluru has witnessed a decline of vegetation and water bodies by 62% and 85%, respectively, in recent period. The urban area keeps expanding the last 60 years, especially past decade.

iii **Industrial and commercial transactions:** Study conducted in the ten peri-urban villages showed that there is an active non-agricultural land transaction leading to changes in the land use and land value. Primary data survey showed that 15.2% industrial and 25.6% commercial land transactions in the periphery.

iv **Residential land transaction:** There are innumerable residential land transactions in the periphery. It is around 51.2% as per the survey. The more residential land transactions show the high demand for land in the peripheries and consequent increase in the land value.

v **Land acquisition:** According to a National Highways Authority of India (NHAI) official, 80% of land acquisition process for the road-widening work has been completed. Government has acquired land in the peripheral village, Kolathur in Hoskote region for the proposed road widening purpose of NICE Corridor and consequent changes in the land use and land value.

vi **Land fragmentation:** Peripheral areas are undergoing rapid urbanisation, vegetation clearing and fragmentation. Although greening is taking place in the landscape surrounding the city limits, this appears to be short term largely consists of fast-growing water-hungry exotic species, and large scale development as the city expands even further.

vii **High market value of land:** There is 66% of the land sale is due to high land value in the periphery.

viii **Low income and productivity:** Lack of productivity is a major problem in the periphery; 18.4% land sale in the study area is due to lack of agricultural productivity. Irregular rainfall in Bengaluru has caused the failing yield of crops, causing the agricultural population to move to an urban centre in order to find another source of income. People in India migrate to cities "not due to urban pull but due to rural push" (Datta, 2006, 12).

ix **Distress sale:** Water scarcity is a major reason in the East periphery of Bengaluru especially Hoskote; farmers are unable to cultivate productively and to get sufficient returns that led to more of distress sale 15.6%. The real-estate agents acquired land in such areas especially in the periphery of Hoskote and used for residential land transactions.

x **Growing job markets:** Bengaluru has become a land of opportunities and growing ideas for various job markets. There has been an extreme growth in the industrial sector and IT sector in last couple of years and migration of people to these places for housing and work has brought severe pressure on the environment. Being a major IT hub of South India, the vibrant city of Bengaluru invites people from far and wide. Over the years, it has attracted millions of people from India and abroad who have settled here permanently due to various reasons. Bengaluru is now the commercial centre of new technology of India. Approximately, 35% of professionals are engaged in IT and related industry works in Bengaluru, and many international IT companies are hiring people from other cities in India. Four new companies start business in this state every week and they create 50,000 new jobs in one year (Silicon India 2005). The economic and industrial growth is mainly due to IT parks which are set up in the peripheral areas that encouraged three export-oriented industries software and other manufacturing industries.

xi **Quality of life:** Improvements in quality of life with increased proximity to work place, high-quality schools, hospitals, markets and administrative services, which promoted housing projects on surroundings. The above said reasons lead to frequent changes in the land use and consequent changes in the land value in periphery.

Growth of Peri-Urban Impacting Urban Environment of Bangalore

Rural-urban boundary forms a dynamic semi-natural environment from where the whole natural resources of rural settings are sourced into the growing city, transmuting the PUI in return. Urban areas engulf the fringes, and the boundary of the city is ever shifting. The dynamic changes in the periphery lead to multiple transformations of the city in terms of socio-economic characteristics and in terms of its population in Bangalore city. Therefore, the peri-urban growth affects the growth of the city and the vice versa. The major impact of the peri-urbanisation to the urban development is the spatial expansion and ever-changing boundary of the Bangalore city.

These changes cause urban area to encounter high spatial uncertainty resulting in undesirable, complicated LU/LC patterns in the Bangalore city. The resources and energy required for the rapid expansion are actively supplied by peri-urban areas at the cost of its farmlands which leads to reduction in cultivation and consequent reduction in the supply of the agricultural products to the cities.

The wide-ranging building on the peri-urban interface not only devours precious land resources but is largely responsible for the high costs of infrastructure and energy, congestion of transport networks, the increasing segregation and specialisation of land use, and also degradation of the environment in the city life.

Managing the environment of this interface has significant implications on city life, for sustainability of urban and rural development since the ecological, economic and social functions performed by and in the peri-urban interface affect both city and the countryside (Allen, 2003; Narain, 2009). Moreover, the current top-down policies for land acquisition by the land authorities in developing cities do not consider social equity and environmental integrity (Narain & Nischal, 2007). There are more than 200 industries which are located in Bangalore East and South peripheries. The extent of pollution of the industries in the periphery affects the quality of the life of environment in the city.

The importance of urban transition with the peri-urban growth is recognised in the literature, but largely underexplored in developing world cities. There are actual relationships between projections and discussions of spatial growth with urban and regional reality. Many environment and development problems of a city are rooted in the way land use planning is made and governed as outlined in the Master Plan. But in the context of the peri-urbanisation, there is a huge deviation from the existing land use pattern and the proposed land use pattern in the Bangalore city as we seen in the analysis of land cover and the discussion with the officials. Land becomes the tool of "enabling environment" for infrastructure provisions in growing cities, and urban planning appears out of series of crises and social responses to them. The unrestrained expansion pushes too hard in the direction of "bigger cities" with inadequate enabling infrastructure. Consistent with the working of a free market economy, people's and market responses to economic opportunities are mediated by private and public landowners which in turn drive land cover changes, often in an unscientific manner ignoring the long-term ecological and aesthetic impacts of the urban centre (Koomen & Stillwell, 2007). This can create externalities as land development societies in the past have often neglected enabling resources and overall carrying capacity of a region in developing master plans for future growth of the city.

The land market is a major force shaping peri-urban expansion in a way affecting city growth since it set of housing possibilities for families based on their available income. In cities like Bangalore population, growth is exponential; the government and private companies develop housing units that cater to their needs. Realising the complex nature of urban dynamics, particularly in the fast-growing cities of developing countries of Asia, city planning has become crucial to the urban planners and researchers. It is also pertinent from the viewpoint of smart city projects as the basis of successful smart city lies in proper planning and urban growth analysis in the context of ever-growing periphery. Ongoing peri-urban expansion is therefore happening within an environment that lacks adequate information systems and informed data analyses and it affects the urban development of Bangalore city significantly. Liberalisation of land market is a significant aspect both globally and locally; therefore, it is briefly discussed in the background of economics of land price.

Liberalisation of Land Market

Worldwide experience with land market liberalisation provides useful lesson from other countries. Within the agenda of the "Washington Consensus", the World Bank has been advocating liberalisation of land markets not only in Latin America but also in the post-Soviet countries. There are numerous success stories with reasonably functioning land markets do exist; implementation of these policies has turned out to be more perplexing in many countries (Kvartiuk & Herzfeld, 2019). The way in which land markets are designed and the goals the government engage in significantly impact land distribution among the different types of agricultural producers. Improving the infrastructure in land markets will improve access to land for poor, undercapitalised farmers (Williamson, 2000). Land concentration is one of the major matters of liberal land policies and requires careful analysis of the rural political economy. Both domestic and foreign investors have actively sought to acquire large areas of land in the growing metropolitan regions. Market facilitating institutions in common experiencing from corruption typically fail at the privatisation stage. Corrupt practices exist in the scenario of land administration in some of the countries and the issues related to the problems in the land market were visible in the study area.

The discussion on dynamics of peri-urban land transaction pointed out the difference in the land prices in two peripheries. The land prices are very high due to the speculation. Speculation in property values particularly is common in these places of South and East periphery. For example, the information dissemination related to any new investments to the public has a huge impact on land prices. As in the case of announcement of new metro line and extension of it till Art of living Ashram led to the surge in the land prices in the South periphery. The value of land often increases more than proportionately in inflationary situations. This is explained both by economics and psychology.

The extent to which inflation may account for a sustained increase in land values depends on how expectations of continued price increase are shared among agents in the real estate market and the examples of issues in land market are discussed further.

Summary

The dynamics of peri-urban transition is assessed in the case of divergent periphery. The factors that make East and South peripheries different are predominantly the land use pattern. East periphery is known more for residential and mixed land uses, whereas South periphery is known for commercial and residential land uses. East periphery poised for growth, whereas South periphery acting as a major growth corridor by spilling over benefits to the nearby locales. South periphery is known for a social transformation, changing lifestyle and change-makers shows a remarkable social activism which makes the cosmopolitan culture more inclusive whereas the East periphery consist of young professional and attractive destination for individual investors has not led to a significant change in the social life. Eastern periphery is in a gradual transition phase, whereas South periphery is at a faster rate of transition and in the process of absorbing hinterlands quickly. Price is a major parameter used in the study that shows a swift change in both peripheries by 2010. The rate of change of land price is faster in South periphery attributed by the above-mentioned key drivers; price is always influenced by the speculation in the real estate market.

Notes

1 https://www.makaan.com/price-trends/property-rates-for-buy-in-kanakapura-road-bangalore-10451
2 https://twitter.com/_kanakapuraroad
3 realty.economictimes.indiatimes.com/news/residential/credai-members-to-launch-250-affordable-housing-projects/58011988 – 144 page.
4 https://www.thehindu.com/life-and-style/homes-and-gardens/major-growthcorridor/article17644128.ece
5 https://en.wikipedia.org/wiki/Namma_Metro
6 https://www.Namma_Metro
7 Datta, P. (2006). Urbanization in India: regional and sub-regional population dynamic population process in urban areas. European Population Conference, 21–24
    June, 2006, 1–16, viewed March 2, 2016. *Population Studies Unit, Indian Statistical Institute, 203.*

References

Adams, W. (1968). *The Brain Drain*. New York: Macmillan.
Allen, A. (2003). Environmental planning and management of the peri-urban interface: Perspectives on an emerging field. *Environment and Urbanization*, 15(1), 135–148.

Datta, P. (2006). *Urbanization in India: Regional and sub-regional population dynamic population process in urban areas.* European Population Conference, 21–24 June, 2006, 1–16, viewed March 2, 2016. Population Studies Unit, Indian Statistical Institute, 203. https://www.siliconindia.com/; https://pkps.ipb.ac.id › ratification-definition-bwfd › c1

Koomen, E., & Stillwell, J. (2007). Modelling land-use change. In Koomen, E., Stillwell, J., & Bakema, A. (eds.), *Modelling Land-Use Change* (pp. 1–22). Dordrecht: Springer.

Kvartiuk, V., & Herzfeld, T. (2019). *Welfare Effects of Land Market Liberalization Scenarios in Ukraine: Evidence-Based Economic Perspective* (No. 918-2019-1635).

Narain, V. (2009). Growing city, shrinking hinterland: Land acquisition, transition and conflict in peri-urban Gurgaon, India. *Environment and Urbanization*, 21(2), 501–512.

Narain, V., & Nischal, S. (2007). The peri-urban interface in Shahpur Khurd and Karnera, India. *Environment and Urbanization*, 19(1), 261–273.

Sudhira, H. S., Ramachandra, T. V., Raj, K. S., & Jagadish, K. S. (2003). Urban growth analysis using spatial and temporal data. *Journal of the Indian Society of Remote Sensing*, 31(4), 299–311.

Taubenböck, H., Wegmann, M., Roth, A., Mehl, H., & Dech, S. (2009). Urbanization in India–Spatiotemporal analysis using remote sensing data. *Computers, Environment and Urban Systems*, 33(3), 179–188.

Titman, S. (1985). Urban land prices under uncertainty. *The American Economic Review*, 75(3), 505–514.

Williamson, J. (2000). What should the World Bank think about the Washington Consensus? *The World Bank Research Observer*, 15(2), 251–264.

7   Peri-Urban Land Governance – Need for Sustainable Urbanisation

Land Policy and Governance

"Land policy" signifies the measures of public authorities in order to implement their land use policy. This incorporates acquisition and transfer of land impacts on land prices advancement of land ownership and tenure systems in order to meet the objectives of land use policy. "Urban land policy" refers to a policy which deals with particularly urban land. The major goal of it is the advancement of land use planning and implementation of different kinds of urban plans (Virtanen & Verlaat, 1999). While land administration is the process of determining, recording and disseminating information about ownership, value and use of land when implementing a land management policy. It is a process and an instrument for government to offer security of tenure, regulate land market, implement land reform, protect the environment, levy taxes, etc. as well as serve the peculiar development needs of her citizens (United Nations, 1996). In addition, land administration is the way in which the rules of land tenure are applied and made operational. A good land administration system aims at equitable distribution of wealth to encourage economic growth and development. Efficient, equitable, environmentally sound and compatible systems are necessary for any rural and urban economy.

Unplanned development in the periphery is a major menace in the context of Indian cities. The land use policy needs to be undertaken by identifying the key elements that contribute to an efficient policy mechanism including land values and land use planning of peri-urban areas. Different theories show that these elements are interrelated. As discussed, and evidenced in the earlier chapters, the land use determines the land value, and the land market is influenced by both land use and land value. These two factors, in turn, influence the planning of land use and development. The planning and policies decisions are fundamental in aiming the rural-urban dichotomy. The meaningful land policy is needed for managing the expansion of urban sprawl. Despite the efforts by the Government of India and various state governments, India still lacks a comprehensive land policy which considers rural and peri-urban land market. In this background,

DOI: 10.4324/9781003362333-7

an attempt is made to understand the role of government and the policy to deal with the land issues in the rural-urban fringe and the policy instruments so far adopted. One of the major concerns has been the lack of reliable data and that acts as a serious lacuna. State-level adoption and implementation of growth management and planning mandates have received significant attention in the 1990s (Burby et al., 1997), but these efforts have not been accompanied by similar endeavours at the local level. Property rights are not always clearly defined and easy to enforce, measurement of the effects of different kinds of externalities may be costly and the amount of information available to homeowners and developers may be asymmetric. Land markets suffer from market failures due to locational specificity of all parcels of land and welfare loss, often conflict associated with the livelihood, increasing vs. decreasing balance of urban-rural built land. During the urban-rural transformation process, there is a significant intensive land use that leads to land conversion for non-agricultural use.

Government institutions are important in land use because the transaction costs in settling land use conflicts are often high. Local policy decisions reflect a balance of the conflicting interests and responses to economic and political pressures. The findings reported in the previous chapters can have important implications for the study of local land use management. Growth management decisions are inherently political, the results demonstrate that local governance structure plays a critical role in land use management. There is an array of policy instruments, political institutions and land use policy institutional arrangements can facilitate some policy choices. The instruments of land policy are chosen based on the interaction between market forces and government regulations as the market for land is fragmented. The transfer from agriculture to residential, commercial and industrial properties is frequent. Government regulation and intervention serve interrelated and sometimes conflicting objectives, such as the efficient provision of public services, the prevention of adverse externalities or the achievement of particular urban patterns.

To improve a set of controls and regulations, account needs to be taken of a wide variety of interactions between the multiplicity of markets, instruments and aims. The problem in developing countries is that the pressures on land are strong and administrative capacity is low; it is to be expected that strong restrictions on land use is a mandatory norm. There are two broad categories of controls on land use. At first, plans, rules and regulations that set a framework affect urban land use. The second comprises the actions of public authorities that directly determine land use. These two categories do not automatically strengthen one another. The basic features to be sought in government land development are well expressed by Neutze (1973). The policies, regulations and investment in infrastructure that are specifically directed at controlling urban land use do not necessarily have the greatest influence on that use. Countries like Turkey, Brazil and Thailand illustrate the strong effects of government regulation in land market. Clearly, national spatial planning, regional planning and urban planning should be compatible with government activities that strongly influence urban growth directly or indirectly. Yet, this compatibility has rarely been achieved even in developed countries. In developing countries, the shortage of professional skills and the urgent need to cope with rapid development diminish the practical possibility of such reconciliation.

The analysis of peri-urban land market based on the field survey and observations has led to the two important areas where government intervention is required.

First, there is a significant change in the land use pattern in peripheries. Analysis based on dummy variable regression conducted for LU/LC time series data showed structural break in the land use pattern in the Hoskote Taluk and visible structural break is observed for Harohalli village in the South periphery. This is an important aspect where planning authorities should focus on planned city development because changes in the land use pattern are rapid in the periphery.

Second, the change of land use from agricultural to non-agricultural use results in the creation of additional land value simultaneously. Land prices have shown a continuously rising trend in space and time across periphery. No credible record of land prices is available across the sources from which prices are obtained. In addition, there are issues of lack of proper titles adding to the problem. This is another area where the government intervention is necessary for fixing land prices and making technological interventions in the land market. Hence, it is important to discuss that the role of local government in the context of land market is significant. Local governments have considerable autonomy in approaches and policy instruments for land use and comprehensive planning. Previous studies have not addressed the role of local authorities in the land market and major debatable questions related to land policy in the backdrop of the peri-urban land market. These questions include what factors account for local government land use practices among land management policy instruments? How the land market framework establish land use policy in metropolitan cities are shaped by institutional features of governments? What factors account for local government land use practices and growth management initiatives?

To understand the role of government in the land policy formulations, we examine the role of parastatal bodies, fiscal policy, land legislation in BMR and the need of technological interventions in peri-urban land policy and administration in the context of changing land value and land use in the periphery.

Role of Institutions in Land Policy

Economic activities and the growth of IT sector induced a leapfrogging pattern of development in the Bengaluru periphery. Various policies were formulated to control the growth through planned development. It is apparent that urban planning and city growth were relatively cohesive during public sector development. The spatial development completely diverged jurisdictions of all the planning authorities. But as the city developed, the disparity in urban planning started during IT phase since 2000. Bengaluru as a result, at this point, has several authorities and parastatal agencies engaged in planning in order to establish coordination among these authorities, and to provide a regional level planning; the role of parastatal agencies in the city planning and land administration is discussed.

Bengaluru Metropolitan Region Development Authority (BMRDA)

The Bengaluru Metropolitan Region Development Authority (BMRDA) is an Authority established under the Bengaluru Metropolitan Region Development Authority Act, 1985.[1] The major purpose is of planning, coordinating and supervising the proper and orderly development of the area within the Bengaluru Metropolitan Region. The BMRDA Act declares that the Authority shall be a body corporate with power to acquire, hold and dispose of property and to enter into contracts, etc. (section 3).[2]

The detailed tasks required to be performed by the BMRDA (section 9) of the Act include conducting survey of the Bengaluru Metropolitan Region and to prepare reports, formulation of Structure Plan for the development of the Bengaluru Metropolitan Region, carrying out works specified in the Structure Plan, formulation suitable schemes for implementation of the Structure Plan, coordinating implementation of the town planning schemes for the development of the Bengaluru Metropolitan Region, raising fund for any project or scheme for the development of the Bengaluru Metropolitan Region and to extend assistance to the Local Authorities for its execution, delegating to any Local Authority the work of execution of any development plan or town planning scheme, organising the activities of the Bengaluru Development Authority (BDA), the Bruhat Bengaluru Mahanagara Palike (BBMP), the Bengaluru Water Supply and Sewerage Board (BWSSB), the Karnataka Slum Clearance Board (KSCB), the Karnataka Power Transmission Corporation Limited (KPTCL), the Karnataka Industrial Areas Development Board (KIADB), the Karnataka State Road Transport Corporation (KSRTC) and such other bodies as are connected with developmental activities in the Bengaluru Metropolitan Region. The Act also delivers the nomination by the Government of individuals representing labour, women, scheduled castes, scheduled tribes, members of the State Legislature and representatives of the Local Authorities from the Region and to do such other acts that may be entrusted by the Government.

The Section 9 (ii) of BMRDA Act, 1985 stipulates for preparation of Structure plan. The Structure Plan is a regional level perspective plan supporting a long-term vision for development and related spatial perspective for integrated development in the area without compromising on its ecology and natural environment. Structure plan is a framework that guides development of a particular area. The plan provides the overall strategy for development. The plan does not assign use to each land parcel; it gives broad zoning of organisable area. The plan has to be further detailed into area level plans for execution/enforcement. Structure plan provides policy measures to encourage the concentrated decentralisation from the BMA to strategic satellite towns, growth centres and nodes in the periphery of the Bengaluru Metropolitan Region, thereby alleviating the excessive burden of demand on urban services and resources of the BMR. BMRDA initiated preparation of the plan in 1998. The Draft approval has taken place on 02-06-2004. And, the final approval was on 21-09-2005. As per the plan area suitable for Urbanisation has been classified as Area Planning Zone (APZs). Areas where agriculture is a predominant, forestry is abundant, conservation has been stressed more and such areas have been classified as Interstitial Zones. In order to improving Regional accessibility, the following is planned – STRR, IRR, ITRR & RR, Satellite Towns and New growth centres.

Proposed Area Planning Zone (APZ) is as follows (1) APZ1 – Ramanagaram and Chanapatna Urban Development authority. (2) APZ2 – Nelamangala Local Planning Area. (3) APZ3 – Doddaballapur–Devanahalli–Bengaluru International airport planning authority. (4) APZ4 – Hoskote. (5) APZ5 – Proposed Anekal Local Planning Area. And there are two corridors, Peri-urban Corridor Development Control Zone and Green Belt Corridor Development Control zone.[3] Purpose of revision – Plan period ended in 2011, New plans and Policies, changing global trends & Liberalised economic environment is a dire requirement. The revised plan preparation started in the year 2008.The Draft Approved on 24-02-2011. The Revised Structure Plan-2031 is proposed before the Meeting of BMRDA under the chairmanship of Hon'ble Chief Minister held in 2014 and the subsequent submission to the Government for final approval. It is approved in the year 2015; the pathbreaking step as per the plan is the development of STRR and ITRR.

Directorate of Town and Country Planning

The key role of Directorate of Town and country planning is conversion of land. The legal entity of the land needs to make an application, to the competent Revenue Authority (Tahsildar or the Assistant Commissioner or the Deputy Commissioner, by and large, contingent upon on the area to be converted). The revenue authority requests the Department of Town and Country Planning for issue of No Objection Certificate or opinion for conversion of land for various uses (Residential/Commercial/Industrial/Others) demand the Department of Town and Country Planning for the issue of No Objection Certificate or assessment for the transformation of land for different uses (Residential/Commercial/Industrial/Others).

The following records must be submitted by the applicant with the application. (1) Record of Rights and Tenancy Certificate (R.T.C) in original issued by the Revenue Authorities of the Taluk. (2) Photocopy of the Atlas of the land (survey number), duly signed by the competent authority of the Department of Survey Settlement and Land Records, showing the dimensions in meters with scale and boundary of the land proposed for conversion. (3) Photocopy of the Revenue Survey Map of the village demonstrating area of the land proposed for conversion. (4) The proposed change is for development of locales. (5) Site Plan drawn at scale not littler than 1:1000, indicating the details of existing encompassing advancements, cadastral limits of encompassing review numbers, contours, spot heights, the developments in the adjoining areas of the proposed land including approach road with width, power transmission line, telephone line, railway line, nearby water reservoirs, nalas and so on if any. (6) Any other information required by the authority. (7) The concerned Revenue Authority, subsequent to confirming the reports, will advance the application and furnish the opinion to the concerned Revenue Authority.

The Department of Stamps and Registration

It is the third most noteworthy income producing division for the Government of Karnataka with an income assortment of Rs. 10845.04 crores for 2018–19 and Documents enlisted – 19.99 lakhs. Authorised staff quality of the office including officials and staff is 1662.[4] The office has a huge frontline association with people. The following include the acts are significant to the land organisation. Document Registration Act 1908 is for the electronic adaptation of the rule is for individual use and not allowed for the purpose of resale. Formatting of this electronic version may contrast from the printed version. Arranging of this electronic rendition may contrast from the authority, printed adaptation. Next, the Registration Act solidifies identifying with the Registration of Documents.

It is convenient to unite the enactments identifying with the registration of documents and Registration through Computerization Process – Kaveri to the E-registration process which replaced the manual system of registration. Any transaction involving two or more parties has to be registered for legal proof. When transaction is done the document becomes public record. When a property has to be transferred, the public record is scrutinised to know whether the said property has been previously encumbered or not. Karnataka Valuations and E-Registration Integrated or KAVERI handle the entire registration process. It was developed based on the principle of public-private participation on a BOT basis. Another significant initiative is the integration of KAVERI and Bhoomi. The computerisation of land records in Bhoomi has made the procedure easy for registration since the details regarding survey number, extent of land, name of the seller, ownership pattern, partitions, etc. This information is accessed by KAVERI for registration. Hence, the integration between these two makes the process easier.

Revenue Department/Department of Survey, Settlement and Land Records

The Department of Survey, Settlement and Land Records conducts study, attracting of portrayals to shape the Village maps. Conservation of Survey Records in the State is the obligation of the Revenue officials under the supervision of Survey Department after the practical merger with impact from May 2005. District is the Principal Authoritative Unit under the State and in regard of all the review related issues the Technical Advisor and ex-officio Deputy Director of Land Records at the District Level under the direction of Deputy Commissioner handles the issues. In the District, a village is the fundamental Administrative Unit and as such all-survey related archives are maintained village wise.

The different activities under Revenue Department Karnataka include Bhoomi, Mojini and UPOR. Bhoomi is a lead venture of Karnataka State Government and is a Land Records the board framework. The venture was initiated in the year 2000. Under this undertaking, all the manual RTCs which prevailed at the time of data entry were digitised and made available to the citizen. The major objectives of the projects are (i) Smoothen the process of maintenance of land records; (ii) Timely updating of land records; (iii) Tamper-proof records; (iv) Easy access to land records for citizens generation of database pertaining to land revenue, cropping pattern, land use, etc.; (v) making use of the information for planning and devising development programmes; (vi) providing data base access to other stakeholders like courts, banks and companies, etc. the illustration of Bhoomi the revenue department has computerised more than 20 million land records.

Next Mojini, Mojini means measurement. It involves electronic measurement and computerisation of survey sketches. Land was measured or surveyed after the mutation process leads to litigation. There were instances when the actual dimensions of land differed widely from that of land records. The Government initiated the Mojini system to avoid mismatch between RTC and survey sketch. Mojini programming process the whole permutation sketch is made transparent, computerised by sourcing and integrating the relevant information from Bhoomi. Mojini was brought into existence in 2007 with the specific objective of correcting the data available in revenue records with the data in survey department. Functions of Mojini include (i) Digitisation of akarband,[5] (ii) RTC mismatch, (iii) resurvey in case of disputes, (iv) hardware and software management, (v) Phodi[6] issues and boundary fixation, (vi) selection of surveyors, (vii) complaint redressal system, (viii) complaint redressal and (ix) integration with Bhoomi data.

UPOR is another landmark initiative at this context. It is a computerisation task to keep up urban properties which precisely records both the spatial details of the property just as non-spatial record of rights information for the land parcels, structures and streets and so on. Property records is a confided in record for all transactions. This property record created through this venture will confirm property proprietorship for all administrative and legitimate reason. The property record will keep on staying precise perpetually through the procedure of change. All property record-related transactions and administrations will be dealt with through this venture. The main objective of Urban Property Ownership Record (UPOR) is assurance of ownership title to urban households and providing fresh data base for urban mapping. The secondary objectives include (i) measuring and mapping of all non-agricultural land and urban properties, (ii) creating and maintain records and (iii) preservation of existing land records by the revenue department. Under UPOR property, records will be recreated. At present a PPP model is followed for city survey and it is a commercial mode of service delivery. It is a robust system with a fair degree of accuracy.

Land Policy and Legislation

In exploring the role of institutions in local growth management of periphery of the specific context of this study, I need to address the role of land legislation in BMR. The most significant constitutional provision in relation to Urban Land Policy is Article 19(1) (f) which confers on individuals the right to property. The working of this provision is restricted by article 19(5) which empowers the state to place reasonable restrictions on property rights in public interest. There are several policy choices that follow from the analysis undertaken based on the field study of peri-urban land market. It is also obvious that policy correctives may have to be taken on multiple fronts and may require synchronisation and specific sequencing. I analyse the need of policy interventions with a specific spotlight on following direction of outgrowths in Bengaluru City. One of the principal instruments of land use policy is urban and regional planning. In practice, one of the fundamental objectives is the promotion of land use planning and implementation of different kinds of urban plans. Along these lines, the urban policy existing in the states is to a great extent is laid out in the national five years plans and other policies and programmes of the central government.

1 The first kind of urban intervention the application of various types of fiscal devices, includes policy instruments such as the property tax, controls on the pricing of urban goods and services and direct governmental subsidies and grants.
2 The second kind of urban interventions are legal restrictions on land uses such as official plan provisions, zoning ordinances, subdivision controls, building codes, etc.

Fiscal Policy

Government intervention in urban and fringe land market can be with the assistance of fiscal policy. The role of fiscal policy with regard to Urban

Land Policy (Ravindra, 1996) is to give general revenue to the local government deliver revenue to finance expenditure for public services, provide incentives for efficient allocation of resources in the urban land market, motivating forces to productive portion of assets in the urban land advertise and to lesson inequities in the distribution of land ownership. Taxation is a source of revenue to the government and an instrument of land policy. It is one such tax in India is the property tax which is based on yearly rental value of land and buildings. It is a powerful mechanism to enhance supply of land needed for urban development to promote efficient allocation of land. Various kinds of land tax systems are developed in course of time. Various kinds of land charge frameworks are created at present. These systems include Site Value Taxation, General Property Taxation and Betterment Levies. The different taxes levied on Land and Property at present are property tax which is required on all structures and land arranged in the metropolitan area and furthermore, the designs created by BDA, tax on vacant land in respect of vacant land, KMC act has not laid down any precise method of assessment, Betterment fee aims at the expansion in land value must be taxed.

In Bengaluru, the authority of such duty is derived from the arrangements of segment 18 of Karnataka Town arranging act. According to this, the planning authority may impose a charge at whatever point it awards authorisation for an adjustment in the utilisation or advancement of any land or constructing and such change or improvement is fit for yielding a superior pay to the proprietor. Next, Stamp Duty and registration charges when ardent property is moved in the BMR two sorts of duties are pulled in – Stamp Duty and Registration charges. The State Government determines significant measure of income from these two. Yet, these charges are imposed on various sorts of exchanges. Tax collection is a powerful instrument of Land policy. Property Tax keeps on involving a focal spot in the area. Property charge keeps on possessing a focal spot in the arrangement of nearby tax collection in India despite the fact that it's anything but a significant wellspring of land revenue. The lack of land has prompted issues identified with land use, lawful rights and increment in land prices. Along these lines, there is a need of government mediation in land market. The regular changes in land use are an after effect of different forces. Henceforth, the detailing of independent land policy is a difficult process. The premise of strategy is found in theories identifying with land use, land values.

Instruments of Land Legislation

In order to deal with the development of the city, several authorities were established to provide necessary services. Sprawling of the fringe areas beyond the planned boundary is caused by IT industries and movement of individuals. It was noted that the built-up area outstripped the master plan boundaries. The urban peripheries experienced rapid growth due to industrial clusters and

IT parks in Bengaluru. Accordingly, there are a number of authorities, policies, actors, laws, procedures and processes in Bengaluru to manage proper planning of rapid growth of the city (Sundaresan, 2013).

The first phase of the urban policy was characterised by the absence of a complete vision on urbanisation or urban processes in India. The plans arranged during this period to a great extent had an impromptu and piecemeal methodology towards urban issues. During the subsequent phase: 1969–84 the plan enunciated the requirement for urban land strategy at the state level and gave explicit rules to the definition of the same. It suggested the optimum utilisation of land, making land accessible to weaker sections, checking the concentration of land ownership, rising land values and speculation of land. The Fifth Plan (1974–79) was essentially concerned with introducing measures to control land prices in cities. The Tenth Plan (2002–07) was set up in the background of the Union Budget of 2002–03 which had reported radical measures to push cities into carrying out comprehensive urban reforms. Five-year plans are significant strategy as to urban development. The Sixth five-year plan concentrated on urbanisation policy and the seventh plan focused on metropolitan areas and the need for preparation of regional and sub region urban development plans.[7] Other sources of urban land policy are reports brought out by the Central and State Governments: (a) Report of the Committee on Urban Land Policy, (b) Task Force on Housing and Urban Development, (c) National Housing policy, (d) National commission on urbanisation, (e) Background paper on Urban Policy in Karnataka (Ravindra, 1996).

A significant aspect in this regard is master plan; as cities expanded into metropolises, master plans revised to accommodate changes with new policy regimes for the service provision. In order to understand if the evolution of policies matched the growth pattern of the city, the development process of master plans and the role of institutions are discussed in this chapter. Master plans is prepared by the parastatal agencies assisted by the state governments in order to control land use planning. The Master plan helps to plan the development within the city core, and for the future, in peripheral areas (Karmakar, 2015). It aims at the deliberate growth of land use and development is accomplished through it. Land Use planning of master plan is depending on population forecasts. Masterplan incorporates development control measures such as land use regulation zoning, subdivision and building regulations. Masterplans have a physical edge of land use for a projected city population over a period of 15–25 year. The instrument of master plan has to include all aspects of urban living.

Land Acquisition and Disposal is a major instrument. The principal legal instrument[8] to aims at the supply of land for a public purpose is the Land Acquisition act 1894. The significant outcome of public acquisition of land is to offer land at very cheap prices. After land is obtained, it is developed as per rules and guidelines. The land distribution policy has favoured the rich segment of the society than the poor. Third, Urban Land Ceiling – the Urban Land Ceiling Act was formulated in the year 1976 so as to bring the equitable distribution of land in urban areas.

Under the Karnataka Town and Country Planning Act of 1961, the state government constituted a local planning authority to prepare the outline development plan (ODP) for the local planning areas. It has mainly three components, i.e. ODP, CDP and town improvement schemes. Outline Development Plan is an important part of the Act. The objective of this is to afford directions in regulating the land use and improvement of undeveloped areas and vacant plot in built-up areas. It is a short-term instrument of regulating land use. It incorporates a general land use plan and zoning of land use for residential, commercial, industrial, agricultural, recreational purposes.

The ODP was prepared consisting of zoning policies and permitted land uses in each zone. The outline development plan was prepared as a precursor to the master plan giving general guidelines for land development and was later detailed out into a comprehensive development plan (Gowda, 1972). The ODP was submitted in 1963 and obtained final approval in 1972, which was a significant decision towards providing planned and healthy development (Ravindra, 1996). The creation of the CDP is in the second stage. In this stage, preliminary surveys are conducted. The CDP incorporates recommendations for comprehensive zoning of land use with zoning regulations. It includes the following. (a) Acquisition of land; (b) Financial obligation; (c) Both ODP and CDP, there is a procedure to publish the plan. Henceforth, the plan is submitted to government for its final approval. The third stage includes the detailed town improvement schemes. Such schemes provide for laying out new streets, improvement of infrastructures. The Act accommodates the expenses of Town planning Scheme. A significant policy objective enunciated in the CDP is controlling the development of BMR and empowering other urban centres in the state. Location, accessibility and commutation costs are significant factors in determining the growth of a metropolitan city. In European cities, location planning has been based mostly on transportation systems resulting in spatial expansion. With such systems in Indian cities like Bengaluru give rise to some problems. It is highly capital intensive which our cities cannot bear.

A major difficulty in the articulation of urban land policy is the plenty of existing enactments and guidelines which administer the land market.[9] These laws relate fundamentally to land use regulation which confines private rights and direct intervention to deal with the land. The constitution of India vests the ability to authorise laws identifying with land with the state Government. Given the existing institutions and legislation, there are issues related to the land policy, administration and management in Bengaluru. The attempt to integrate various departments related to land policy is already conducted. However, it needs further strengthening. The gaps are identified in the process of field survey and it is discussed.

Field Insights and Need for Peri-Urban Policy

Land governance in the southern Indian province of Karnataka is portrayed by both dark spots and genuine cases of worry since there is no specific administrative mechanism for fringe land markets. The state has been in the cutting edge of modernising land administration by utilising data innovation for as far back as two decades, and it has propelled a couple of profoundly effective ventures to improve the conveyance of land-related administrations. Karnataka has a record of having executed one of the most dynamic land changes laws in India. There is an expanding interest for equitable distribution of land. There is a need of productive arrangement of urban land records, land use and arranging. In spite of the fact that different governments have endeavoured to address these issues, the outcomes were not agreeable. Key obstacles to land arrangement identified include absence of data quality, missing data and inadequate benchmark information, inadequate financing for mindful government elements, institutional complexities, absence of institutional will, individual/institutional debasement, absence of technical standards and capacity to share data, lack of prepared work force, significant expenses of maintaining software, hardware and frameworks, advancement of frameworks that coordinate the different tenure forms (World Bank's Land Governance Assessment Framework 2013–14).[10] The land use analysis, land market survey led to the insights where policy intervention is required based on the field experience.

Situation 1: Non-DC Converted Sites are Used for the Residential Buildings

It is evident nearly 20% in the study area. Land conversion is a significant issue in the changing scenario of the South-East periphery. The Deputy Commissioner is allowed to grand such conversion under the Land Revenue Act. It is observed that government has been granting permission for conversions without reference to the planning authority.[11] This leads to the expansion of residential land uses. Land under green belt is being converted for non-agricultural uses resulting in built up developments. According to Karnataka Land Revenue Act 1984, no consent will be allowed for using agricultural land lying within the confinement of green belt. The zoning regulations clearly specify the uses permitted in each zone. The Master Plan emphasises the proper utilisation of land. These proposals are based on projected populations.

Situation 2: Dispute in Ownership

Survey reveals the traces of dispute in ownership by 15% of respondents and there are cases of multiple owners for the land in the study area. Field survey encountered this particular problem innumerable times. This is an area where the government intervention is required when multiple owners compete for the same land. The manipulation of land records is still prevalent in the study area. Lack of proper land records is a matter of adequate attention in the context of land administration. There were issues of litigation, lack of property rights in South-East Bengaluru; however, the number of cases is less in the advent of technology.

Situation 3: Speculation

It is a major problem throughout various years in land markets of Bengaluru especially in the South periphery. Land speculation can drive land prices beyond the productive value of the land, causing a "bubbly" land price and property market. Land speculation happens when the demand for land, at present or in the near future, outstrips the supply of land. This can be brought about both on the demand side and on the supply side. Empirical result shows the exponential growth of land prices in the periphery. The land price is fixed due to the free-market forces and there are other factors that influence the land prices in the periphery. For example, the Government announcement of the new investments or business or infrastructural development leads to increase in the land prices swiftly. Hence, there is a huge exponential growth in the land prices in the periphery with the dissemination of information to the public.

Situation 4: High Stamp Obligations

Field survey showed high stamp obligations debilitate land transactions, and as an outcome diminish the supply of land. There is an immediate connection between Registration Act and Stamp Duty Act. Stamp obligation should be paid on all records, which are enlisted, and the rate shifts from state to state.

Situation 5: Joint Ventures – Conflicts between Farmer and Builder

This is another observation from the field where conflicting interest is found in the joint venture process between farmer and builder in the selected periphery. They both agree on the 60:40 ownership and profit sharing. This leads to conflicts as the original owner of the landlord does not get the profit share as the real estate builder earns his high profit share. This is one of the peculiar problems identified in the field survey of peri-urban land market.

Situation 6: Large Institutional Land Holdings

It is major loophole come across in the survey; we pointed out land acquisition in the selected periphery is 7.5%. Government acquisition of land was evident in South East periphery for the infrastructural purposes in Hoskote. Government or parastatals, for example, Railways, CPWD and PWD regularly possess huge tracts of land in urban areas. Land can't be sold in the market to the advantage of the proprietor, it is frequently underused or utilised in a route inconsistent with its genuine market value. Huge numbers of the land property have been acquired from frontier times and are situated in peripheral areas. Government and parastatals are required to make a full stock of their property possessions and to assess them at market value. Government elements and parastatals ought to be permitted to sell land, and hold the returns, at whatever point they feel that the money estimation of land would be more significant to them than the utilisation of land.

The existing policy has disadvantages than the advantages. Land use control appears to have practised disadvantages than the efficient management. Given this backdrop of various issues related to land administration in the state, there arises a need of peri-urban land policy.

Government interventions have a direct impact on urban land supply and on the demand for land. Land prices are abnormally high in the city centre and there is more demand for land in the periphery. Some regulations have

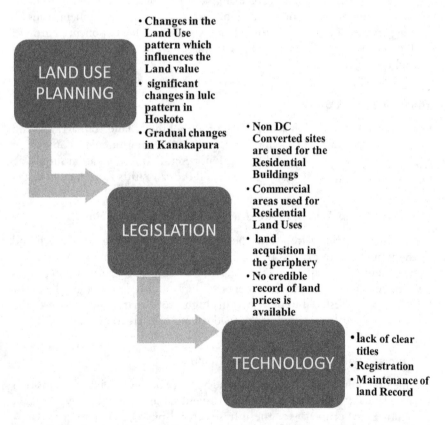

Figure 7.1 Peri-urban land policy framework. Compilation by the author.

a negative impact on the spatial structure of cities. Land regulations are necessary to the efficient functioning of markets, but when poorly managed, it hampers economic development. The following conclusions are drawn from the analysis of price trend of peri-urban land and land use changes (from three analytical objectives of the study) which requires the attention of the state government through effective implementation of policy.

The need of the peri-urban land policy is understood based on the study. Figure 7.1 shows the need of integrating major tools in the policy. LU/LC analysis and the field survey showed frequent transitions in the land use pattern, active land transactions which necessitate the efficient land use planning, legislation and the need of technological interventions in the land market. Though there are neglects for peri-urban, there is a need for peri-urban land policy which integrates the above elements while addressing the challenges faced by the peripheral land markets. Technology plays a major role in the land management and policy.

Technological Interventions in the Land Administration – A Way Forward

The E-governance in the context of complicated land management practices is an innovative remedy in the context of rapid growing complexities in land transaction in India. This is a dire requirement of policy revision because rapid urbanisation resulted in complications in land administration. It is further exacerbated by migration, industrialisation and frequent land use changes with the expansion of the cities. Land continues to be a major source of income to government through stamp duties and is a key element in implementing a wide range of government programs. Experts such as land administrators, lawyers and surveyors are involved in the process of creating and defining land parcels and land rights, but the land registration process does not guarantee title ownership, though the right to property is a legal right in India. The land-related conflicts lead to court cases and litigations resulting in social cost, creation of fake documents where single property is sold to several persons, encroachments, illegal constructions are the major loopholes. Hence, more control at the official level is required to tackle these irregularities.

E-Governance plays an important role in providing these facilities to citizens by making speedy service delivery in efficient and transparent way. Karnataka has been among the front ranking states in adopting e-Governance. The state has adopted the innovative model of Public Private Partnership (PPP) for implementation of e-Governance projects. Projects like Kaveri, e-procurement, Nemmadi and KSWAN[12] are implemented in a PPP Model. Bhoomi is another landmark project through technology by computerisation. Bhoomi implemented in 2002 and was honoured by UN, public service award in 2007. The Bhoomi Model is adopted by the Central Government Department of IT as model for replication across all the states of the country.

The RTC is a major document delivered at these kiosks.[13] Another such valuable facility for citizens under Bhoomi is to affect the mutation on the land. Mutation is a process via possessor's name or specifics like liabilities are changed consequent during various transaction.

KAVERI is an E-registration process which is integrated to Bhoomi to make the registration process through computerisation easier. The Mojini process involves e-measurement which a computerisation process of survey sketches (Manasi et al., 2015). Interestingly, the efforts taken by Government of Karnataka (GoK) via Bhoomi, KAVERI and Mojini projects by integrating is a step to overcome the hurdles of land administration of the state. Most of the States in India now have digital information about land and digital parcel maps. At some places, both are integrated. Computerised land registries are operational in states like Gujarat, Karnataka, Madhya Pradesh, Maharashtra, Rajasthan and Tamil Nadu. To great extent, it helps to overcome weaknesses in the public sector. It has reduced the scope of corruption associated with the land administration. In order to achieve the sustainable and rational outcomes, appropriate laws are required and their implementation will be focus of the land administrators.

Efficient Land Administration in Peri-Urban Land Market

Measures for efficient land administration is suggested with reference to the field observations and the analysis based on land market.

- **Land use planning:** It must be treated as a part of general planning process since it is related to employment, transportation, communication and socio-economic profile of the people living in the city. There is a haphazard growth of land in the periphery of Hoskote. In order to overcome this, there is a need of proper utilisation of land. Existing town planning practices are largely aimed at controlling land use patterns rather than optimising land use pattern with reference to employment and city development.
- **Planned Unit Development Zones:** Land Use development oriented towards regulations at present. These controls prevent urban development to some extent. There is a need of innovative measures like planned unit development zoning like in the western countries.
- **New Business Initiatives and Investment:** At present, industrial development is not based on urban planning. Future policies have to be formulated in a regional and state wise perspective. The land use pattern changes in Kanakapura Taluk show only a gradual change except Harohalli industrial area there is frequent changes. While comparing the transition of agricultural land to built-up in Sathnur village in 2005–06 is around 10%. However, this land is not used for commercial uses. Therefore, the role of government is that of inviting more of

investments, public-private projects or businesses or FDI. All developed vacant land public and private will be put to use if Government invites more investment.

• **Land acquisition must take place in coordination with land use planning:** There is Government acquisition of land for peripheral ring road in selected villages of Hoskote and directly or indirectly it affects the peri-urban farming and livelihood of the people. BDA must stop acquiring vast extent of agricultural land which is leading to peripheral expansion.

• **Technology intervention in the land valuation/land market/records:** Properties are registered on the basis of SR value; this can lead to undervaluation. Therefore, there is a need for efficient mechanism to monitor the land valuations and revisions at Kaveri. The study revealed the fraudulent practices of land registration without the knowledge of the property owners. Hence, efficient measures are required to tackle these issues.

• **Role of government authorities in the creation of credible record of land prices:** The available official data of the land value are from the SRO. However, this value is underestimated figure of the price at which transaction is done. There are no other authentic sources of the market value published by the government sources. Therefore, there is a need of government authorities for the credible record of land prices.

• **Integrated Policy:** The integration of Bhoomi, Kaveri and Mojini is a path breaking effort by the Karnataka Government. But there are issues at present hampering the proper implementation and integration of Bhoomi, Kaveri and Mojini. However, changes should be brought about keeping in view the local requirements. An integrated policy includes land use planning, legislation, technology, taxation and public intervention in the land market into a single framework to achieve policy objectives.

• **Instruments for the Effective Land policy**: (1) Legitimate and regulatory measures: Master plan which incorporates zoning, building guidelines and sub-division guidelines. (2) Fiscal Measures-Taxes and Levies. (3) Development measures: Land acquisition (4) Urban Land Ceiling

• **Measures for Effective planning:** Direct intervention by government by acquiring land and providing infrastructural facilities and restricting private land use by zoning subdivision and building controls. The land use policy for Bengaluru that has to operate within the legal framework of Karnataka Town and Country Planning Act came into force on 15 January 1965.[14] Major instruments under the policy are as follows: (a) Declaration of a Local Planning Area, (b) Constitution of a Planning Authority and (c) Preparation of Development Plan.

Urbanisation leads to the conversion of agricultural land to urban land, mostly in the periphery. A large majority of the new urban population does not have easy access to land and that much of the new development is not adequately serviced resulting in unauthorised and haphazard development particularly in the urban fringe areas. Current practices and policies regarding urban land use and development cannot manage the situation efficiently and major efforts are required to improve land market efficiency. Furthermore, there is a need to control land speculation. The magnitude of the urbanisation and the limited resources call for devising an efficient urban land management system. Since land is the most crucial input for development, the formulation of these programmes and the implementation process is highly dependent on the larger availability of developed land at appropriate locations. Efficient land policy aims land use planning and legislation which address imperfections in the land market considering rural-urban dichotomy of the metropolitan cities of India.

It is difficult to define land parcels and to describe associated rights especially in the metropolitan cities since the cities are expanding to the fringe areas at a rapid rate. Land administration and policy has not clearly demarcated land markets both in urban, rural areas as well as the peri-urban areas in most of the Indian cities. Illegal transfers of land and lack of coherent management of restrictive land and their updated information, boundary dispute, ownership rows, land re-measurements, payment of land taxes, land possession and non-encumbrance certificates are vexatious issues in Indian context.

In most of the countries, land administration is one of the most corrupt public services. Bribes paid annually by users of land administration services are estimated at $700 million in India.[15] Moreover, rural land transacted after 1882 are maintained by both the revenue department and the stamps and registration department. This overlap further increases transaction costs and frauds in the records.

The land-related conflicts lead to court cases and litigations resulting in social cost, creation of fake documents where single property is sold to several persons, encroachments, illegal constructions are the major loopholes. Hence, more control at the official level is required to tackle these irregularities. The integration of Bhoomi, KAVERI and Mojini projects by GoK is a promising approach at this context.

Countries like Australia are advanced with E-land. The advent of technology and pressures on land administrators created by increased population and land use changes necessitated E-land administration. The latest concept is I-land. I-land is integrated, spatially enabled land information available on Internet which facilitates government policies by information such as people, interests, rights, prices and transactions. Proper execution is required so that each state makes a fast journey from on-line to E-land and I-land administration.

The commodity "Land" has the power to transform the governments and institutions of the economies of modern societies and their functioning. Land information with spatial data infrastructure has the power to transform economies and societal functions through the ways in which tax is collected, services are delivered, spatial expansion, etc. Effective land administration system is the sole motive of an efficient land market. Hence, better land management policies are required for the land markets of modern economies. Therefore, the challenges ahead for the administration and policymakers are to capitalise the opportunities of modern world for better service delivery.

The analysis reveals divergent nature of Bengaluru periphery. Challenges arise from the ways that cities grow and change especially the emerging mega-cities in developing countries. The above two dynamic clusters of South East Bengaluru explore physical and socio-economic dynamics of change and help to understand different levels of change in the peri-urban systems in city's context.

Scope for Future Research

The important aspect of the study envisaged is to develop an integrated policy on land legislation, land use planning and technology. There are chances for the future research since peri-urban always is in transition and it faces various developmental challenges. Long-term studies in this aspect is aimed to provide a solution to farmers, policymakers and planners while practically investigating the consequence of spatial-temporal development in land use and land value. Since peri-urban context are different across countries, the discussion on the land use and land value in different periphery is relevant and suggestion of integrated land policy in other countries and metropolitan cities is important.

The frequency of peri-urban changes is very high; therefore, the latest studies are relevant for the policy purpose. There is a need for the national government to formulate broad policy for planned spatial growth of megacities to ensure sustainable development in peri-urban areas. The future of the cities changes frequently; therefore, there is a scope for policy-based research to manage the urban transition.

Next, inability of the rural-urban governments to deal with the changing circumstances in the peri-urban area is the scope for further research. Inadequate planning and governance of peri-urban areas by specific government result in various problems. The adoption of regional planning and development approach is an alternative strategy to address this issue. There is a need of state-specific policies. Therefore, more regional specific future research can give more relevant policy suggestions.

Urban agglomeration in India will continue to attract people and investment. Therefore, pressure on dynamic periphery will grow further. There is a scope for in depth future research amidst global environmental changes in the peri-urban. There are discussions on different notions on sustainability in the context of peri-urban. Drawing examples largely from south Asia is common in the literature. Particular challenges posed by South Asia are similar however not that of western world.

In the previous two decades, peri-urban have received special attention in research and development as areas with distinct characteristics that need to be addressed on their own terms. Despite an expanding collection of literature, no common explanatory theory or definition has been developed, due to different disciplinary traditions and approaches, and the debate as to whether a fuzziness of the peri-urban concept can be measured and compared. In the context of the increasing interest in holistic, a number of researchers have centred the requirement for a general system for peri-urban areas, including definitions, measurement and interpretation tools. The theoretical, conceptualisation peri-urban and empirical research in the context of sustainability goals needs to be reviewed as conceptualisation of peri-urban fluctuate across time and space. Friedmann et al. (2016) contend against the formulation of general theories of peri-urbanisation for the purpose of policy and planning as related strategies should always be specific to given places and times as well as institutional contexts. On the other hand, planning and policies are de facto based on existing planning models, oftentimes reflected in administrative, dichotomous entities of "urban" and "rural" that do not satisfactorily reflect the real-world situation in many cities.

Indian cities are in transition, continuous growth of built-up areas leads to lack of ownership of peri-urban areas by rural urban administration. Therefore, there is a need of India's national government a planned strategy for the spatial and temporal growth of megacities to ensure the sustainable urbanisation. Urban sprawl in the form high density, discontinues and dispersed urban development is now a common phenomenon throughout the metropolitan cities. Some of the challenges addressed are particular for the context of India, still there are global environmental changes affecting the peri-urban in developing countries demanding sustainable urbanisation.

Global Environmental Changes and Sustainable Urbanisation

Global environmental changes are critical in the transformation of landscapes and peripheries worldwide; these changes are associated with urbanisation and industrial developments. Issues of peri-urban zones, particularly economic, environmental and social challenges affecting the loss of peri-urban landscape are matter of debates in many European research forums. Global environmental changes necessitate sustainable development of peri-urban zones, as the urban growth leads to physical transformation of landscapes. Global environmental changes are major challenges to sustainability. Notwithstanding land use planning as a particular tool for sustainable land use in peri-urban, it has impact on the reduction of pressure on land resources; hence, global factors responsible for challenges to peri-urban areas and urban development which require policy attention. Rapid urban development has environmental impacts; these include decline in agriculture, fragmentation of farmlands, industrial pollution and variability of climate, lack of waste-water management and sanitation. Excessive urban growth, demographic pressure, proliferation of infrastructure and shopping complexes and industrial pollution have destroyed protected areas and interrupted the ecology and climate. In the field survey, I analysed the aspects of peri-urban land, but there are issues pertaining to peri-urban development in the developing country context; these challenges require local governance and solutions. In the backdrop of the peri-urban research, the challenges of peri-urban landscape are related to sustainability of agriculture, water resources, peri-urban environment – sanitation and waste management. I urge solution to the developmental challenges of peri-urban via sustainable urbanisation. Sustainable urbanisation focuses on the reversal of these problems and the future towards sustainable urbanisation; consequently, I identify the challenges to the peri-urban landscape and sustainability.

Peri-urban areas have special set of socio-economic, political and ecological features; the impacts of conversion of rural areas to urban are likely to have an effect on ecosystem and ecosystem services (Ojima et al., 2005). At this context, land use-land cover (LU/LC) change deserves special mention in environmental impact literature with the increasing pressure of urbanisation and climate change induced by industrialisation. LU/LC changes have significant impact on the socio-economic vulnerability (Azqueta et al., 2013); it creates increasing pressure on rural-urban interface. It destroys the main ecological corridors that connect core protected natural areas, by reducing the scope for agriculture. Inadequate management of LU/LC results in detrimental effects on environment, including biodiversity loss, habitat destruction (Shalaby & Tateishi, 2007), as an increase in greenhouse gases (Barson et al., 2004) and loss of agricultural land (Wu et al., 2006), degradation of soil quality (Dunjó et al., 2003; Ali, 2006; Cebecauer & Hofierka, 2008). The loss of agriculture is a challenge for sustainable urban development and planning. Industrialisation and unsustainable production practices of landscape fragmentation, and changes in drainage systems and soil fertility create unfavourable conditions for sustainability. Better land-use planning is needed to consider the effects of land-use change on the increasing vulnerability of ecosystems.

Impact of Climate Change on Peri-Urban Agriculture

Global environmental change has triggered concerns over peri-urban areas and farmlands in the varying climate. Emissions associated with production and industrial development are irreversible and it is a highly visible anthropogenic force worldwide. Climate change-induced factors consider agriculture is no longer viable, thereby the scope of land conversion increases due to active land sale for attractive returns. Land conversion leads to commercial and industrial building, and infrastructural developments. Industrial clusters are located in the periphery including California and Bangalore, India's Silicon Valley. It leads to pollution, decrease in forest cover and global warming.

Emissions from these industrial houses located in the peripheries of industrialised countries are responsible for vulnerability-induced climate changes.

Field insights show that peri-urban agriculture does not increase resilience to climate change. The main cause of climate change currently being experienced globally is human induced through the burning of fossil fuels and the release of greenhouse gases. Rural-urban dichotomy has left the transitional space with climate vulnerability and less productivity. As found in the land transaction survey, farmers responded climate change is a cause of decline in farming and income from agriculture; it leads to the land sales amidst the real estate boom in the cities of developing world. Temperatures have increased, rainfall seasons are inconsistent and that droughts increase its frequency. Due to industrialisation, increasing atmospheric temperatures and diminishing precipitation directly affected their agricultural activities. Farmers in the study area failed to adapt to the effects of climate change; there is a need to take actions against climate change and its detrimental effects on agriculture and the environment. Mitigation strategies reduce the emissions of climate-changing gases responsible for global warming. I look into the climate variability and need for interventions for climate change adaptation in rural-urban fringes.

Agriculture in the periphery is threatened by limited water availability, land degradation, biodiversity loss and air pollution, but climate change makes the scenario more vulnerable. Agricultural yields and livelihoods are affected by climate-related impacts on the quantity and quality of water resources. As temperatures increase, the need for irrigation will rise in those areas projected to become drier, especially the semi-arid region. Especially South Asia is known for increasing water stress, expressed as a high ratio of water withdrawal to renewable water resources (IPCC, 2007). Seasonal changes in rainfall and temperature have an impact on agroclimatic conditions, growing seasons, planting and harvesting calendars as well as on pest, weed and disease populations.

Droughts, wildfire, ocean acidification and other climate-related disturbances will increase the stress on forests, vegetation and farmlands with negative consequences cultivation and income from agriculture. Variability of rainfall and higher temperatures could impact livelihood in the periphery. Weather extremes and greater fluctuations in rainfall affect farming. Food security, health, livelihoods and access to basic services of water, sanitation, energy and shelter of farmers is severely affected in the unplanned fringes of the cities. High-population densities and the region's climate variability make developing world vulnerable to the consequences of climate change. Climate change exacerbates development problems and impact sustainable future growth and growth of the cities. Therefore, we explore the potential impact of climate change on agricultural sector and livelihood.

Impact of climate change includes both biophysical and economic impact. Biophysical impact of climate change includes higher temperatures, changes in precipitation and higher atmospheric CO_2 concentrations which may affect yield, growth rates, photosynthesis and transpiration rates, moisture availability, through changes of water use and agricultural inputs such as herbicides, insecticides and fertilisers. Environmental effects such as frequency and intensity of soil drainage, soil erosion, land availability, reduction of crop diversity may also affect agricultural productivity in peri-urban areas. The evidence shows a decline in the yields of cereal crops like rice and wheat under changing climate change conditions.

The economic impact of climatic change on agriculture is a major challenge. There are two broad approaches for assessing economic impacts – the agronomic-economic and the Ricardian. In the first approach, the physical impacts in the form of yield changes and area change are introduced into an economic model exogenously as Hicks neutral technical changes. First Approach in the Indian context, Kumar and Parikh (2001) have estimated the macro-level impact of climatic change using such an approach. They have showed that under the doubled carbon dioxide concentration levels in the latter half of the twenty-first century the GDP would decline by 1.4–3 percentage points due to climate change. The second approach suggests the scope for incorporating adaptation into the agronomic-economic approach. The approach is based on the argument that

> by examining two agricultural areas that are similar in all respects except one has a climate change on average (say) 3 degree Celsius warmer than the other, one would be able to infer the willingness to pay in agriculture to avoid 3-degree Celsius temperature rise.
>
> (Kolstad, 2000)

Climate change is aggravated by the incomplete combustion of fossil fuel, excessive fertiliser use. Nitrous Oxide (N_2O) emission from excessive use of fertilisers by farmers in the periphery is significantly adding to global warming.

Pollutants from burning fossil fuels like coal, oil and gas burning in power stations and automobile transport include carbon monoxide; methods of reducing carbon monoxide pollution affect the environment and reduce the fertility of the soil, thereby the land is not suitable for cultivation in rural and peri-urban. Livestock sector waste is dumped into the periphery. Animal rearing is an alternative occupation of farmers in the rural-urban fringe. Beef and dairy cattle are the greatest methane emitters from enteric fermentation that are attributed to anthropogenic activities and lead to pollution and unhealthy living conditions in the periphery.

Enteric fermentation and its corresponding methane emissions take place in the environment. Such a quantity of waste and its complexity not only have a significant adverse environmental impact, causing pollution, greenhouse gas emissions and posing threats to human health but also waste a huge amount of material and energy resources.[16] Adaptation measures are to be undertaken in the informal settlements and substantial help from local institutions in adaptation to climate change is mandatory. Peri-urban communities suffer from water insecurity caused by urbanisation and climate change impacts. Scenarios of peri-urban environment in the context of increasing challenges of water crisis are traced.

Peri-Urban Water Resources and Environment

Developing countries, particularly with economically and politically marginalised societies with cheap labour and low prices, attracted export-oriented industries to their peripheries (Dicken, 2003). Many peripheral locations have encouraged hazardous chemical and other manufacturing industries. In the most urbanised cities, emissions via toxic substances, the improper disposal of hazardous wastes and materials with the rapid population growth and increased human activity creates unsustainable living conditions. It contributes to the environmental damages in the peripheries. These damages are of various forms such as groundwater pollution and depletion, contamination of rivers and coastal regions. The emergence of new industrial and manufacturing activities in the fringes leads to physical and environmental changes. Increasing economic activities in association with the migration creates the massive changes in the built-up structure which affects the service availability with respect to water resources. Water availability is affected by the depletion of surface water sources, such as rivers and lakes to meet water requirements in the urban areas. Demand for water for a variety of purposes within peri-urban areas and the conditions of drought and water dress also reduces the quantities available for cultivation and agri-businesses. Vulnerability of the peri-urban households includes the damage of the cultivation, floriculture and farmlands due to the disposal of industrial effluents in the canals in the peripheries. It is common for metropolitan cities of India, such as Delhi, Chennai and Bangalore (Narian et al., 2013) where untreated sewage affects livelihood in the peri-urban communities. Outskirts of these cities are known for the contamination of the peri-urban water resources and environment. The flow of urban wastewater to the periphery also creates unfavourable conditions for living and it has significant amounts of health impact in the households.

Drilling of borewells in the urban settlements also creates a challenge to the sustainability of the environments in the periphery. Excessive numbers of bore wells are common in Bangalore. Population pressure and pollution deteriorate the quality of drinking water to great extent. The excessive drilling affects irrigation-water availability for the peri-urban farming. Apart from that increasing competition for local groundwater sources and water sources depletion, the contamination of peri-urban water sources due to industrial wastes is a matter of concern. The nature and dynamics of these intricacies vary on social, economic and political factors. The complexities include

1 Shortage of water for agricultural purpose – irrigation
2 Excessive demand to cities and peri-urban households

3 Water demands for agri-businesses
4 Water demand in real estate constructions
5 Demand for water for industrial houses

Indian cities severely affected by huge demand and supply gaps, poor operation of water supply system and intra rural and urban disparity are a problem (Aijaz, 2010). Water resources are critical in the peripheries and the sustainability of the environment, where there is land utilised for agriculture. The increasing household and industrial demand for water require need a clear policy attention in the growing cities of developing countries. There is a need for better policy mechanism at the global level and at the local level because poor governance leads to world's water crisis (Rogers & Hall, 2003). Ineffectiveness of water governance is an issue of peri-urban development. There is a need for appropriate institutions to tackle these issues of unplanned development affecting the lives and livelihoods of people in periphery. Better policies improve the periphery of large cities that bear rapid expansion and developmental challenges. Peri-urban governance largely covers the issues of climate change, water resources and waste disposal.

Wastewater Management in Peri-Urban

The contradiction of peri-urban development pattern is identified through the land-related issues (Allen, 2003; Arabindoo, 2005; Narain & Nischal, 2007), but there are important scenario of wastewater management and sanitation in the peripheries of the developing countries; there has been little attention paid to the existing service provisions of sewage and wastewater. Water resources situated in the peri-urban areas of the cities of Global South are affected by rapid urbanisation (Mundoli et al., 2015). The rapid increase in urban land use for real estate purposes is affected by land degradation which affects water availability for local citizens and livelihoods of peri-urban users. In Indian cities like Bangalore, Delhi and Ghaziabad, peri-urban transformation involves the establishment of IT parks, commercial centres, hotels and restaurants, malls and infrastructure projects, industrial pollution leading to water pollution. These densely populated cities have slums located in the outskirts and less provision for wastewater management and urban sanitation.

Example of these cities illustrates the problem of current policies in managing these issues of related to sanitation and wastewater management. The scenario is not different from developing economies like Nepal, especially Kathmandu is known for great amounts of pollution and very low mechanism to tackle wastewater with poor sanitation facilities. Developing economies in common suffer from the issues of better life due to the lack of better provisions for poor and marginalised peri-urban communities. Existing studies indicate that untreated domestic wastewater that enters in the fringes is a major source of contamination of drinking water sources. According to Allen (2006), the key to improvements in water and sanitation lies in the identification of nonconventional practices and their articulation.

Research from major metropolitan cities of India, pointing to both ever-increasing rainfall and high temperature variability, intensifies the need for wastewater management. Lack of adequate water and sanitation compromises hygiene of the peri-urban poor. The rural-urban dichotomy has always aggravated the problems of resource management as the entangled jurisdictions negatively affect the service delivery of water and sanitation, which disproportionately affect poor communities (Allen, 2010). Marshall et al. (2009) point out the rapidity of the landscape transformation as "frequently accompanied by the downgrading of water services and waste removal". These transforming peri-urban landscapes create demands on resources which push the needs of the peri-urban poor to the margins and the lack of adequate water and sanitation compromises the hygiene of the peri-urban people. In many of the cities, the innovative strategies are needed for transforming wastewater for irrigation and to avoid significant health impact due to lack of clean drinking water. Wastewater reuse and management in peri-urban situations need to have better approaches that give opportunities for better management and resource recovery. Improvements in water and sanitation are needed for the sustainable development of the periphery. This requires urgent policy solution for the better management of peri-urban in the developing economy context.

Policy Interventions in the Developing Countries

Conventional economic approaches to urban growth ignore effects on land by changes in use, for example, the loss of agriculturally productive land to urban development as well as the aesthetic or other social values of land (Brueckner et al., 2001). Usual approaches to land-use planning and peri-urban development have its own limitations. Peri-urban landscape needs to be treated meaningfully as changes are rapid. To create truly sustainable strategies, a different approach to land-use planning is needed in developing countries. The proposed pattern of land use planning for sustainable and the planned growth of the peri-urban shall focus on the following policy perspectives based on the European model of city planning. Innovative approach is required to curtail the haphazard nature of sprawling in the Indian peripheries. The city planning system in the advanced countries often depends on operates with a balance of private and public control over land ownership and development. There are the important policy interventions for the suitable outcomes. These planning approaches utilise the law, science and economics McFarland (2015) as part of the planning process as we deal with the aspect of specific aspect of social demographic and economic impact of challenged development patterns. By integrating legal, technological and economic approaches, we formulate a sound policy regime with the help of planning agencies. The possible measures are

1 A long-term strategy of Master plan which ensures the match between existing land use pattern and the proposed land use pattern.
2 Strict and coherent demarcation and "ownership" of the principles for land.
3 Balancing peri-urban land and with urban land growth and the appropriate policy using appropriate rules the process of land conversion in the periphery.
4 Genuine co-operation between local and state planning authorities for water management and sanitation in the periphery.
5 Technology integration with efficient land use planning and legislation
6 Public-private partnerships in the management of infrastructure growth and the planned city development.

Urban land use assimilates a small proportion of the land area, population growth exacerbates the physical space to cater for the socio-economic needs of that increasing population from the perspective of the built form (McLoughlin, 1992). The peri-urban life is affected by the quality of landscape and the living, regional landscape qualities have a major influence in determining the quality of life as it provides multiple functions, including conservation, mental health, physical health, outdoor recreation, social, cultural and economic functions. Hence, these policies contribute to the community's quality of life, liveability and sustainability (Low Choy, 2008). Considering peri-urban as an integral part of a metropolitan strategy, we further look into some measures to remove the challenges of peri-urban. They include

1 Regulatory Measures for Efficient Land Use Planning
2 Green Infrastructure
3 Sustainable Drainage Systems for wastewater management
4 Innovation for Sustainable Urbanisation

Regulatory Measures for Efficient Land Use Planning

The regulatory measures for the efficient land use planning include the measures such as Land Use Control, Zonal Regulations and Building Byelaws. These are essential for retaining an efficient land use measures and sustainable scenario of agriculture as cities often face uncontrolled conversion and the boundary keeps changing. Land use control imposes a regulation on the land uses such as residential, commercial, industrial and agricultural uses in the fringes. The regulation on land use is imposed. Zonal Regulations are important for the efficient planning of the cities. Zonal regulations are part of Development plan for cities like Bangalore. According to Output Development Plan, there is a division of planning area for the purpose of land use. Zoning refers is spatially separating incompatible land uses. Zonal regulations define the purpose for which the use of land is permitted in each zone. There are reasonable limitations on the use of land and buildings so as to prevent congestion and control population densities and lead to the development of the city in accordance with the land use plan. The utilisation of land that is allowed in various zones has been set down in the zoning guidelines. Another step in this regard is the Building Byelaws. The building byelaws form part of the zoning regulations endorse the setbacks, maximum plot coverage and Floor area ratio for different areas. In light of these guidelines, the Bengaluru city corporations have outlined separate building byelaws. The city has been divided into the following three areas for the regulation of the construction of buildings. (A) Intensely populated area, (B) Central administration area and its surroundings, (C) Sub-division Regulations. These are effective measures in the practices of sustainable land management and city planning; nevertheless, innovative methods are needed.

Green Infrastructure

Green infrastructure refers to a shift in the way local and state governments think about green space for the sustainable growth of the cities. The notion of green infrastructure symbolises a spectacular shift in the way local and state governments assume green space (McMahon and Benedict 2000). Increasing urbanisation leads to enormous socio-economic and environmental pressures, pollution and housing crisis. As urbanisation contributes to climate change, the increase in emissions results in the less quality of air, water and land resources in developing countries. To address these issues related to the global challenges, nature-based solutions are required. Green Infrastructure is a method providing alternative solutions for human well-being and protection of the environment. Green infrastructure set up has been increasing worldwide; green infrastructure planning is required to meet today's reality and future prospects regarding environmental and urban planning (Davies et al., 2017; Mell, 2017). Green infrastructure is thus referred to as "a strategically planned network of natural and semi-natural areas with other environmental features designed and managed to deliver a wide range of ecosystem services". It combines green spaces and other physical features in terrestrial and marine areas. European Commission promoted green infrastructure in order to enhance green planning and an integral part of spatial planning and territorial development in all its member states (Dunn, 2010).

Urban sprawl has triggered the rapid fragmentation of land, on the fringes of major metropolitan areas. People have demanded policy measures to tackle the challenges of urbanisation; green infrastructure is one such measure which takes various infrastructures including corridors which are common in advanced nations like Sweden. The strategies followed are for urban and peri-urban revitalisation and promotion of sustainable development (McMahon & Benedict, 2000). Its emphasis on multi-modal transportation planning, funding for bicycle and pedestrian facilities and policies aimed at reducing fossil fuel consumption as we see most of the European countries. The United States is the fastest urbanised country in the world; statistics shows that the loss of farmland and other open space to development has more than doubled in recent years. Between 1992 and 1997, the rate of loss grew to 3.2 million acres a year.[17] How the green infrastructure is portrayed is illustrated by Dr. Mark Benedict, green infrastructure comprises a wide variety of natural ecosystems and landscape features. For the purpose of urban planning and revitalisation, green infrastructure takes various shapes such as Reserves, Managed Native landscapes, Regional Parks and Preserves and Reserves.

1 **Reserves** refers to large, protected areas, including national wildlife refuges or state parks, for the conservation of biological diversity.
2 **Managed Native Landscapes** includes large publicly owned lands, such as national and state forests, for resource extraction and recreational values.
3 **Regional Parks and Preserves are** less extensive hubs of regional importance which provide ecological benefits and preserve biological diversity.
4 **Trailhead**s occur surrounded by rural natural areas and working landscapes or within urban areas ranging from large metropolitan areas to small communities and it serve as human hubs within greenways systems.
5 **Conservation Corridors** are linear protected areas, such as river and stream corridors, serve as biological conduits for wildlife, and they also provide opportunities for compatible outdoor, resource-based recreational activities.
6 **Greenbelts**: Protected natural lands or working landscapes serve as a framework for development while also preserving native ecosystems and/or productive farms and directing urban and suburban growth.

These forms of green infrastructures commonly found in the Europe and the United States; India is in the initial stages of adopting green infrastructures. Adoption of such measures in the rapidly growing developing countries is needed for mitigating global environmental challenges. The implementation of green infrastructures is helpful for removing environmental problems in the emerging peri–urban areas.

Sustainable Systems for Water and Wastewater Management

Developing countries face a major problem of industrialisation and rapid urban agglomerations resulting in ever-increasing problems of wastewater (Minhas & Samra, 2004; Corcoran et al., 2010). This is particularly common in the growing metropolitan areas of Ghaziabad, Delhi and Bangalore. Studies show a number of cases, who have no access to formal clean water supplies and essential service to the poor peri-urban dwellers (Dardenne, 2006). The water and sanitation requirements of the peri-urban poor are met neither by conventional policy; hence, informal approaches are employed (Allen et al., 2006). The issue of water and wastewater services to peri-urban areas is a significant challenge for providing services to cities in developing countries. Therefore, sustainable solutions are important, to solve the environmental and health risks posed by failing wastewater management. The safe and sustainable use of wastewaters in agriculture is a low-cost option and it helps in avoiding uncontrolled dumping of wastewaters into the environment (Drechsel et al., 2010). The sustainable solution includes reuse options, and it minimises impacts on the local and global environment (Sharma et al., 2010).

Sustainable wastewater systems and technologies are needed to improve public health and environmental conditions in peri-urban. Considering the need for better water and wastewater management in the peri-urban, we inspect several solutions.

Decentralised approaches extend opportunities for wastewater reuse and resource recovery, and it improves in local environmental health conditions in peri-urban (Otterphol et al., 2002; Parkinson & Tayler, 2003). It is argued that the key to structural improvements in water and sanitation lies in the recognition of nonconventional practices and their articulation to the formal system under new governance regimes (Allen et al., 2006). Innovative technologies are required for decentralised water management, wastewater and biowaste management in urban and peri-urban areas. By applying effective technologies for treatment of used waters, it is possible to have better strategies to deal with urban wastewater. The essential and innovative idea of integrated water concepts is based on the principle of separating the different flows of domestic wastewater according to their characteristics. Innovative methods found in Netherlands and Germany include vacuum technology for the collection of slightly diluted black water is useful. The treatment technology for black water is yet another method of wastewater management used in advanced countries. Common technologies for a source control wastewater management are used in urban areas (Winblad, 1998). Understanding the scope of the innovative methods of waste management is inevitable in the developing economies.

Innovations for Sustainable Urbanisation

Sustainable urbanisation, technological innovation and the concept of sustainable cities have increasingly become a pervasive trend on a global scale. The scope of sustainable urbanisation and technological innovation discussed is both at the government level and the firm level. Various governments try to address urban sustainability challenges (Evans & Karvonen, 2010; Marvin et al., 2018). Many city governments embarked on innovative measures to reduce their impact on climate change. Successful sustainable urbanisation necessitates accountable governments with the management of cities and urban expansion, and efficient use of technologies. European cities are successful with good governance and adopted sustainable urban planning in order to tackle sustainability issues related to land use, climate change, water, waste management and sanitation by integrating technologies of sustainable urban development and innovation. This indicates that city governments have set out to address urban sustainability issues on a global scale (Bulkeley, 2010).

Collaborative arrangements, which are co-funded by local, national or European subsidies, suggest the growing interests of governments to support the digital technologies to drive sustainable urbanisation. Utrecht adopted Green Structure Plan for the period 2017–30 focusing sustainable urbanisation with climate- and energy-neutral construction, efficient water management and green areas for healthy urban living, it is a way forward to sustainable urbanisation adopted by the European cities with the support of the government.

"Sustainable City" refers to an innovative city that practises information and communications technologies to improve living standards, efficiency of urban management and urban services.[18] Deployment Technology solutions to address urban sustainability issues is an integral part of smart and sustainable cities. At the firm level, we understand the technology adoption for the sustainability of the cities. IT cities of the developing countries have attracted significant number of firms to their peripheries which leads to fast urbanisation. These technology firms increasingly placed themselves as strategic partners for city governments and policymakers to address urban sustainability issues (van den Buuse & Kolk, 2019). It created prospects for these firms, developed solutions based on digital technologies for cities. Firms such as IBM, Cisco, Google and Philips developed a variety of solutions based on digital technologies for cities. It is more of a technology-centric approach to urban development (Joss, 2017). For firms, experimental settings such as the urban living labs (Evans & Karvonen, 2010; Voytenko et al., 2016), urban transitions labs and climate change experiments and sustainable solutions are inevitable. Smart city programs are the way towards sustainable urbanisation; these are initiated by city governments for smart administration such as Amsterdam Smart City in Amsterdam, and Copenhagen Cleantech Cluster in Copenhagen. Firms use internal R&D activities of firms to improve solutions based on digital technologies for cities. It is possible to explicitly link sustainable city programmes and pilot projects for solving sustainability issues in the urban environment in developing countries. Technologies and urban innovations influence the way of organising sustainable environment for the better future of cities. Developing world requires urgent remedies for sustainable urbanisation and city planning as the peri-urban acts as a litmus test of change and transition not just locally but in the whole city region or the "rural urban region".

Summary

Developing countries face major challenges of industrial development and known for rapid urban agglomerations. IT boom in Bangalore led to swift transformation of peripheries, real estate development and active land transactions leading to ambiguity albeit enormous growth in the state economy. Often, challenges in the peri-urban are due to the fuzziness with respect to the role of institutions in the land policy. The dichotomy between the rural and urban administrative institutions fails to address the problems of land administration; corrupt practices in the land markets leads to significant grey spots amidst the exorbitant growth of the real estate sector in India. The role of administrative institutions in the land management of Bangalore is expounded with the various institutions like Bengaluru Metropolitan Region Development Authority (BMRDA), Directorate of Town and Country Planning, The Department of Stamps and Registration, Revenue Department/Department of Survey, Settlement and Land Records. An integrated policy incorporating land use planning, legislation and technology is suggested in the context of increasing property conflicts and litigation in India. The issues of peri-urban are largely associated with the land, but the problems are exacerbated by the environmental changes in the peri-urban in the developing countries. The global environmental changes that affect the peri-urban are climate change, contamination of water resources and wastewater management. In order to tackle these issues related to the peri-urban, policy interventions by genuine co-operation between local and state planning authorities, technology integration with efficient land use planning, legislation and public-private partnerships for infrastructure and planned city development are needed. Policy measures include regulatory mechanisms for efficient land use planning, green infrastructure, sustainable drainage systems for wastewater management and innovations for sustainable city planning; thus, sustainable urbanisation is a remedy and an alternative path to deal with urban sustainability challenges.

Notes

1 Karnataka Act No. 39 of 1985.
2 BMRDA Report 2017.
3 BMRDA Report 2017.
4 https://karunadu.karnataka.gov.in/karigr/Pages/Home.aspx
5 Akarband Extract is issued by the Survey Department, it indicates total extent, boundaries and classification of property in question.
6 Issues pertaining to land grants, mutation, and land reform files received by the Revenue Department for measurement.
7 Five-year plan.
8 Land Acquisition Guidelines issued between 1963 and 1980 Revenue Department, Government of Karnataka, Bangalore.
9 Planning Commission, 1983.
10 Land Governance Assessment Framework: Implementation Manual for Assessing Governance in the Land Sector Version: October, 2013, Implementation Manual.
11 The Karnataka Town and Country Planning Act. Draft, 1961. Chapter IA.
12 Karnataka State Wide Area Network.
13 RTC or Pahani is a very important revenue record which is issued through computerization. It contains valuable data related to a piece of land.
14 The Karnataka Town and Country Planning Act. Draft, 1961. Chapter IA.
15 Transparency International (2006).
16 European Commission, 2010.
17 U.S. Department of Agriculture's National Resources Inventory, 1997.
18 International Telecommunication Union, 2015.

References

Aijaz, R. (2010). *Water for Indian Cities: Government Practices and Policy Concerns*. policycommons.net

Ali, A. M. S. (2006). Rice to shrimp: Land use/land cover changes and soil degradation in Southwestern Bangladesh. *Land Use Policy*, 23(4), 421–435.

Allen, A. (2010). Neither rural nor urban: Service delivery options that work for the peri-urban poor. In Kurian, and M., McCarney, P. (eds.), *Peri-Urban Water and Sanitation Services* (pp. 27–61). Dordrecht: Springer.

Arabindoo, P. (2005). Examining the peri-urban interface as a constructed primordialism. In Dupont (ed.), *Peri-Urban Dynamics: Population, Habitat and Environment on the Peripheries of Large Indian Metropolises*, 44, no. 14, Publication of French Research Institutes in India.

Azqueta, D., Rodrígues, M., & Román, M. V. (2013). Methodological approach to assess the socio-economic vulnerability to wildfires in Spain. *Forest Ecology and Management*, 294, 158–165.

Barson, M. M., Randall, L. A., & Barry, S. C. (2004). Modelling greenhouse gas emissions from land cover change: Linking continental data with point/patch models. *Mathematics and Computers in Simulation*, 64(3–4), 329–337.

Brueckner, J. K., Mills, E., & Kremer, M. (2001). Urban sprawl: Lessons from urban economics [with comments]. Brookings-Wharton Papers on Urban Affairs, 65–97.

Bulkeley, H. (2010). Cities and the governing of climate change. *Annual Review of Environment and Resources*, 35(1), 229–253.

Burby, R. J., May, P. J., Berke, P. R., Kaiser, E. J., Dalton, L. C., & French, S. P. (1997). *Making Governments Plan: State Experiments in Managing Land Use*. Baltimore and London: JHU Press.

Cebecauer, T., & Hofierka, J. (2008). The consequences of land-cover changes on soil erosion distribution in Slovakia. *Geomorphology*, 98(3–4), 187–198.

Corcoran, E. (Ed.). (2010). *Sick Water?: The Central Role of Wastewater Management in Sustainable Development: A Rapid Response Assessment*. UNEP/Earthprint.

Dardenne, B. (2006, November). The role of the private sector in peri-urban or rural water services in emerging countries. In *Background Paper for OECD Global Forum on Sustainable Development*.

Davies, C., & Lafortezza, R., Spanò, M., Gentile, F. (2017). The DPSIR framework in support of green infrastructure planning: A case study in Southern Italy. *Land Use Policy*, 61, 242–250.

Dicken, P. (2003). *Global Shift: Reshaping the Global Economic Map in the 21st Century*. Sage.

Drechsel, P., Bahri, A., Raschid-Sally, L., & Redwood, M. (Eds.). (2010). *Wastewater Irrigation and Health: Assessing and Mitigating Risk in Low-Income Countries*. IWMI.

Dunjó, G., Pardini, G., & Gispert, M. (2003). Land use change effects on abandoned terraced soils in a Mediterranean catchment, NE Spain. *Catena*, 52(1), 23–37.

Dunn, A. D. (2010). Siting green infrastructure: Legal and policy solutions to alleviate urban poverty and promote healthy communities. *Boston College Environmental Affairs Law Review*, 37, 41.

Evans, J., & Karvonen, A. (2010). Living laboratories for sustainability: Exploring the politics and epistemology of urban transition. In H. Bulkeley, V. Castán Broto, M. Hodson, and S. Marvin (eds.), *Cities and Low Carbon Transitions* (pp. 142–157). London: Routledge.

Friedmann, D. Low, B., Carter, M. R., Wood, E., Mitchell, C., & Proietti, M. (2016). Building an urban arts partnership between school, community-based artists, and university. *Learning Landscapes*, 10(1), 153–172.

Gowda, K. R. (1972). *Urban and Regional Planning: Principles and Case Studies. Prasaranga, University of Mysore* (pp. 1–11). New York: Palgrave Macmillan.

Joss, S. (2017). *Sustainable Cities: Governing for Urban Innovation*. Bloomsbury Publishing.

Karmakar, J. (2015). Encountering the reality of the planning process in peri urban areas of Kolkata: Case study of Rajarhat. *Archives of Applied Science Research*, 7(5), 129–138.

Kumar, K. K., & Parikh, J. (2001). Indian agriculture and climate sensitivity. *Global Environmental Change*, 11(2), 147–154.

Low Choy, D. (2008). The SEQ regional landscape framework: Is practice ahead of theory? Practice review. *Urban Policy and Research*, 26(1), 111–124.

Marvin, S., Bulkeley, H., Mai, L., McCormick, K., & Palgan, Y. V. (Eds.). (2018). *Urban Living Labs: Experimenting with City Futures*. Routledge.

Marshall, L. A. Jencso, K. G., McGlynn, B. L., Gooseff, M. N., Wondzell, S. M., & Bencala, K. E. (2009). Hydrologic connectivity between landscapes and streams: Transferring reach- and plot-scale understanding to the catchment scale. *Water Resources Research*, 45(4), 1–16.

McFarland, P. (2015). The peri-urban land-use planning tangle: An Australian perspective. *International Planning Studies*, 20(3), 161–179.

McLoughlin, J. B. (1992). The case for a legal basis for land-use planning systems. *Built Environment (1978-)*, 18(3), 214–220.

McMahon, E. T., & Benedict, M. A. (2000). Green infrastructure. *Planning Commissioners Journal*, 37(4), 4–7.

Mell, I. C. (2017). Green infrastructure: Reflections on past, present and future praxis. *Landscape Research*, 42(2), 135–145.

Minhas, P. S., & Samra, J. S. (2004). *Wastewater Use in Peri-Urban Agriculture: Impacts and Opportunities*.

Mundoli, S., Manjunath, B., & Nagendra, H. (2015). Effects of urbanisation on the use of lakes as commons in the peri-urban interface of Bengaluru, India. *International Journal of Urban Sustainable Development*, 7(1), 89–108.

Narain, V., Anand, P., & Banerjee, P. (2013). *Periurbanization in India: A Review of the Literature and Evidence*. Report for the Project: Rural to Urban Transitions and the Peri-Urban Interface. SaciWATERs. India First published in.

Narain, V., & Nischal, S. (2007). The peri-urban interface in Shahpur Khurd and Karnera, India. *Environment and Urbanization*, 19(1), 261–273.

Neutze, G. M. (1973). *The Price of Land and Land Use Planning: Policy Instruments in the Urban Land Market*. Environment Directorate, Organisation for Economic Co-operation and Development.

Ojima, D., Moran, E., McConnell, W., Smith, M. S., Laumann, G., Morais, J., et al., 2005. *Global Land Project—Science Plan and Implementation Strategy*. IGBP Report No. 53/IHDP Report No. 19. IGBP, Stockholm, Sweden.

Parkinson, J., & Tayler, K. (2003). Decentralized wastewater management in peri-urban areas in low-income countries. *Environment and Urbanization*, 15(1), 75–90.

Ravindra, A. (1996). *Urban Land Policy. Study of Metropolitan City*. New Delhi: Concept Publishing Company.

Rogers, P., & Hall, A. W. (2003). *Effective Water Governance* (Vol. 7). Stockholm: Global Water Partnership.

Shalaby, A., & Tateishi, R. (2007). Remote sensing and GIS for mapping and monitoring land cover and land-use changes in the Northwestern coastal zone of Egypt. *Applied Geography*, 27(1), 28–41.

Sharma, A., Burn, S., Gardner, T., & Gregory, A. (2010). Role of decentralised systems in the transition of urban water systems. *Water Science and Technology: Water Supply*, 10(4), 577–583.

Sundaresan, J. (2013). Urban planning in vernacular governance land use planning and violations in Bangalore (Doctoral dissertation, The London School of Economics and Political Science (LSE)).

United Nations. Economic Commission for Europe. (1996). *Land Administration Guidelines: With Special Reference to Countries in Transition*. United Nations Publications.

van den Buuse, D., & Kolk, A. (2019). An exploration of smart city approaches by international ICT firms. *Technological Forecasting and Social Change*, 142, 220–234.

Virtanen, P., & Verlaat, J. (1999). *Urban Land Policy-Goals and Instruments*. International Federation for Housing and Planning.

Voytenko, Y., McCormick, K., Evans, J., & Schliwa, G. (2016). Urban living labs for sustainability and low carbon cities in Europe: Towards a research agenda. *Journal of Cleaner Production*, 123, 45–54.

Wu, Q., Li, H. Q., Wang, R. S., Paulussen, J., He, Y., Wang, M., & Wang, Z. (2006). Monitoring and predicting land use change in Beijing using remote sensing and GIS. *Landscape and Urban Planning*, 78(4), 322–333.

Winblad, U. (Hrsg.) (1998). *Ecological Sanitation*. Stockholm: SIDA.

Appendix

Land Transactions in the Peri-Urban Land Markets in Bengaluru Questionnaire

1	Category of **Seller (Farmer)**
	(1) Marginal, (2) Small, (3) Semi-Medium, (4) Medium, (5) Large
2	Location of the parcel
3	Farm income
4	Source of non-farm income
	(1) Rental, (2) Salary, (3) Pension, (4) Other
5	Non-farm income of the farmer
6	Year of transaction
8	Quantity of land sold in parcel lot (size of land transacted) in sq ft/ha
9	Price of land sold
10	Pre-sale total owned land area of seller
11	Post-sale total owned land area
12	Distance from national highway
	(1) less than 1 km, (2) 1 km to 2 km, (3) km to 5 km, (4) 6 km to 10 km
13	Reasons for sale
	(1) Distress sale, (2) High market value, (3) Low income and productivity
14	Market value of the property per sq ft
15	Do you have a land title?
	Is there a record of land registration?
	Have you entered into any property conflict or litigation?
	Did you face any hurdles for land registration?
	Was it undeveloped land or built property when you acquired it?
16	Type of land use at present
	(1) Agricultural, (2) Residential, (3) Commercial, (4) Industrial
17	How did you utilise the money after selling the land?
	(1) Agricultural, (2) Residential, (3) Investment, (4) Bank deposit, (5) Other
18	What is the present income generating source of farmer after sale?
	(1) Agriculture, (2) Rental, (3) Both, (4) Bank deposit, (5) Other
19	Whether sale of land helped you to earn sufficient income?
	(1) yes (2) No

1 Category of buyer
(1) Farmer, (2) Real estate agent, (3) Individual buyer peri-urban resident, (4) Individual buyer business purpose
2 Location of the parcel
3 Source of income
(1) Agriculture, (2) Rental, (3) Salary, (4) Pension, (5) Other
Income in Rs
4 Year of transaction
5 From whom
6 Quantity of land purchased in parcel lot (size of land transacted) per sq ft
7 Price of land bought in Rs
8 Pre purchase total owned land area of the buyer per sq ft/ha
9 Post purchase total owned land area of the buyer per sq ft/ha
10 Distance from National Highway
(1) Less than 1 km, (2) 1–2 km, (3) 3–5 km, (4) 4.6–10 km
11 Cost of registration
12 Time taken for registration
(1) 1–30 days, (2) 31–60 days, (3) 61–90 days, (4) Over 90 days
13 Source of finance
(1) Personal savings, (2) Commercial credit, (3) Informal plan, (4) Other
14 Purpose for which it lands bought
(1) Agricultural, (2) Residential, (3) Industrial, (4) Commercial, (5) Real estate, (6) Other
15 Do you have a land title?   Yes/No
Is there a record of land registration?
Have you entered into any property conflict or litigation?
Did you face any hurdles for land registration?
Was it undeveloped land or built property when you acquired it?
Is there any traces of non-DC converted sites used for residential construction?
What are the factors complicated the land management practices?
Did you sell land to government for infrastructural purposes or any?
16 Market value of the property per sq ft in Rs
17 Type of land use at present
(1) Agricultural, (2) Residential, (3) Commercial, (4) Industrial
18 What is the present income generating source?
19 Whether the purchase of land has improved your income?
(1) Yes, (2) No

Table 1 Kanakapura Taluk LU/LC statistics (area in hectares)

Observation	Agriculture	Built up	Others
2000	73,916	704	38,866
2001	74,165	954	39,115
2002	74,415	1,204	39,365
2003	74,665	1,454	39,615
2004	74,915	1,704	39,865
2005	69,654	1,724	39,858
2006	69,654	1,747	39,880
2007	69,676	1,770	39,903
2008	69,722	1,792	39,925
2009	69,744	1,815	39,948
2010	67,661	2,585	40,878
2011	67,629	2,553	40,846
2012	67,598	2,522	40,815
2013	67,571	2,495	40,788
2014	67,545	2,469	40,788
2015	67,510	2,434	40,727
2016	67,475	2,399	40,692
2017	62,237	2,674	46,433

Table 2 Hoskote LU/LC statistics (area in hectares)

Observation	Agriculture	Built up	Others
2000	32,580	1,524	15,901
2001	33,005	1,949	16,326
2002	33,431	2,375	16,752
2003	33,856	2,800	17,177
2004	34,282	3,226	17,603
2005	35,978	1,400	10,835
2006	35,894	1,315	10,301
2007	35,809	1,230	10,216
2008	35,724	1,145	10,131
2009	35,639	1,060	10,046
2010	29,060	2,834	16,081
2011	28,882	2,657	15,903
2012	28,704	2,479	15,725
2013	28,527	2,302	15,548
2014	28,349	2,124	15,370
2015	28,172	1,947	15,193
2016	27,994	1,769	15,015
2017	25,064	3,153	21,325

Table 3 Harohalli LU/LC statistics (area in hectares)

Observation	Agriculture	Built Up
2000	1,221	36
2001	1,238	39
2002	1,256	43
2003	1,274	46
2004	1,292	49
2005	1,309	53
2006	1,309	55
2007	1,308	58
2008	1,307	62
2009	1,307	66
2010	1,306	65
2011	1,288	71
2012	1,271	76
2013	1,253	82
2014	1,236	88
2015	1,218	94
2016	1,201	100
2017	1,183	105

Table 4 The number of land transactions

Sellers (250)	Buyers (250)
Marginal (152)	Real estate agent (88)
Small (26)	Farmers (20)
Semi Medium (31)	Individual buyer (peri-urban resident) (84)
Medium (35)	Individual buyer (Business purpose (58)
Large (6)	

In that case, the latest transaction by the respondent is used in this study. This is true for all the agents in the land transactions except real estate agent where a real estate agent is an agent in the land market who is known for the multiple land transaction. However, it was difficult to get more response from the real estate agent; therefore, the number of transactions by them in land purchase is restricted to 88 transactions from the recent transactions of 11 real estate agents. There are 11 real estate agents in the buyer category of 250 respondents.

Table 5 Peri-urban villages and distance

Village	Distance from NH	Distance from District Headquarters	Distance from Commercial Centre
Devanagundi – Hoskote	3–5 km	33 km	23 km
Tavarekere – Hoskote	3–5 km	25 km	20 km
Bhaktharahalli – Hoskote	Less than 1 km	28 km	1 km
Samethanahalli – Hoskote	2–3 km	33 km	19 km
Kolathur – Hoskote	Less than 1 km	35 km	16 km
Harohalli – Kanakapura	Less than 1 km	41 km	28 km
Sathanur – Kanakapura	6–10 km	64 km	30 km
Taralu – Kanakapura	3–5 km	33 km	21 km
Somanahalli – Kanakapura	1–2 km	32 km	22 km
Nettigere – Kanakapura	2–3 km	33 km	26 km

Note: The commercial centre of the villages in Hoskote is K R Puram, whereas for villages in Kanakapura, it is Banashankari.

Table 6 Relevant information – peri-urban villages

Peri-Urban Village	Geographic Area (Hectare)	Distance from District Headquarters	Population	No of Households	Significant Developments
Devanagundi	578	33 km	2,004	472	Railway station, oil refineries
Tavarekere	356	25 km	2,481	–	Manufacturing units
Harohalli	1675	41 km	13,044	3,121	Industrial
Sathanur	596	64 km	4,966	1,162	Mixed development
Kolathur	439.46	35 km	1,568	332	Agrarian
Samethanahalli	463.87	33 km	4,102	999	Residential
Bhakatarahalli	259.38	28 km	1,105	245	Mixed developments
Somanahalli	539.78	32 km	4,655	1,158	Mixed developments
Nettigere	472.19	33 km	1,847	443	Mixed developments

Note: The information related to Taralu Village, Kanakapura, was not available in village directory.

Table 7 SR value and market value of Kanakapura periphery

Year	Average SR value (in Rs)/ Sq Ft	Average Market value (in Rs)/ Sq Ft	Average SR value (in Rs)/ Sq Ft	Average Market value (in Rs)/Sq Ft
	Hoskote periphery	Hoskote periphery	Kanakapura periphery	Kanakapura periphery
2000–01	28	200	–	100
2001–02	28	270	–	150
2002–03	28	300	–	175
2003–04	28	325	–	200
2004–05	29	350	–	250
2005–06	29	380	487	300
2006–07	29	400	487	500
2007–08	34	500	654	600
2008–09	230	600	719	650
2009–10	230	900	719	750
2010–11	310	1,000	719	1,000
2011–12	290	1,100	748	1,100
2012–13	390	1,200	1,060	1,300
2013–14	440	1,200	1,182	1,500
2014–15	530	1,375	1,182	1,600
2015–16	530	1,750	1,260	1,700
2016–17	732	2,250	1,503	2,000

Table 8 SR value for Kanakapura peri-urban villages

Year	Harohalli	Sathanur	Somanahalli	Nettigere	Tharalu	Average
2004–05	40	17	890	760	730	487
2005–06	40	17	890	760	730	487
2006–07	250	50	1,100	990	880	654
2007–08	500	125	1,100	990	880	719
2008–09	500	125	1,100	990	880	719
2009–10	500	125	1,100	990	880	719
2010–11	500	125	1,100	990	880	719
2011–12	650	120	1,100	990	880	748
2012–13	650	450	1,400	1,400	1,400	1,060
2013–14	650	450	1,590	1,590	1,630	1,182
2014–15	650	450	1,590	1,590	1,630	1,182
2015–16	938	450	1,690	1,590	1,630	1,260
2016–17	938	929	1,800	1,900	1,950	1,503

Table 9 SR value for Hoskote peri-urban villages

Year	Samathanahalli	Devanagundi	Tavarekere	Bhaktarahalli	Kolathur	Average
2000–01	30	20	30	30	30	28
2001–02	30	25	30	30	25	28
2002–03	30	25	30	30	25	28
2003–04	30	25	30	30	25	28
2004–05	30	25	30	30	30	29
2005–06	30	25	30	30	30	29
2006–07	30	25	30	30	30	29
2007–08	50	40	40	30	10	34
2008–09	300	200	150	200	300	230
2009–10	300	200	150	200	300	230
2010–11	300	300	400	200	350	310
2011–12	300	300	300	200	350	290
2012–13	400	400	500	300	350	390
2013–14	500	500	400	400	400	440
2014–15	600	600	500	450	500	530
2015–16	600	600	500	450	500	530
2016–17	720	720	840	840	540	732

Index

Note: **Bold** page numbers refer to tables; *Italic* page numbers refer to figures and page numbers followed by "n" denote endnotes.

Printed in the United States
by Baker & Taylor Publisher Services